FABULOUS VOYAGE

FABULOUS VOYAGE

by

FLEMING MacLIESH

and

MARTIN L. KRIEGER

LONDON
VICTOR GOLLANCZ LTD
1963

Grateful acknowledgment is made for the use of the following quoted matter: extracts from "Gerontion" and "The Waste Land" from *Collected Poems 1908–1935* by T. S. Eliot, published by Faber and Faber; extracts from "I Wake and Feel the Fell of Dark" and "No Worst, There is None" from *Poems of Gerard Manley Hopkins*, published by the Oxford University Press; and extracts from Preludes (24), "I think continually of these . . ." from *Collected Poems 1928–1953* by Stephen Spender, published by Faber and Faber.

Made and printed in Great Britain by
William Clowes and Sons, Limited, London and Beccles

TO

Gavin, John, Katherine, Melissa,

Nancy AND *Susan*

It is not the desirer of desires who attains peace but he into whom all desires enter, as the waters enter the ocean, which is full to the brim and grounded in stillness.

THE BHAGAVAD-GITA, II, 70
(*Translated by Swami Nikhilananda*)

They that go down to the sea in ships, that do business in great waters; these see the works of the Lord, and his wonders in the deep.

PSALM 107:23, 24

Authors' Notes
and Acknowledgments

The primary sources on which we have relied throughout are, of course, Woodes Rogers' *A Cruising Voyage Round the World*, and Edward Cooke's *A Voyage to the South Sea*, both published in London in 1712. Rogers' account is the more generally important, as well as the more interesting, and the one to which we have most frequently referred.

There has never been, so far as we can determine, any subsequent edition of Cooke's two volumes; but a modern edition of Rogers' book—a transcript lacking only the original introduction—was published by the Seafarers' Library in 1928, with an excellent introduction and footnotes by G. E. Manwaring. While we have consulted the original, we have chiefly used the 1928 edition by Manwaring as our working copy.

For other references, quotations and background material from late seventeenth and early eighteenth century sources, we have drawn largely from the writings of William Dampier published in various volumes between 1697 and 1701. John Masefield's two-volume, collected edition of *Dampier's Voyages*, published in London in 1906 with an invaluable introduction, notes and extensive appendices, is the edition upon which we have principally relied.

The remaining author among the chief officers of the *Duke* and *Dutchess* is, of course, Captain-Doctor Thomas Dover, whose *Ancient Physician's Legacy to His Country* was published in 1732. Other studies and accounts which have a direct bearing on the voyage and/or its principals, which appeared a few years before it or in the era immediately following, and which might be singled out from the general bibliography are: *A Complete Collection of Voyages and Travels* by John Harris, 1744; *A Voyage round the World* by J. F. Gemelli Careri (Vol. IV of *A Collection of Voyages and Travels* by Awnsham and John Churchill, 1704); *Terra Australis Cognita* by John Callander, 1768; *A Chronological History of Discovery in the South Sea* by James Burney, 1803; *Journal du Voyage fait à la Mer du Sud, avec les Flisbustiers de l'Amerique en 1684 et anneés suivantes* by Raveneau de Lussan, 1689; and the essay on Selkirk by Richard Steele in *The Englishman*, 1714.

Among modern sources, we have had most frequent recourse to the following: W. H. Bonner's *Captain William Dampier*, 1934; Kenneth Dewhurst's *The Quicksilver Doctor*, 1957; R. C. Leslie's *Life Aboard a British Privateer in the Time of Queen Anne*, 1889; John Masefield's *On the Spanish Main*, 1925, and his edition of *Dampier's Voyages*, already noted; W. A. McEwen and A. H. Lewis's *Encyclopaedia of Nautical Knowledge*, 1953; J. W. Damer Powell's *Bristol Privateers and Ships of War*, 1930; Louis H. Roddis' *James Lind, Founder of Nautical Medicine*, 1950; William Lytle Schurz' definitive work, *The Manila Galleon*, 1939; and Clennel Wilkinson's *William Dampier*, 1929.

We are particularly and personally indebted to Dr. Dewhurst for many letters and for his having forwarded us from England on his own initiative some of the research material for his own book, including transcripts of records and documents in the House of Lords, as we are indebted to Mr. John Masefield, Professor Schurz and Dr. Roddis, Captain U. S. Navy Medical Corps, Retired, for correspondence providing additional leads and information and various confirmatory facts and references.

We are also deeply indebted to the following libraries, institutions and organizations for their coöperation, not only in making various rare and otherwise unprocurable volumes available to us but also in generously tracking down and corresponding with us about numerous obscure details and references: Bank of England; Bristol Public Library; British Museum; Hakluyt Society; Huntington Library; Library of Congress; Los Angeles County Medical Association Library; Los Angeles County Museum; Los Angeles Public Library; National Library of Medicine; Nassau Public Library, British West Indies; Scrips Institute of Oceanography; U. S. Naval Academy; University of California, Los Angeles, bio-medical and general libraries; University of Southern California; Hancock Library; Yale University, Medical Library, Cushing Collection.

It ought to be added that, in respect to general background material from modern sources, we owe much to the works of Rachel Carson, Louis Kronenberger, Felix Riesenberg and Allan Villiers. In this connection—and for additional specific information—Bryan Little's recent biography of Woodes Rogers, titled *Crusoe's Captain*, deserves a particular acknowledgment; it is mentioned last only because it was the most recent work consulted, having been published in England after our book had been in the hands of the publisher and we were engaged in final rewriting, corrections and revisions. When we began on this history, early in 1958, no full-length biography of Woodes Rogers had apparently ever been done. Mr. Little's scholarly study is the first to our knowledge to appear and has clarified many hitherto obscure or ambiguous details about Rogers' later life, following the completion of the voyage.

Finally, we owe a conspicuous debt of thanks to Mr. Harry E. Maule, our editor, whose interest from the beginning, critical advice and extensive suggestions for specific cuts and changes have been more valuable and more appreciated than we can say; to Mrs. Clare Ryan Talbot, librarian and ex libris authority, who originally typed a considerable portion of the first manuscript and recommended a number of important leads and sources during the early stages of our research; and lastly to Mrs. Lucille Bowers, who typed and retyped the entire manuscript through its several rewritings and revisions and who, in the process of transcribing faithfully and accurately a great bulk of often nearly illegible material, frequently served in a kind of editorial capacity.

In view of the fact that when quoting from early sources we have retained the original spelling, punctuation and capitalizations, it may be parenthetically noted that if the usage often seems arbitrary and inconsistent it is because the writers of the time were themselves highly inconsistent.

FLEMING MACLIESH
MARTIN L. KRIEGER

Contents

Part Three: The Requiem Sharks

Part One

THE
PURSUERS

1

POINT
OF
DEPARTURE

ON AUGUST 2, 1708, two privately owned men-of-war sailed from King's Road, Bristol, bound first toward Cork. With their sailing, the great cruising voyages began again for the first time in England since the days of Elizabeth. But, in fact, there never was a voyage quite like this one.

There were, to begin with, two ships, both frigates, the *Duke* and the *Dutchess*. Each carried a commission in the form of Letters of Marque and General Reprisal from Prince George of Denmark, Lord High Admiral of England and husband of Queen Anne. They were out, under sealed orders known only to the captains, the owners and the Admiralty, to strike the Spanish and the French in the remote Pacific.

England had been at war for six years, allied with Austria, Holland and, later, Portugal against France and Spain in the War of the Spanish Succession. War had become more or less inevitable when Louis XIV put his grandson, the Duke of Anjou, on the throne of Spain, as Philip V. This temporarily united two empires under the actual rule of Versailles, and upset, to say the least, the balance of power in Europe. The precipitating event was the occupation of Spanish fortresses in The Netherlands by French troops; a contributing factor was Louis' public recognition of James Stuart as the legitimate King of England.

The war had so far largely been fought in Europe. The guns of Blenheim and Ramillies could still, in a sense, be heard, with Malplaquet yet to come; and the slaughter, for those times, had been terrible. But if the war had been fought in Europe and European waters, it was also, as Louis said, a war for the trade of the Indies, a term which then included Spanish America.

The gold and silver of Mexico and Peru, the riches of the Orient funneling through the entrepôt of Manila, almost solely and entirely financed the Franco-Spanish war effort. Any Englishman who could hit the enemy there, in that area of seventy-odd million square miles known as the Great South Sea, could be certain of substantially helping his country and would also stand a good chance of getting rich himself.

The *Duke* was a ship of 320 tons, mounted thirty guns, and had, at the time of clearing from King's Road, a crew of 117 men. The *Dutchess*, somewhat smaller, was of 260 tons, with twenty-six guns, and a crew of 108. Both ships had been particularly designed and adapted for their mission. Both were three-masters, frigate-built. As frigates they corresponded to what would be cruisers in our day, and at the time of their launching were equivalent to fifth-rate and sixth-rate men-of-war of the Royal Navy.

As they sailed from Bristol, they flew the Union Jack and the Red Jack of the privateer. Privateers had been, and would continue to be, described—particularly by the Royal Navy—as pirates operating with a license. But this expedition attacked no neutral ports and shipping, much less allied ones, and it scrupulously adhered throughout its operations to all the Articles of War and the commissions it had been given. Furthermore, in the greater part of the seas for which it was bound—seas still largely unknown—no Royal Navy ship had ever yet sailed, and none would for more than another thirty years.

A young man named Woodes Rogers, of considerable experience and exceptional ability, commanded the expedition and was captain of the *Duke*. He had made the original proposal and drawn up the first plans for the voyage. But a lot of backing was needed, capital to build and equip the ships and underwrite the costs of the expedition; investors had to be convinced of some possibility of success—solid citizens, businessmen, professional men, men of property, who had no intention of risking their necks on any venture and would not risk a pound without the prospect of large returns.

This was to be a raid on Spanish possessions and Spanish commerce in the Great South Sea. Even the Spaniards, who knew most about the Pacific, did not know much; and nobody, temporary enemy or temporary ally, had succeeded since the days of Elizabeth in accomplishing what this expedition proposed to do.

However, Rogers, his officers and the other captains had prepared themselves long and carefully and planned well. They unmistakably understood what the chances were and what they were about.

The matter was clinched for the last cautious speculator when, in March of 1708, Parliament passed a new Prize Act. Formerly the Crown had demanded a fifth of the profits of all privateering voyages, then reduced that to a tenth. Now it renounced any percentage; everything went to the owners and private investors, with a smaller share for the captains and chief officers, and a still smaller share for the crews.

The financing and fitting out of the *Duke* and *Dutchess* was accordingly underwritten by a few prominent citizens of Bristol, then the second city in England. Their investment, for the times, was heavy; but the promise of returns was enormous. Rogers had persuaded them, and though they did not, as owners, altogether trust him— they set up an elaborate system of checks and balances— they were fortunate in him as commander. He knew how to lead men and how to hold them together, his discipline was strict but never harsh, and he looked scrupulously to the needs, interests and well-being of those who served under him.

Rogers rarely lost his temper, did not boast, and could not be swayed in his opinion by flattery. Conventionally religious, he was tolerant of others' convictions, and always allowed his prisoners full liberty of worship, including the services of their priests, which was rare at that period. Moderate but not mild; humane but decisive in action, which he could plan and execute brilliantly, he had, together with a fine, dry sense of humor, a high degree of moral and physical courage.

During one engagement he saw the younger brother he loved killed before his eyes, "to my unspeakable sorrow," but did not falter in the action or in his responsibility to the men he led. Later, in another sea fight, he had part of his jaw shot away and, lying in blood on the deck where he had fallen, continued to fight his ship by writing out his commands.

At the time of this voyage he was about thirty. Three years earlier in London he had married the eighteen-year-old daughter of Rear-Admiral Sir William Whetstone, of Bristol, Commander-in-Chief of the West Indies. If the marriage was advantageous to a young seaman who was listed simply as "Mariner" and "Merchant," there is no reason to suppose it was simply opportunistic. His family had been prominent in the affairs of Bristol for several generations, and his father before him had followed a career at sea.

Rogers was, of course, neither a poet nor a philosopher and no more deeply reflective than the rest of the age of reason, but, like so many in his age, he wrote very good English prose, and he wrote about what he knew. His account of this expedition, published in London in 1712 as *A Cruising Voyage Round the World,* went into several editions, was translated abroad, and became the most popular book of voyages of the time. He sat, with his son and daughter, for a portrait by Hogarth. Addison and Steele were among his friends. It was said that even the Spaniards he fought never parted with him on anything but good terms.

The second ranking officer on board the *Duke* was not a seaman at all but a graduate physician of Oxford and Cambridge, Thomas Dover, who ranked as a second captain.

Captain-Doctor-Pirate Dover, as he was sometimes called by his contemporaries, had been to sea before on several voyages to Africa and the West Indies—voyages about which little is known except that they were apparently profitable. There is a darkness here which is not merely the darkness of obscurity; somewhere in the back-

ground there is the telltale, abominable stench of the
blackbirder—in keeping with the coasts for which he
sailed and the fact that one of the chief sources of the
prosperity of Bristol was the slave trade.

Dover abandoned a long-established and highly lucrative medical practice ashore to sail with Rogers. Even
so, this hardly qualified a man to be ranked as a captain,
the commander of all the marines and president of the
ship's council, who knew next to nothing about navigation and nothing about handling a ship or commanding
military operations ashore. What did conspicuously qual-
ify him was the fact that he had been one of the principal
investors, the second largest, in the whole enterprise.

That he insisted on going along and in such a capacity, rather than sit safely ashore and wait for his dividends,
if any, is an indication of his character.

He was a solid citizen, and at the same time an ad-
venturer; contentious, imaginative, intelligent, obstinate
and intractable, a man of stature and reputation, so rash
—or alternatively so mulish—in his opinions and actions
as to endanger everyone and everything; courageous but
scarcely likable, endowed with the conviction, shared by
so many physicians before and after him, that he knew
practically everything there was to be known about everything.

As a physician, however, he was certainly ahead of his
time, and in an age of incredible quackery whose remedies
included concoctions of ground-up vipers, bat's dung and
the saliva of a fasting man, he developed a specific, Dover's
powder, which was in general use until a few years ago
and is still prescribed today.

The smaller frigate, the *Dutchess*, was commanded
by Stephen Courtney, a gentleman of "birth, fortune and
very valuable qualities." Earlier in the war Courtney had
been captain of a 220-ton, sixteen-gun privateer, the *Reso-*

lution, which operated successfully in European waters. He had contributed a considerable sum toward the costs of the present voyage and took an active share in it, partly, it was said, "that he might see how it was managed, and be able either to prevent miscarriages, or at least to make a faithful report of them." He was a highly capable officer, had an amiable disposition and appears to have been very well liked.

His second-in-command was Captain Edward Cooke, a mariner who had lost to the French a couple of ships, of which he was commander and part owner, and suffered a good deal at the hands of French privateers cruising out of Dunkirk. Cooke, too, could write, though not as well as Rogers, and he, too, kept a journal, later published in London as *A Voyage to the South Sea and Round the World.*

The impression is that of an experienced and efficient seaman and executive officer—honest, level-headed and observant. More stolid than Rogers', his account lacks Rogers' color, humor and eye for important details; but it does present what happened when, in a somewhat clearer and more chronological sequence. (Rogers is inclined to jump around and often includes under the heading of one date, as a sort of afterthought but without noting the fact, something that actually took place many days earlier.)

In any event, Cooke's journal is a companion piece to Rogers' and complements it. The two together—since Cooke's account presents actions and events as viewed from the decks of the *Dutchess*—give the effect of a sort of binocular vision.

Rogers, Courtney, Dover, Cooke—these were the principals, all but one and that one notable anywhere; the only one, aside from Hogarth's painting of Rogers, of whom a contemporary portrait has come down. He was William Dampier, the expedition's pilot, whose picture by Thomas Murray hangs in the National Portrait Gallery.

Dampier was certainly, at the time they set out, the most famous, strange, varied and colorful of them all—the foremost navigator, explorer and hydrographer in England and perhaps in the world.

He was also a naturalist, botanist, zoölogist, anthropologist and historian; and very little of everything he learned was learned from schools. He had already made his way twice around the world and been three times to the South Sea. As a young man he had crossed the Isthmus of Darien with the buccaneers—. . . *knee deep in the salt marsh, heaving a cutlass,/Bitten by flies, fought*—and cruised the western Pacific with the first pirates to break into those waters. After a brief period in the West Indies and Virginia, he joined another buccaneer task force, sailed around the Horn and into the Pacific again, where, under various captains, he raided and explored for several more years. He sailed to Guam; languished on Mindanao; was marooned on the Nicobar Islands in the Indian Ocean; made gunpowder for the Christian missionaries in Tonkin.

And through all this, in the free moments of happy uproar when the men he was with were boozing and whoring and gambling and quarreling, he carefully redrew the maps and set down those notes and observations which he kept in a watertight bamboo tube and which were to interest ordinary men, literary men, seamen, scientists and specialists for a couple of centuries to come; observations on winds, tides, currents, charts, magnetic variations, on men, plants, mammals, reptiles and fish.

Dampier returned to England from these adventures in 1691, after an absence of twelve years, and published the first volume of his *Voyages*, which Masefield has called the best book on voyages in the English language. He dined with Samuel Pepys and John Evelyn, and kissed the hand of Queen Anne. In his own time his books were combed by Defoe and Addison and Steele and, above all, by Swift.

The very beginning of *Gulliver's Travels* speaks of "my cousin, Dampier." And his fame and his influence extended far beyond his own time. James Cook, the great explorer of the Pacific, studied him; so did Lord Nelson. Sir Walter Scott read him with delight and, writing of Gulliver, said, "The character of the imaginary traveller is exactly that of Dampier, or any other sturdy wanderer of the period, endowed with courage and common sense." Coleridge said of him that he was a man "of exquisite mind." And as a naturalist he influenced Charles Darwin.

Sensitive, brilliant, original, spare, strange, and, in respect of fortune, fickle. He planned great enterprises that would make him rich, and returned from all his voyages with next to nothing. He dreamed of taking ships loaded with pearls and silk and ingots of silver and chests of gold, and kept capturing prizes loaded with tons of marmalade.

It was not only his luck. He could not handle men or enforce proper discipline—such discipline as he administered was sporadic, gratuitous, often disproportionate—and he frequently proved himself in moments of crisis fatally irresolute. After his days of buccaneering and the first publication of the *Voyages*, he received command of a King's ship, the *Roebuck*, and was sent on an expedition around the Cape of Good Hope to explore Terra Australia Incognita.

It was not a happy ship or a happy voyage; nevertheless, Dampier discovered all that was to be known for another hundred years about the west and northwest coasts of Australia.

He also discovered New Britain and a number of smaller islands, the Straits of Dampier, the Dampier Archipelago, Shark's Bay and Roebuck Bay. On the return voyage the ship was in such rotten condition that she sank at anchor off Ascension Island, in the middle of the South Atlantic. Dampier and his crew were marooned on Ascension for five weeks. When he got back to England, he was court-martialed by the Admiralty and found, because of his treatment of one of his chief officers, unfit ever to command a King's ship again.

His fame, however, was brighter than ever. His *Discourse on the Trade Winds,* published in 1699, had proved him the most informed mariner of his day. Meanwhile the War of the Spanish Succession had just begun. Dampier was put in command of two privateers, the *St. George,* of which he was captain, and the *Cinque Ports,* captained by a choleric type named Stradling. They sailed down through the South Atlantic, around Cape Horn and up the coasts of Chile and Peru. Abandoned, after a series of quarrels, by Stradling and the *Cinque Ports,* Dampier operated in the Pacific fairly effectively for a period but eventually his ship, honeycombed by marine worms, sank under him. He and his crew transferred to a captured vessel and crossed the Pacific to the Dutch East Indies, where they were all thrown into prison as pirates because Dampier had lost his commission along the way.

That cruise was almost uniformly referred to as Dampier's "late unfortunate" or "last disastrous" voyage. He had been back in England about a year when he was offered the position of navigator for the *Duke* and the *Dutchess.* He was fifty-six and he accepted—fortunately for him and fortunately for everybody else concerned, in view of his skill as a navigator and the fact that he knew at first-hand and from long experience all the coasts and oceans toward which they were headed.

These then were the chief officers and these were the ships—horribly overcrowded, overloaded with a weight of

guns and cargo and too-tall masts and too much canvas—
the *Duke* herself the bigger, barely eighty feet long in
keel length and twenty-five feet in beam, not much larger
than a big boat.

The Bristol privateers intended, before they were
through, to circumnavigate the globe, for the third time in
the history of England, following Drake and Cavendish;
for the sixth time in the known history of the world, following Magellan.

They intended, against enormous odds, to break into
the Pacific and harry Spain there, to strike at least some
of her towns, to raid her shipping. They hoped to add to
the hydrographic, topographic and navigational knowledge of their time and to reopen the major part of the
Pacific to English enterprise and exploration.

They hoped, and by no means incidentally, to capture
a prize so fabulous, so wrapped in purposeful confusion
and misrepresentation, that its true value was beyond accurate calculation; it was, at any rate, the richest prize of
any ship on any ocean of the world.

They had prepared themselves long and carefully;
they had mastered all the information available to them
and studied extensively the accounts of others who had
probed before them into the Great South Sea—yet the
outcome of the least they intended and hoped to do was
highly problematical, wildly uncertain.

The voyage, the attempt itself, would have considerable repercussions in its own age and influence many different fields of human endeavor. Among the indirect and
unforeseeable consequences, it would affect, if not alter,
the course of the English novel and provide the central
character in one of the most popular stories ever written;
it would also be indirectly responsible for one of the biggest financial bubbles of all time—a bubble whose cata-

strophic collapse nearly wrecked the economy of all England.

This voyage was launched in an age full of savagery and cruelty and much misery everywhere, an age which could nevertheless not afford to look too deeply into all that, if it were still to retain its pretensions to a noble objectivity, classic, Augustan. It was an age that produced among its leading figures many conspicuous madmen who at all points praised the rational; an age that always considered it better not to look awkwardly too far down or up but to trust to the safe planking and keel beneath, of reason and order and logical procedures.

These voyagers would encounter terror and devastation and violent death, nightmares and delusion and despair of mind; they would confront the unknown and the unnamable. But it did not pay to reflect upon this too long, because the very act of contemplation might have incapacitated them entirely. The age, in that sense, upbore them. The depths were, of course, always present yet never profoundly scrutinized.

But it began ordinarily and conventionally enough, as such crossings almost always begin, with a certain amount of natural disorder, a few elements of the always unpredictable, safely contained and neutralized in the logical anticipation of the odds. It began more or less by the book.

2

OUTWARD
PASSAGE

THE FIRST NIGHT OUT, in the Irish Sea, the *Dutchess* sighted
a possible prize, a large ship, and immediately gave chase.
By a stroke of luck she lost the enemy in the darkness. A
French warship, the *Jersey*, of forty-six guns, was reported
to be cruising between Ireland and England, and if they
had come up with her, anything might have happened,
because neither of the two frigates had been properly
shaken down. Rogers noted that they did not sail well, to
say the least: ". . . our Masts and Rigging being all unfit
for the Sea, our Ships out of trim, and everything in disorder, being very indifferently mann'd; and not with-
standing our Number, we had not 20 Sailors in the Ship,

and it's very little better on board the *Dutchess*, only we hope to get some good Sailors at Cork."

The crews were, indeed, mixed. About a third were foreigners of various nationalities; and among Her Majesty's subjects could be counted: "Tinkers, Taylors, Haymakers, Peddlers, Fidlers," plus one, John Finch, "late wholesale Oilman of London." This closely knit group included a pet bulldog, apocryphally known as Lord Harry, who was later to engage in a foot race with the most famous castaway in history.

At Cork a number of their problems were solved— after they finally got there, having overshot the port and being delayed a day at anchor near Kinsale, off the two large rocks called the Sovereigns Bollacks, presumably christened before the time of Queen Anne. They reached Cork four days after clearing from King's Road, Bristol, and immediately several of the crew jumped ship, having already had enough of the nautical life in the drenching darkness below decks of wooden ships, bound on a voyage nobody knew how long, toward destinations known only to the officers and owners.

Many of the men who had been shipped were landsmen, as was inevitable at that period. A folio broadside, circa 1695, attributed most of the diseases of seamen to the fact that a quarter of all crews consisted of landsmen without "sea-legs and sea-stomachs," who "cannot forbear vomiting, nor have command of their legs to go upon the Deck and do it over the Gunnel of the ship, but empty themselves every way, either between Decks or in the Hold, to the great annoyance of all the rest of the Crew."

A number of these landsmen were now happily gone, some having jumped ship, others having been cleared out and replaced by better sailors recruited at Cork, while the frigates were overhauled and provisioning completed. Additional supplies were loaded and stowed in great amounts and variety: flour and water and meat, spare tackle and spars, needles and sails and wine, hammers and tongs and forges, wood, cables, canvas and tar, beer, butter, vegetables, thread, cloth, trade goods, staves, leather, grindstones, knives, saws, screwdrivers, awls, chisels, braces and bits, nuts, bolts and oakum, tallow pulleys and blocks, more powder and shot, and on and on.

The crews spent their time ashore swilling flip—beer laced with whiskey or rum, sweetened with sugar and heated; it is supposed to have got its name from a saying that after two pots of it a man could vault over the mizzenmast and after four pots, over the mainmast.

Going over the mainmast, suitably loaded, was presumably safe; but they did worse; they also spent the time vaulting or flipping into marriage. "Our Crew were continually marrying whilst we staid at *Cork*, they then expected to sail immediately. Among others there was a *Dane*, coupled by a Romish priest to an Irish Woman, without understanding a word of each other's Language, so that they were forc'd to use an Interpreter; yet I perceived this Pair seem'd more afflicted at Separation than any of the rest; the Fellow continu'd melancholy for several days after we were at Sea. The rest understanding each other, drank their Cans of Flip till the last minute, concluded with a Health to our good Voyage, and their happy Meeting, and then parted unconcern'd."

They sailed from Cork on September 1st, proceeding in a convoy with one of Her Majesty's men-of-war, the *Hastings*, until they were clear of British and French waters. "We had now about double the number of Officers usual in Privateers, and a large Complement of Men to each Ship." They had, in fact, 100 more men in the crews than they sailed with from Bristol. "We took this Method of doubling our Officers to prevent Mutinies, which often happen in long Voyages, and that we might have a large

Provision for a succession of Officers in each Ship, in case of Mortality."

Mortalities, of course, there were bound to be, and mutinies also. Just as, before very long, the water in the casks would stink, the peas would be full of maggots, the dried beef would be hard as mahogany (tobacco boxes could, in fact, be made from it: it had the color of mahogany and took the same high polish), the biscuits would be full of weevils. Sailors banged their biscuit against anything handy to knock the insects loose; and, after a decent interval at sea, anyone finding a weevil-free biscuit threw it overboard, the incontrovertible fact being that if it wasn't fit for weevils, it wasn't fit for men.

The *Duke* and *Dutchess*, after the repairs and overhaul at Cork, with cargo and gear properly stowed, and better manned, now sailed well, just as well as the man-of-war, which pleased Rogers, particularly since he quoted: "Our Holds are full of Provisions; our Cables, a great deal of Bread and Water-casks between Decks: and 183 Men aboard the *Duke*, with 151 aboard the *Dutchess*; so that we are very much crouded and pester'd Ships. . . ."

Crowded and pestered. In his book on Cape Horn, Felix Reisenberg notes that the great clipper ship, *Edward Sewell*, with a displacement of 6,000 tons at loaded draft, was manned by a crew of twenty hands, and points out that Drake's *Pelican* later rechristened the *Golden Hind*, with a displacement of about 200 tons and a crew of eighty-seven, would have had, on a comparable basis, a crew of two thousand. On a comparable basis, the *Duke*, if she had displaced the tonnage of the great clipper, would have been manned by 3,395 men.

But these frigates needed not only an extra complement of officers to handle mutinies, as Rogers explained: not only men to replace those who would inevitably die by accident and disease and in battle, but men to undertake landing assaults while others guarded the ships, and men to serve as prize crews for all the vessels they hoped to capture.

On the evening of September 5th, the frigates parted company from the *Hastings* and the rest of the convoy. A small galley, headed for Madeira, sailed with them to be under their protection. Before leaving the convoy, the officers at last let the men know that they were bound for Cape Horn and the Pacific—"that if any Disorders should have risen upon it, we might have exchang'd our Malcontents whilst in Company with one of her Majesty's Ships. But I found no Complaint on board the *Duke*, except from one Fellow who expected to have been Tything-man that year in his Parish, and said his wife would be oblig'd to pay Forty Shillings in his Absence; but seeing all the rest willing, he was easily quieted, and all hands drank to a good Voyage."

With the number of toasts that had apparently been going round ever since they left Cork, it is not surprising that they presently found themselves running low on liquor. Considering the length of the voyage ahead of them, the various climates they would pass through, and the excessive cold around Cape Horn, they decided to head for Madeira to lay in some stores.

The business of fortifying themselves against the Horn went on for quite a while. A little later they decided to "cruise among the Canary Islands for Liquor." Two weeks after leaving the Canaries, they were laying in casks of brandy at the Cape Verde Islands; and by the time they got to Brazil, the supply had just about run out again. "Seamen," said Samuel Pepys, when he was Secretary of the Admiralty, "love their bellies above everything else." And Rogers noted that though the men were "but meanly clad, yet good Liquor to Sailors is preferable to Clothing."

En route to Madeira they overhauled and captured their first prize and were treated to their first mutiny, only nine days out of Cork. The prize was a twenty-two gun ship flying Swedish colors and said to be carrying contraband: gunpowder and cables. However, no contraband could be found aboard, and to take the vessel into a harbor where it could be determined whether or not she were a legitimate prize would have cost them time they could not afford. Rogers, therefore, "let her go without the least Embezelment," after he and her captain, a Scots-Irishman, had exchanged courtesies and presents of hams, dried beef and cider.

Sailors on the *Duke*, led by the boatswain and three petty officers, at once mutinied, claiming the prize was theirs by right and demanding that it be given them to plunder. Rogers, unlike Dampier in similar circumstances, settled "this Disorder" fast. He broke out arms for his chief officers, secured the quarter-deck and poop, had one of the ringleaders whipped and, along with nine others, tossed into irons, where he kept them to cool off on bread and water.

He knew very well the long, sad history of previous voyages where the captains had compromised or vacillated; and ahead of these men, who had as yet undergone nothing, endured nothing, there lay some thirty or forty thousand terrible sea-miles, where effective discipline would mean the difference between life and death for everyone.

The crew of the *Dutchess*, who were also stirred up and making threatening gestures, quieted down immediately when they saw what happened on board the *Duke*. But there were still, though the back of this first mutiny had been broken, a few lingering spasms. A number of the men came up to Rogers with a demand that the boatswain, the original ringleader, be freed at once. The spokesman was soundly whipped and the rest tossed into irons with the other mutineers. In a few days, upon their promise of correction, all of them were released and reinstated. Rogers had also intended to reinstate the boatswain, Giles Cash; but Cash continued intractable and was a focal point for trouble. He was therefore kept in irons and put aboard the accompanying galley headed for Madeira, when the *Duke* and *Dutchess,* faced with contrary winds and a further loss of time, decided to by-pass Madeira and proceed to the Canary Islands.

Rogers had reason to be happy about his additional complement of officers. "This Mutiny would not have been easily lay'd, were it not for the number of our Officers, which we begin to find very necessary to bring our Crew to Order and Discipline."

Some, like his younger brother, John Rogers, second lieutenant on board the *Dutchess,* were capable and courageous and could be counted on, as could others, like Samuel Hopkins, an apothecary, who was Thomas Dover's nephew, served as Dover's assistant aboard ship and also as his lieutenant on landing parties. Hopkins was a quiet man, with a certain quiet piety—if actual piety can be anything else; not canting, not proselytizing, unobtrusive. He endured what he had to endure to the end, and remained cheerful.

But there were several officers whom Rogers presumably would not have deeply missed if they had been washed overboard in a heavy sea, or fallen from the maintopgallant mast (except that they never went aloft).

One of these was Carleton Vanbrugh, merchant, the agent and representative of the owners. Vanbrugh was pompous and callous; a businessman inflated with self-importance, who could not help acting the fool when out of his element and who lacked any sense of humor; a man of audits and annual reports and returns per share on investments risked; a man who was overbearing and inept, who confused mere violence and heartlessness with aptitude in action; an apoplectic, unintentional clown who later turned murderous when laughed at. He was not fit for the sea and whatever there was of his character deteriorated rapidly, at least in the beginning.

He precipitated himself into trouble almost at once— two days, in fact, after the remaining mutineers had been discharged from their irons. On September 18th, when the ships were in sight of the Peak of Teneriffe, the *Dutchess* overhauled and captured a small Spanish bark which proved to be a legitimate prize. There were some forty-six passengers on board the bark, bound out of Oratava on Teneriffe for the Island of Forteventura. For some unaccountable reason these passengers labored under the acute misapprehension that they had been captured by Turks, and were immensely relieved to find that they had merely fallen into the hands of the English.

Rogers stood in for Oratava to see what he could get by way of ransom for the bark, after appropriating her small cargo, which consisted of two butts of wine and a hogshead of brandy. "Amongst these Prisoners were four Fryars, and one of them the Padre Guardian for the Island of *Forteventura*, a good honest old Fellow. We made him heartily merry, drinking King *Charles* the Third's Health." As for the others, Rogers bleakly noted: "the rest were of the wrong sort." Charles III was that Austrian Archduke the English-Dutch coalition had proposed putting on the throne of Spain in place of the Bourbon incumbent, Philip V.

The ships came to anchor at Oratava the following day. The master of the Spanish bark and a few prisoners were sent ashore with the ransom demands. Carleton Vanbrugh insisted, against Rogers' objections, on going with them in order that negotiations might have the incalculable benefit of his personal supervision. The minute Vanbrugh stepped out of the boat he was seized by the local authorities and locked up.

These authorities at Oratava then sent word to Rogers that unless the bark and remaining prisoners were freed and returned to them at once, Mr. Vanbrugh, merchant, man of affairs, would—as far as anyone could tell—languish in durance vile for the rest of his unnatural life.

They also contended that—according to agreements in their possession made by Queen Anne, by His Catholic Majesty, and by the most gracious Christian King—the seizure of the bark had been completely unwarranted and illegal and, what was worse, would prove very bad for trade.

This letter was signed by four Englishmen in the town, among them the Vice-Consul, who were equally concerned about reprisals against themselves and their businesses. Rogers and Courtney replied: "We have yours and observe its contents; but having no Instructions given us with our Commission relating to *Spanish* Vessels trading among these Islands, we can't justify the parting with this Bark on your single Opinions. It was Mr. *Vanbrugh's* misfortune to go ashore; and if he is detain'd we can't help it . . . If Mr. *Vanbrugh* is unjustly detain'd we'll carry the Prisoners we have on board to the Port we are bound to, let the Consequence be what it will . . . We shall wait but a short time for an Answer, having Water and Provisions for ourselves and our Prisoners to the *English* Settlements, where we are bound . . . Your Humble Servants, *Woodes Rogers, Stephen Courtney.*"

They were not, of course, bound for any English settlements at all, but Spanish intelligence functioned quite efficiently enough in all the ports of Europe and all along their route without making things easy for it.

The town continued to delay, trying to prolong negotiations until a large Spanish ship and a smaller vessel, which were expected, might come up. Another day went by. That night Rogers warned the negotiators that if they didn't come to terms, he would sail, and, before clearing the harbor, "tho' we could not land our Men, would visit the Town with our Guns by Eight next Morning . . ."

That settled it. Bright and early, and well before eight, a boat put out from shore carrying wine, grapes, hogs and other necessaries for the ransom of the bark— also carrying Carleton Vanbrugh, and one of the English merchants at Oratava, a J. Crosse, who supervised the exchange.

The prisoners were given back such of their personal belongings as could be found—"particularly to the Fryars, their Books, Crucifixes, and Reliques. We presented the old *Padre* Guardian with a Cheese, such as were strip'd, with other Clothes. So that we parted very well satisfy'd on all sides. Mr. *Crosse* told us the *Spaniards* ashore were very inquisitive whither we were bound; and understanding by the Prisoners, that our Ships were sheath'd and so full of Provisions, they suspected we design'd for the South-Sea: and he inform'd us that four or five French Ships, from 24 to 50 guns, sail'd thence about a month before on the same Voyage. But we did not think fit to own there, that we were bound to any other place than the *English West-Indies*."

This large French squadron was to be a looming menace for months to come—its position unknown, its orders enveloped in mystery—a menace that hung always a point below the horizon, and might at any moment come blindly up on them. Now it had proceeded on its way. It had been swallowed up in the enormous distances and ambiguity of the ocean—as they, too, were about to be swallowed up—but as they neared their objectives, the courses would converge; and then hour by hour, over a period of weeks and months, they would have to be constantly prepared.

Vanbrugh hadn't any room in his head for all that, at the moment. He got back on board boiling; he had spent two days and a night in confinement, when, by simply giving in to the Spaniards' demands, Rogers could have freed him, and—what was even more unthinkable—the dickering had reached the point of threats to sail without him. He had been made a cat's-paw, a pawn; he had been lightly regarded. He wanted Rogers censured by the council—which consisted of the chief officers and representatives of the crews of both ships. The council unanimously voted—Rogers and Vanbrugh abstaining—to censure Vanbrugh. He was to be up before it a number of times, and with even worse results, before his race was run.

The council itself had been set up by the owners in Bristol and incorporated in the "Constitution" of the voyage: all major decisions, "all Attempts, Attacks and Designs upon the Enemy," as well as all "Discontents, Differences, or Misbehavior," had to be submitted to it for majority Vote.

The advantages and disadvantages of this arrangement were fairly balanced. As a democratic body it prevented usurpation of power by a single individual; the owners recognized that anyone with the habit of power, even Rogers, begins to grow intolerant not only of any restrictions put upon his use of it but even, eventually, of any major differences in judgment or opinion with his own. The council also prevented any small clique or faction among the officers taking over and diverting the expedition to missions and adventures—for example, plain piracy —never intended or authorized by the owners. Finally, it served as an outlet for grievances and resentments which otherwise might simmer and steam and explode into wholesale mutiny. The will of a ship's captain at sea was absolute enough, and these men were to be at sea for more than three years.

The disadvantages of the council were the familiar ones of unwieldiness and divided counsels at moments when speed of decision and action were essential. Often Rogers' hands were tied by the margin of one vote; often by the same margin, a plan or course of action, which he and his better officers knew to be the only strategically sound and practical one, was shelved in favor of some harebrained design which brought "Enterprises of great Pith and Moment" to next to nothing. If, therefore, the council played a major part in the success of the voyage, it was also responsible for many fumbled opportunities and for most of the conspicuous failures.

Captain-Doctor Thomas Dover had two votes. Everybody else—Rogers, Courtney, Dampier, Cooke, Vanbrugh and the other seven members—had one. Dover got two because he was president of the council. He did not, obviously, achieve this eminence through sheer popularity or experience. He achieved it because he was the second largest shareholder in the expedition and by far the largest one afloat—having put into the venture 3,312 pounds, which was then a tidy fortune. Where did he get it? There is, again, a darkness in the background, and the whiff is a whiff of the slave ship that, when to windward at sea, could be smelled miles away. But Dover also had a lucrative practice; and successful and capable physicians enjoyed considerable status and big incomes. A contemporary, Dr. John Radcliffe, at one point dropped 5,000 pounds of the realm—an enormous sum then—in some West Indian venture and dismissed the loss, saying that he had only to climb so many flights of stairs to make himself whole again. He left endowments for two medical traveling fellowships, for building the Radcliffe observatory, hospital and library at Oxford and for enlarging St. Bartholomew's Hospital in London.

Another contemporary, Richard Mead, had a library of 10,000 volumes in his house in Great Ormond Street and exchanged extravagant gifts with the kings of Naples and France. Still another, the famous Irishman, Sir Hans Sloane, a friend of Dover, Rogers and Dampier, was the first medical practitioner to receive a hereditary title, bought the manor of Chelsea and, through that, gave his name to a street and a square in London; he accumulated such an enormous collection of books, art and antiques that when he bequeathed it to the nation, it became the foundation of the British Museum.

Dover's practice, in the period preceding this voyage, was of course in Bristol, not London; but Bristol being then the second port as well as second city in England, its prosperity was prodigious. And in Bristol he did not have to face competition from men of his own caliber—if, indeed, there were any of quite that caliber anywhere.

He was sure of himself, to say the least, and independent in judgment. But the very qualities and abilities that made him a success ashore and in his own profession also worked, at sea, in a kind of reverse. The courage of his convictions became, in matters about which he knew next to nothing, plain, ruinous obstinacy; the faith in himself, in his own knowledge and experience, became faith in opinions rooted in ignorance and intemperately sustained against all reason and logic; and the general all-around courage with which, whatever his faults, he was certainly endowed, became mere headlong recklessness—proceeding from the absurd to the nearly fatal.

At the moment, however, all was serene, and the council functioned smoothly. The ships cleared from Oratava on September 23rd and set course for the Cape Verde

Islands, to lay in water, wood and other supplies against the long haul across the South Atlantic.

On September 26th they crossed the Tropic of Cancer. "This day, according to custom, we duck'd those that had never pass'd the Tropick before. The manner of doing it was by a Rope thro a Block from the Main-Yard, to hoist 'em above half way up to the Yard, and let 'em fall at once into the Water; having a Stick cross thro their Legs; and well fastned to the Rope, that they might not be surpriz'd and let go their hold. This prov'd of great use to our fresh-water Sailors, to recover the Colour of their Skins which were grown very black and nasty."

About sixty men were plunged into the briny. Others bought off, those who refused the ducking being obliged to pay half a crown apiece into a common fund which was being built up to underwrite a mammoth beer, gin and rum celebration when the crews returned to England. A number of the Dutch and English sailors had themselves dropped overboard eight, ten and even twelve times to build up credit and their shares in the treat—though the long-range odds against any single one of them surviving to collect were fairly high.

And inevitably the accidents, the fatal mischances, had begun. On September 29th there is a brief entry: "Betwixt nine and ten at night, a Sailor going up to furl the Main-Top-Gallant Sail, fell suddenly without any noise from the Main-Top over board, occasion'd as I suppos'd by a Fit . . . fair Weather, smooth Water, fresh Gales at N.E. Lat. 17. 5. N. Long. W, from London 23.16."

The following day they anchored in the Bay of St. Vincent, one of the Cape Verde Islands owned by Portugal, their ally. Here they could buy provisions in just about the variety and quantity needed, and from nearby St. Antonio they obtained water, wood, limes, tobacco, poultry, potatoes, bananas, oranges, brandy.

The value of citrus fruits and fresh vegetables in preventing or curing scurvy was not yet recognized and would not be for almost another fifty years, until the famous Royal Navy physician, James Lind, published his work establishing their anti-scorbutic effect. And even after that—while the mortality rate from scurvy continued higher than the combined mortality from battles, wrecks, accidents, other diseases—in fact from all other casualties of the sea put together—the Admiralty waited a further forty years, until 1795, before issuing rations of lemon juice to the British Navy. Yet sour juices had been advised by Solomon Albert in 1593; and in the same year Sir Richard Hawkins cured his crew of scurvy with lemon juice.

It is likely that Rogers and his captains—almost certainly, Dover—knew of these and other precedents. Wherever they could, they stocked up plentifully on vegetables and fruits, and at sea Rogers was continually recommending punch as a preventative therapy; the punch, of course, was well and properly laced, but its indispensable vehicle and base was fruit juice.

In any case, they knew and applied much that their predecessors and contemporaries ignored. And it was one of the great advantages of the expedition that its captains were more or less free to use the best knowledge and experience available.

The squadron may have lacked, to a degree, the organization and discipline of the Navy; Rogers complained about that sometimes. On the other hand, it was not tradition-bound, rule-bound, wrapped in prejudice and red tape; imagination and intelligence were at a premium. Embarked on an operation no Royal Navy ship had yet attempted, this force was commanded by resourceful and inquiring minds, who had read just about everything available on every subject that was in any way connected with their voyage and its objectives and who were at liberty to apply what they knew.

The loading continued; more limes, melons, oranges, hogs, fish, tortoise and black cattle. Dampier had been here before, as he had been to just about every other harbor and coast they were to reach. About one of the Cape Verdes, Mayo, he had written: "The inhabitants of this Island, even their Governour and Padres, are all Negro's, Wool-pated like their African Neighbors, from whom it is like they are descended; tho' being subjects to the Portugueze, they have their Religion and Language. They are stout, lusty, well-limb'd people, both Men and Women, fat and fleshy; and they and their Children as round and plump as little Porposes . . ."

And again, concerning immensely valuable ambergris: "We stay'd here three days: in which time one of These Portuguese offered to some of our Men a Lump of Ambergreece in exchange for some cloathes, desiring them to keep it secret, for he said if the Governor should know it, he should be hanged. At length, one Mr. Coppinger, bought for a small matter; yet I believe he gave more than it was worth. We had not a man in the ship that knew Ambergreece; but I have since seen it in other Places, and am therefore certain it was not right. It was of a dark color, like Sheeps Dung, and very soft, but of no smell, and possibly 'twas some of their Goats Dung."

Rogers' officers and crew made out better than Dampier's, by and large. However, they lost their linguist, a man named Joseph Alexander, proficient in at least two tongues, who went ashore to negotiate the buying of provisions and never came back. This was the first time the man's feet had hit land since Cork, and for him that was it; he had all he was ever going to want of *Roll on, thou deep and dark blue ocean, roll!*

Even after the ships were ready to sail again, Rogers

and Courtney waited for him and kept sending him messages to come aboard, but from the purlieus into which he had crept, Joseph Alexander returned no word; eyeing the safe, dry, motionless prospect of these islands, he maintained a crafty and impenetrable silence.

They gave up and abandoned him: ". . . we consulted with the Officers of both Ships, and all unanimously agreed, that we had better leave him behind, than to wait with two ships for one man that had not followed his Orders."

They weighed anchor on October 8th. But first they had a meeting of the council to make rules about plunder and proportionate shares—something which had not yet been properly settled and which had caused considerable friction among the crews after taking the small ship ransomed at Oratava. The original agreement drawn up by the owners ashore proved—as any such instrument drafted ashore by parties exclusively interested in their own maximum profits was bound to prove—somewhat inadequate and unrealistic at sea. As for the men, "They all insisted that there was never any Privateers Crew hinder'd from Plunder, so that we were forc'd to agree on the following Instrument of a Dividend, when we should meet with any Prize . . . For we found it would be next to a miracle to keep the Men in both Ships under Command and willing to fight resolutely on occasion, if we held 'em to the Letter of Agreement with the Owners, which was not duly consider'd of at home."

The council reserved to the chief officers and agents the right to determine what was plunder that individuals might keep for themselves and what belonged to the owners and the expedition as a whole. In the interest of general harmony, Rogers and Courtney gave up their right, as captains, to the cabin plunder, retaining only a 5 percent share.

Other stipulations included: ". . . that if any Person on board either Ship do conceal any Plunder exceeding one Piece of Eight in value, twenty-four hours after the Capture of any Prize, he shall be severely punish'd, and lose his Shares of the Plunder. The same penalty to be inflicted for being drunk in time of Action, or disobeying his superior Officer's Commands, or concealing himself, or deserting his Post in Sea or Land-Service; except when any Prize is taken by Storm in Boarding, then whatsoever is taken shall be his own, as followeth: A Sailor or Landman 10£. Any Officer below the Carpenter 20£. A Mate, Gunner, Boatswain, and Carpenter 40£. A Lieutenant or Master 70£. And the Captains 100£ over and above the gratuity promis'd by the Owners to such as shall signalize themselves . . .

"That a Reward of twenty Pieces of Eight shall be given to him that first sees a Prize of good Value, or exceeding 50 Tuns in Burden."

It was, considering what lay ahead, a very timely agreement for the morale of the crews. As Rogers noted, ". . . without their being easy, we must unavoidably have run into such continual Scenes of Mischief and Disorder, as have not only tended to the great Hindrance, but generally to the Total Disappointment of all Voyages of this nature, that have been attempted so far abroad in the Memory of Man."

They sailed from St. Vincent at seven o'clock in the evening. The *Dutchess* cleared the bay first and then stood by with a light until the *Duke* came up. The course was almost due south. Ahead of them, as the wind rose and they pitched and the stars tilted and swung, spread night and the Atlantic.

3

THE MERIDIAN OF ALEXANDER VI

A CONTEMPORARY COMPILATION of voyages, the famous and definitive *Harris' Voyages,* said of this one: "It has been universally allowed by such as are proper Judges of such Expeditions, that there never was any Voyage of this nature so happily adjusted, so well provided for in all respects, or in which the Accidents that usually happen to Privateers were so effectually guarded against."

In the great cabin of the *Duke,* under the swaying lanterns, the captains unrolled the maps. They had been over it all before. The main strategy, plans, procedures had all been carefully laid down far back in Bristol before the ships were even launched, and would have to have been, to convince the investors that they stood a chance.

In the cabin light, gently rising, falling, swinging, the scene must have been as it had been often before and would be often again: Rogers, Courtney, Dampier, Dover, perhaps Cooke, bent over the charts, studying, talking, fingers pointing, the compasses describing arcs. There was always a good deal of visiting among the chief officers of the two ships—for dinners, for conferences and return invitations; and the fact that they made these continual visits between ships in boats that had to be lowered and hoisted, often at night and often with high seas running, as a matter of course and without ever any serious accident or mischance, was no mean evidence of their seamanship.

Sailing south by west, they had now crossed that meridian drawn 370 leagues west of the Cape Verdes, by which the Borgia pope, Alexander VI, had divided the world, giving all newly discovered or unknown lands on one side of it to Spain and on the other to Portugal. From the time of Magellan, Spain had claimed the entire area of that major part of the Pacific known as the South Sea for her closed sea, or private pond.

A law issued in 1540, reiterated in 1558, 1560 and 1563, stated: "No foreign ships shall pass to the Indies and such as do shall be seized." In respect to operations in the Pacific, the interdict applied not only to European ships but to those of China and Japan as well. For European trade these nations dealt, or were told to deal, with Spain and through Spain at Manila, or not at all.

For more than two hundred years Spain monopolized the commerce and possessed the only halfway accurate charts and maps of an expanse of ocean extending north from the Philippines to the coasts of Japan, east across the high latitudes to the Americas, south to Cape Horn. In this area she was entrenched and almost impregnable; and as the first and chief line of defense for the sources of her wealth—for the gold and silver of Mexico and Peru: the silks, jewels, spices, cloths, manufactures of China, Japan and India—she counted on this enormous barrier of the seas, on the fact that few men and ships could survive the voyage required even to come against her, much less to operate there.

Rogers and his officers knew all about the odds and the alternatives; they had put in months or years of study, and Dampier, of course, knew them by experience. There sat Spain, secure in Manila, secure along the thousands of miles of west American coastline from Mexico to the tip of Chile, while the terrible distances of the misnamed Pacific heaved and foamed: and it was almost as if the subjects of his Catholic Majesty, Philip V, were saying in their complacency: "Come and try it."

There were, of course, only two sea routes. One was down around the Cape of Good Hope and up across the Indian Ocean. Any ship that got that far might refit and restock at the Dutch East Indies; but beyond there it was hopeless. How could anyone make the terrible eastward crossing of the Pacific, north from the Philippines to the high latitudes and east to what is now the coast of California—the longest unbroken voyage in the world—to attack American coasts and shipping? What chance, supposing that somehow, impossibly, such a ship succeeded, would she stand on arriving at the extremes of everything: men, food, water, seaworthiness, supplies—on a coast where there was no port or place open at all, everything barred and closed up tight to her like the bare cliffs and rocks?

The other route was down the South Atlantic and around South America. That meant, for ships weakened by rot and disease after months at sea, the weather of Cape Horn—with the most consistently violent seas in the world—or the Strait of Magellan with its winds, rocks and crosscurrents, in which some ships labored for weeks and many for months before being wrecked or turning back. And if one or two did break through, if storms, seas, rocks, rudimentary navigation and inaccurate maps didn't finish them, time and distance would. There were few if any places available and open to them off the Pacific coasts of Spanish America, to refit and careen spongy worm-eaten hulls, to lay in essential supplies of water and food and firewood: they would arrive at the same closed coasts, manned and alerted against them.

So, as the weeks and months passed, what was left of the brick-hard or maggot-filled food would run out. What was left of the poisonous water would run out. Time and distance, starvation, thirst, scurvy, dysentery, typhus and the other diseases would inexorably finish all who tried that way, as time and distance so often defeated or finished the Spaniards themselves, with all their advantages.

This could be counted on. And before that, even before it came to that, it was just about certain the survivors of crews subjected to the hell of such voyages would mutiny. Finally, there were overwhelmingly superior Spanish manpower and armament; squadrons based at Valparaíso and Callao and Panama, that could be launched against the solitary enemy operating in a hostile ocean without allies or bases or sources of supply.

But, obviously, the odds were not completely insuperable, the defenses not foolproof, as the Spaniards knew very well. More than a century earlier Drake had broken through, shaken and blasted them, and passed on —west across the Pacific to the Ladrones and on home. The treasure he brought back is said to have amounted to more than the entire annual budget for the Kingdom of

England at that time. Nine years later Cavendish made it, following Drake's route. They said that when Cavendish came up the English Channel his sails were of China silk.

After that, there were a few more attempts, but no more successes. The King's ocean was not seriously troubled by Englishmen for almost another hundred years.

The Dutch tried next, but after a few forays they, too, gave up, and stuck to their business empire around Batavia, where they distinguished themselves for greed, murder and oppression. And then there was nothing for years, no enemy anywhere on the Great South Sea, until the buccaneers appeared, crossing the Isthmus of Panama toward the end of the seventeenth century. The buccaneers were trouble all right; but trouble in more or less discontinuous packets, like the quanta of wave mechanics. They shot and slashed their way up and down the western coasts, sporadically, almost haphazardly, and they killed a number of people and took a number of ships; but the total dent in the Spanish economy was just about nil; and then the buccaneers, too, were gone with the closing of the century, back to the Caribbean, never to return.

The last threat had been Dampier in the *St. George*, but that hapless expedition was so poorly conducted that when everything was over and done with, it was, for the subjects of His Catholic Majesty, to laugh.

However, what had been done once or twice before could obviously be done again; and just to make assurance double sure, Spain had long ago established a highly organized and effective intelligence system in the principal ports of Europe and in several of those of the Far East, to give warning of any ship or ships that might be "designing against her in the Spanish Sea," before the attempt was even properly launched.

And still time was catching up. If the attempts had

been very few, and the successes even fewer, each one added something to general knowledge of the ocean and the coasts which the Spaniards wanted to keep wrapped in mystery and silence—a mystery so profound that even to probe for it would be like probing into a whistling nowhere.

The buccaneers in particular—precisely because their operations were so sporadic and haphazard—tried everything, went almost everywhere. And a few of them were not only literate but curious and observant. They kept records; they wrote reports. Dampier's *Voyages*, his charts and notes and observations, were, of course, outstanding. But others, too, published accounts with much valuable and supplementary information—Basil Ringrose, Bartholomew Sharp, Ambrose Cowley, Lionel Wafer, a surgeon. Wafer, in addition, at the request of the Duke of Marlborough, had drawn up around the year 1700 a secret memorandum on places fit for settlement in the South Sea.

These reports, observations, journals and memoranda Rogers and his officers had by heart. And what counted more, they had the principal author and observer standing there beside them in his long, dark-brown curling wig, in silk and lace and leather, with his long nose and dark, thoughtful eyes and long slender fingers—who could handle pistols and pen and sword, compass and quadrant, but could not handle men.

The same fingers pointed at the charts, most of which he had himself revised as long ago as when he dined with Samuel Pepys and John Evelyn "with a new map of the Pacific in his pocket"; the scene was as it had been, had to be, if not on this occasion then before, as it would be many times again: in substance if not in detail, since the facts no longer had to be spelled out for any of them.

There are a few key points left unaccountably open and undefended in the Great South Sea. And moving from one to another with care and seamanship and courage and the essential degree of luck, one ship or two ships could make it, should make it.

Here, gentlemen, in the Pacific some 2,400 miles north of the Horn and lying almost due west of Valparaíso, are the Islands of Juan Fernández and one in particular, Más a Tierra. The finger stops, the compass describes its circle, the island is in focus: plenty of food and water and tall trees for masts and other repairs. Only rarely visited by a Spanish squadron, maybe not once in a couple of years, it lies open, deserted and inviting.

Más a Tierra had been settled in the sixteenth century by a Portuguese, Juan Fernández, who established a small colony. When Chile was more or less opened up, he and his colonists departed for fresh fields and pastures new on the mainland. They left behind a few goats, which multiplied prodigiously. So there was an abundance of fresh meat, there was an abundance of cabbage palms which provided a good and nourishing food; there were berries and fruits and legumes and streams of fresh water and so many seals and sea lions that it was almost impossible for a man to come ashore without stepping on them. Dampier, who had been there in 1681, in 1684, and again in 1704, said: "Seals swarm as thick about this Island as if they had no other Place in the World to live in." Obviously, where seals and sea lions existed in such numbers, the waters must be full of fish.

Here, during the preceding century, a number of battered and distressed ships had put in: first the Dutch, then the buccaneers, until by this time it had become known among the Spaniards as the "Thieves Kitchen." But for *Duke* and *Dutchess* it would be more than just a welcome or convenient kitchen; it would be the difference between life and death in the race against time and distance and disease.

So far so good, if they got that far; what then? North of Juan Fernández stretched the locked and guarded coastline with the precipitous, snowy Andes rising beyond. North from Juan Fernández, a thousand and two thousand miles, were the waters in which Rogers' command would have to operate for months.

But there, gentlemen, almost providentially, less than a hundred miles off the coast of northern Peru, is the Island of Lobos de Afuera, also deserted, where there is again food and firewood to be had, where ships can be emptied and heeled and careened and men can recuperate. And a few hundred miles northwest of Lobos lie the Galápagos, where there are enough giant land turtles and sea turtles to provision a fleet and, again, incredible quantities of fish.

For an alternate base, in the same general area, they could count on the uninhabited island of Gorgona, a few leagues offshore from what was then part of the Vice-Royalty of Peru, but is now Colombia. Unlike the Galápagos—where nothing grew but scrub and brush—Gorgona had stands of good timber for spars and masts, it provided decent anchorage, and there was all the water they would need. But it was dangerous. Unlike the Galápagos, it might be visited by the enemy.

These were the bases which would make it possible for the two cruisers to operate in the South Sea, bases to which, after raiding the coasts and shipping of Chile, Peru and Panama, they could retreat and lose any pursuing Spanish squadrons.

One more key point remained: the Islands of Tres Marías, north of Cape Corrientes in Mexico, near the mouth of the Gulf of California. They could put in there to stock up and repair before starting the long homeward passage, following Drake's and Cavendish's route, westward across the Pacific. But the Tres Marías were also essential if they were to stand any chance of achieving their maximum objective: to capture the ultimate prize of the seas, the Manila Galleon. This galleon set out once a year from the Philippines, bound for Mexico. She carried a year's accumulation of the trade and treasures of the Spice Islands, India, China and Japan. From Acapulco a sister galleon sailed annually for Manila, loaded with millions in American gold and silver, to buy at discount from the Orient what the Manila Galleon brought back.

The line had been in operation nearly two hundred years, and in all that time, although many of the galleons had been lost to the sea, only one had ever been captured. Cavendish—the slight, courteous, witty and somewhat murderous boy—took that one in 1587 off Cape San Lucas, at the tip of Baja California.

Such later historians as have written anything at all about the expedition have almost unanimously assumed that Rogers and his officers did not decide to try for the galleon until they had already been at sea for a great many months. In any event, it was a mistake that Spanish intelligence, which could not afford the same lapses as scholars, did not fall into. As soon as the two English frigates left Cork, warnings of the possibilities were sent to the government at Madrid and to the colonies. Even more conclusive, instructions as to the treatment and disposal of the galleon—if he were lucky enough to come up with it—had been embodied in Rogers' orders from his owners, before he ever left Bristol.

Dampier, as usual, knew a great deal about the line. And he had done more than just learn and write about the galleons, he had engaged one. On December 6, 1704, when he was in command of the *St. George*, he intercepted the monster off Cape Corrientes. Far from being able to capture her, he was battered and smashed and barely escaped being sunk by the tremendous weight of metal she threw at him. And the galleon did not even have all her guns out; if she had, the career of William Dampier—navigator, hydrographer, pirate, explorer, author, privateer, naturalist—would have ended right then and there, some cool, clear bubbling fathoms down.

This was the ultimate whale, breaching the seas; fabulously hunted for nearly two centuries and seldom ever sighted. They could only hope, at best, for a chance. Even to break into the Pacific, rip at the power of Spain there and prove it could be done with some success, even this would take much luck. And all the other odds against them were compounded in a kind of arithmetical progression with the odds against intercepting at one small point in time and space a galleon that would be sailing, nearly a year after they had left Bristol, from the opposite side of the earth, to make the longest unbroken and most terrible crossing in the world.

In the captain's cabin on the *Duke,* Rogers and his officers plotted the course as they sailed down the South Atlantic. Whatever the odds, they were determined, using all the skill, knowledge and ingenuity they possessed, to try first for the minimum and then, just possibly, for the maximum objective.

Meanwhile, the strictest secrecy was maintained. Beyond the fact that their general destination was the Pacific, the seamen were informed of nothing that, in event of capture or desertion, they could give away. Talking in ports, however, would not be a problem. The last such port had been Cork, now two months back, and there would not be another for nearly a year and a half. Desertion, of course, could be counted on, at even the most isolated places, after the men had suffered the putrid darkness and torments of the wooden walls for weeks at sea.

To guard against it, the captains had intended to

make as the last point for supplies and repairs, before attempting the Horn, the small, uninhabited island of Trinidad in the South Atlantic, 680 miles east of Espírito Santo on the coast of Brazil. But considering the state of the charts and the inaccuracy of the best methods of navigation, they despaired of hitting so small an island—unlike its namesake in the Caribbean, it is only four miles long by two miles across—and decided instead to put in at Grande, a sparsely settled offshore island lying some 100 miles safely distant from the temptations of Rio.

Toward Grande, then, they pitched and rolled week after week, knowing that after Grande there would be, for any certainty, nothing—a kind of leap into space. Sunlight and cloud-cover, the sea-supported boards beneath their feet; a future, after the sum total of human effort and ability, as far beyond human government and control as the immensity on which they floated. Overhead stood the fixed stars and the usual constellations—no better known, but more to be determined and depended on in their regular rising and setting than what lay ahead; and everywhere, around, above, below, were the turbulent oceans; the earth's hydrosphere; the ocean of air; the ocean of space; infinite, closed, with its numberless galaxies, of which nothing was known at all.

On October 28th, after crossing the equator, the *Duke* and the *Dutchess,* considering the sum total of human courage and knowledge and endurance, went to regular morning and evening prayers.

4

HELL
FOR A
PASTIME

THE CROSSING TO Grande was more or less uneventful.
There were storms and squalls; they encountered "several great Riplings" as of a strange current, and one moonlight night the sea "seem'd to be in a Breach" on all sides,
to the limits of visibility. They hurriedly heaved the lead,
but could find no bottom and relaxed, concluding later
that the phenomenon was due to the spawn of fish floating on the water.

Another night Courtney was dining with Rogers
aboard the *Duke* and they sent the boat across to the

Dutchess for Captain Cooke "with Orders to bring Mr. Page, second Mate, with him to be in the room of Mr. Ballett, that we exchang'd out of our Ship."

Mr. Page refused to obey, which "occasion'd Capt. *Cooke,* being the Superior Officer aboard, to strike him." That occasioned Page to strike Cooke. There was a brisk bout before the reluctant mate was finally forced into the boat and rowed to the *Duke,* where "Captain *Cooke* and others telling us what Mutiny had pass'd, we ordered Page on the Fore-Castle into the Bilboes."

The bilboes were long bars of iron, fixed to the deck, with sliding shackles which were locked around the prisoner's ankles so that he was forced to sit upright or lie flat on his back, his outstretched legs pinned. For mere minor offenses a man might be left that way for a day or a week. Page had no intention of being left that way for even an hour. He asked permission to go to the head. The head consisted of chains under the bowsprit, or occasionally a swinging seat, on which in turns and due order officers and men would balance to relieve themselves. Page, unshackled for this purpose, proceeded to the bowsprit and dived overboard ". . . thinking to swim back to the *Dutchess.* . . . However, the boat being alongside, we soon overtook him, and brought him on board again. For which and his abusive language he was lash'd to the Main-Geers and drub'd; and for inciting the Men to Mutiny, was afterwards confin'd in Irons aboard the *Duke.*"

Page's singular behavior, with no apparent provocation, would seem unaccountable. But his nerves may well have been frayed by the general conditions of life aboard ships of that time, conditions which, no matter how often experienced, never seemed to get any easier to bear and which, after repeated voyages, might become progressively more unbearable as the mind reached a kind of saturation point and endurance its limit.

There was a saying among seamen that "a man who went to sea for pleasure would be likely to go to hell for pastime." Dr. Samuel Johnson delivered, as usual, his own considered opinion: "No man will be a sailor who has contrivance enough to get himself into a jail; for being in a ship is being in a jail, with the chance of being drowned."

Johnson was right on at least a couple of counts: there was the same pestilential overcrowding and several of the same diseases, carried by rats, fleas, lice. Typhus, for example, was known equally as "ship's fever" and "jail fever."

The men slept between decks in hammocks some fourteen inches apart. A sailor coming off watch could not get to his hammock except by crawling to it under the others on his hands and knees. He lay there in his soaking wet clothes in the cold and the darkness—no fires were permitted below—and the darkness dripped, because all the wooden ships, in fair weather or foul, continually leaked. They leaked at the seams, not only below the waterline but above it. Water came in through the upper-deck planks and topside timbers and the hatchways, and all the calking possible could not stop it. The sea splashed through scuppers and ports and through the gun ports, which, even when closed and secured and calked with oakum, could not be made watertight.

As the weeks wore on it got worse, the sea and the weight of the masts and guns working on the seams; and nothing again, even beaching and careening in the blaze of the tropics, would ever properly dry such ships out. Indeed, it might be said that at their very launching and christening they were already oozing water.

Shipbuilders "pickled" the timbers for the hull—a process which was thought to prevent, but actually accelerated, rotting; and other timbers were boiled so that they could be curved and bent into place. Finally, to complete the water-logging, the decks were scrubbed down twice daily, when the weather permitted.

In bad weather, of course, the sea not only splashed or dribbled in, it poured, and the pumps had to be kept going around the watches. Then, with all the ports and hatches tightly closed, often for weeks, the air in the darkness below became almost unbreathable; a darkness broken only by the faint illumination here and there of a few lanthorns, a single candle in each dismally glowing through heavy panes of horn.

There was a stench compounded of the reeking water in the bilge, of an accumulation of rotting refuse which was often swept onto the ballast, of wet, close-packed men, lousy and flea-infested, who practically never changed their clothing, who seldom washed and for whom there were no facilities for bathing—a stench compounded by the decaying carcasses of drowned rats and other vermin down below.

Under such conditions acute respiratory diseases, particularly pneumonia, were common, and crippling rheumatism headed the list of all causes of discharge in the Navy. Men died of typhus and dysentery and, in the tropics, of malaria and yellow fever and cholera and sometimes bubonic plague. They died everywhere and wholesale, of scurvy, after any prolonged period at sea. In fact, it might be said they slowly dissolved; for while the symptoms and progress of the disease took various forms with various individuals, the general pattern was the same: a man's gums would rot and his teeth drop out; his body would be covered with large, discolored spots; his legs would swell and ulcerate; he was alternately subject to helpless torpor and to chills and excruciating pains, to complete weariness and lassitude and to a pathological anxiety. In some cases old, healed wounds would break open and suppurate, and often a man confined to his hammock would get up, feeling better, and after the slightest exertion drop dead.

Scurvy, of course, resulted from a nutritional deficiency, already mentioned, though it had not been established then; and while men learned the cure not many years later, the actual causative factor, a lack of vitamin C, was not established until well into the twentieth century.

But scurvy was only one result, though the most general and devastating, of their diet. Their resistance to infections of any kind was definitely lowered. To sustain them against the conditions in which they lived and against the strains of a punishing labor that never let up, the food they had was horrible.

Their staples were meat and biscuit. Since the only means of preserving meat was to pickle it in brine, they depended on salt beef, salt pork and salt fish, which turned rock-hard as the weeks wore on. The biscuits, made of wheat flour and dried pea flour, cooked into saucer-sized discs, also became hard as stone and could be tossed or skipped like stones.

Ships also carried quantities of dried, ground peas in canvas sacks, in which the rats rioted and the weevils multiplied. Thick pea soup, heavily salted and peppered, was highly esteemed, as was lobscouse—a sort of thick soup or stew containing chunks of salt meat—and into both pea soup and lobscouse, biscuit was broken to soften it. After skimming off as many of the floating insects, rat turds and maggots as they could, the men slurped their bowlfuls gratefully down.

A Dr. Sparman, who sailed with Captain James Cook in the late eighteenth century, observed with unqualified repugnance: ". . . our bread was, and had been, for a long time, both musty and mouldy, and swarming with two different sorts of little brown grubs, *circulio granorius* (or weevil) and the *dermestes paniceus,* which either in that state, or in that of their *larvas* or maggots, had nestled themselves into every bit of bread that we had, so that we could not possibly avoid eating them; and they frequently discovered themselves to us, the former by a bitter, the latter by a disagreeable, cold taste in the mouth. Nay, their *larvas,* or maggots, were found in such quantities in the *pease-soup,* as if they had been strewed over our plates on purpose, so that we could not avoid swallowing some of them in every spoonful we took.

"The pease used for this purpose had been ground a little in England, that they might boil the easier, but had, by this very means, afforded an easier passage to these disgustful insects."

For delicacies the men had "burgoo," oatmeal sweetened with molasses, and "doughboys," dumplings of wet flour boiled in pork fat. As a special treat there was plum duff, a suet pudding containing raisins or prunes. The mess cook, while pitting the prunes for this dish, was required to whistle continually, to prove that he was not eating the principal ingredients. But plum duff was only a treat when properly prepared, which does not seem to have been always or even often. When not properly prepared, it was likened to a "dollop of mortar."

To add to the variety they had cheese, for those who could stomach it when it was finally lifted out of the putrescent hold; they had olive oil or butter that, after months with no refrigeration, Masefield has compared unfavorably to "so much train oil," and beer—which invariably turned sour and acid and produced dysentery.

Even so, the beer—until it was gone—was preferred to the water, which sailors reasonably considered not fit to drink, except as a last resort. The allowance of water per man was three pints a day for all purposes, when supply was sufficient; but on long voyages the supply was almost never sufficient, and the allowance was drastically cut, often to spoonfuls.

Water was carried in charred casks. After a period ranging from a couple of days to a week, it began to stink so foully that no one could gag down a mouthful. However, after another week or two it cleared and became practically odorless though somewhat slimy from the growth inside the casks.

Supplies were replenished by watering parties sent ashore with barrels to be filled from brooks, streams, wells, pools or ponds. If the water seemed reasonably clear, it was dumped into the casks directly. If it seemed stagnant and suspicious, it was strained through a blanket. If it looked particularly bad, it was sometimes, though rarely, filtered through gravel, sand or charcoal. Since the sources were often contaminated, sailors got typhoid, cholera, amoebic dysentery and other waterborne diseases.

Supplies at sea were replenished, whenever possible, by rain water, which was pure, of course, as it fell but, being stored in the same casks, was frequently contaminated by mixture with the bacteria-loaded levels already on hand.

They had, then, this kind of food and drink to keep them going in a routine of work that was in itself nearly enough to kill; four hours on watch and four hours off, and in really bad weather, not even that, each man off watch standing every half-hour to the pumps. There were sails to be hoisted or lowered or furled; men swarming aloft onto yards crazily tilting and swinging across the arc of the sky, their only foothold dripping ropes, their blue hands grabbing and dragging at stiff, soaked, wind-whipped sheets of canvas; and with the storm and the enormous pendulum-sway beating at them on that slippery footing men fell to the deck to smash skulls, ribs, arms, legs, or were lost forever overboard in the foaming blackness.

There were sails to be mended and ropes to be spliced and rigging, often "much damnify'd," to be repaired. There were decks to be swabbed, timbers to be scraped, guns to be exercised and to be continually checked to make sure none worked loose from its lashings to smash between decks with the roll; guns to be lifted out of the hold or put down into it to trim ship. There were morning and evening prayers, drill for general quarters and gun-drill, the sick to be served, food to be prepared, offenders to be flogged, tackle to be fixed, seams to be calked, sides to be painted.

When at anchor or at sea in fair weather, a strenuous effort was made to air and clean the ships. At long last men hung their clothing out to dry all over the rigging. Every port and hatch was opened that safely could be, with strips of canvas rigged to catch the wind and circulate it through the hold.

Iron pots containing a smoking mixture of gunpowder, vinegar and water, or more often just vinegar vaporized by red-hot bars, were carried into every recess that could be reached, as were pans of burning pitch or brimstone, to fumigate everything. The decks were scrubbed with vinegar and sand, sluiced with sea water, scraped with metal scrapers and then swabbed.

Men worked to hold down the lice by going over the seams of their clothing with an iron heated at the galley. They tried to eliminate as many of the rats, beetles and cockroaches as they could.

Bedbugs, however, were an almost insoluble problem; they apparently dined on the fumigants. About the only means of combating them was to paint them into the woodwork, and that only succeeded for a time, until the paint flaked from the constant working of the timbers or until the bedbugs, willy-nilly, beat their way out.

There was the sad case of a captain who took command of a brand-new ship and found the bedbugs already there before him in force: a legacy from the carpenters and dockyard hands who had slept in the hull.

The men who had to suffer all this could look forward to no more shore leaves or celebrations in port. Where the *Duke* and *Dutchess* were headed there would be no ports, except the enemy's, until they reached Batavia nearly two years later, if, with luck, they reached Batavia. And even if there had been any such port en route, the captains would have avoided it, as they were avoiding Rio now, for fear of mass desertions.

The isolated places at which they were to put in would provide the men with a change of diet and some relaxation hunting and fishing. But there, too, the routine of work would go on for everyone except the desperately ill. Tents and shacks would have to be erected ashore; the frigates would have to be unloaded so that they could be heeled over, careened and have their bottoms scraped and cleaned, then reloaded and fresh water and food laid in, together with firewood and such other supplies as might be available.

It should, therefore, hardly surprise anyone that seamen considered sufficient stocks of liquor all-important. This was one of the several advantages of ships over jails —the advantage of free liquor—that Dr. Johnson omitted to mention. One captain noted that he could say, without the slightest exaggeration, that a third of his ship's company was drunk every evening. And if liquor and the sense of being united in common humanity, against a common fate and under continual tremendous stress, didn't hold sailors in line, the discipline would.

The two most common punishments were confine-

ment to the bilboes and flogging. The proceeding at flog-
gings—which the whole ship's company was paraded to
watch—was to strip the offender to the waist and tie him
to a grating, a capstan or the mainmast; the sentence then
being read, at the command, "Do your duty," the boatswain's mate laid on with a cat-o'-nine-tails. "One blow
takes off the skin and draws blood where each knot falls.
Six blows make the whole back raw. Twelve cut deeply
into the flesh and leave it a red mass, horrible to see. Yet
six dozen are a common punishment."

In the Royal Navy men were sometimes "whipped
through the fleet"—the victim being taken in a boat from
ship to ship, at each of which he received a specified number of lashes. This was usually equivalent to a sentence of
death.

Other forms of correction frequently proved fatal,
notably keelhauling. A man was tied by ropes attached to
yardarms on each side of the ship, and thrown overboard.
As he hit the water, a great gun was fired over his head
to give him the full effect of concussion. Then he was
hauled under the keel, either athwartships or from bow
to stern. The keel was deep and he was a good time
under. If he survived drowning, he would emerge half-
dead, a mass of cuts and scrapes from the barnacles.

The usual capital punishment was hanging at the
yardarm, though there was an occasional sentence of
"shooting to death." The buccaneers, and not only the
buccaneers, went in a good deal for marooning. Often
they put a man down on some islet or edge of reef which
was barely above water at low tide, leaving him a pistol
with a single charge of powder and ball to take his
choice when the tide rose.

For the first offense of sleeping on watch, a man got
doused with a bucket of sea water. For the second, he
was tied up by the wrists and water poured down his

sleeves. For the third, he was tied to the mainmast with a heavy bag of bullets around his neck. If he proved incorrigible, he was put out on the bowsprit with a ration of rum, water and food; when this was exhausted, he could either die of thirst and starvation or drop off and drown.

For blasphemy, swearing and dirty talk, a man had to hold a marlin spike in his mouth until his tongue bled. for other transgressions his allowance of food was cut in half, or the allowance of meat and liquor completely cut off. Boteler had written in the seventeenth century: "And the Knaveries of the Ship-boys are payd by the Boat-Swain with the Rod; and commonly this execution is done upon the Munday Mornings; and is so frequently in use, that some meer Seamen believe in earnest, that they shall not have a fair Wind, unless the poor Boys be duely brought to the Chest, that is whipped, every Munday morning." This was actually the origin of the term "Blue Monday."

Few of these punishments, and none of the fatal ones, were administered aboard Rogers' ships. No one was flogged to death, or keelhauled or marooned, or exposed at the bowsprit or hanged from the yardarm.

It is true he complains, once, that he was not permitted, or could not use as a threat, methods of punishment available to captains in the Royal Navy; but he seems to have been merely making a point. His discipline was strict but not harsh, considering the times, and never carried to extremes. Men were drubbed and flogged and put down in irons but were almost invariably released and reinstated, after a due period, upon their promise of correction. He showed himself, indeed, more merciful than the average run of captains and considerably more merciful than courts and judges were ashore. The mutinous Mr. Page, for example, was let out of his irons after a week ". . . on his humble Submission, and acknowledging his Fault, with Promises of Amendment."

"Fair pleasant Weather, with a fresh Gale." That was October 29th. On November 15th they sighted Cape Frio, and two days later dropped anchor at the island of Grande, after forty days at sea.

The island, like Rio some distance to the east, belonged to Portugal. However, when Captain Cooke and a lieutenant proceeded in the pinnace to the one small settlement on the mainland nearby to wait upon the governor, with a present of butter and cheese, and inform him of the ship's arrival, they were instantly fired upon. This, though there is a temptation to think so, was not due to the presumable condition of the butter and cheese but to the fact that the Portuguese mistook them for French.

As soon as they got that straightened out, everything went smoothly. The first request Rogers and Courtney made of the local authorities was for help in hunting down and rounding up deserters.

For all those envying the shipmates who had the foresight to go over the side at Cork more than two months back, Grande was the last chance to jump ship. After Grande there would be an unbroken voyage of six thousand miles around the Horn and toward the uninhabited Juan Fernández islands in the Spanish ocean.

5

GRANDE
TO THE
COMPANIONS
OF THE HORN

GRANDE, some twenty-seven miles long, heavily wooded and with much high land, lies approximately a hundred miles west of the harbor of Rio, along the indented coast. From the bay in which the *Duke* and *Dutchess* anchored, it was nine or ten miles to a small town on the mainland, Angra dos Reis.

On the island itself no one lived. There was dense vegetation and an abundance of animal life, including quantities of monkeys, snakes and birds. Here, after the salt, strenuous Atlantic, men could take their ease under the soft moon and large stars, listening to the noises of the woods, smelling a heavy odor of flowers, of honeysuckle and jasmine and ripening fruit. *"He hangs in shades the orange bright,/Like golden lamps in a green night . . ."*

These were the welcome pauses in a life. But for the crews of the two ships the pause was brief; their short stay at Grande proved, for so comparatively remote and wild a place, singularly eventful.

The third day at the island, Courtney had to put eight of his men in irons for disobeying orders. And the desertions began, as anticipated. "Last night one *Michael Jones* and *James Brown*, two *Irish* Landsmen, run into the woods, thinking to get away from us: tho two such Sparks run away the 25th from the *Dutchess*, and in the night were so frighted with Tygers, as they thought, but really by Monkeys and Baboons, that they ran into the water, hollowing to the Ship till they were fetched aboard again." It was while the alert was on for the two Irishmen that Carleton Vanbrugh again distinguished himself, this time with more serious consequences.

On the morning of November 26th, shortly before daybreak, a canoe from the mainland, loaded with Indians and steered by a Portuguese friar, went skimming past the *Duke*. Thinking it might contain their missing men, the watch on the quarter-deck shouted an order to come aboard and be examined. Instead—Indians all furiously paddling, wind-whipped friar hunched over, steering—the canoe foamed away in the darkness. The *Duke's* yawl and pinnace were sent after it.

Carleton Vanbrugh, without any authority at all, jumped into the pinnace and assumed command. While still some distance off, he ordered the men to fire their muskets, and, as he drew nearer, had the fire poured di-

3*

rectly into the canoe. One Indian was badly wounded.
The friar, who had been carrying a quantity of gold,
beached the canoe and disappeared into the woods, where
he buried or secreted his wealth. It turned out he was a
friendly Portuguese and had mistaken his attackers for the
French.

Eventually everybody was rounded up and brought
back to the *Duke*. The friar lost his gold, either because
somebody finally appropriated it or because he could
never again properly remember where he had hidden it.
The Indian, though treated by the *Duke's* surgeons, died
after two hours. Rogers made what amends he could, but
the gold was gone and, more important, a man's life.

For this, after due investigation, Vanbrugh was again
formally censured by the council before the ships left
Grande; and this time he was removed from his post as
owner's agent aboard the *Duke* and put aboard the *Dutchess*.

The weather turned violently hot. They worked fast.
In the space of a week the ships had been heeled over, the
cargoes unloaded or shifted to produce a violent list, so
that the bottoms could be scraped and cleaned, and then
righted. The crews repaired masts and trestletrees, laid in
fresh water and quantities of firewood, limes, lemons,
fowls; got guavas, oranges, plantains, bananas, pineapples
and fresh fish. From the mainland they brought rum, hogs,
beef, mutton, corn, sugar, sweetmeats and tobacco—
"which they sell very dear, tho not good to smoke, 'tis so
very strong."

Rogers learned that two great French ships, homeward bound from the South Sea and disease-ridden, had
watered here nine months earlier and buried half their
men. ". . . but God be thank'd, ours are healthy."

The news of these vessels may also have served as a
reminder; he had read, long before, a journal published by

a French captain, Beauchesne de Gouin, who had gone in
1698 with two ships to the western coasts of Spanish
America for the purpose of establishing trade under a
Franco-Spanish treaty. As a result, France had in one year
seventeen warships and merchantmen engaged in this
trade; and profits the first year ran to some hundred million dollars, the equivalent of perhaps nearly a billion
today.

Some of the officers of the *Duke* and *Dutchess* attended a celebration at the small town on the mainland.
The town consisted of some sixty houses roofed with
palmetto leaves, two churches, a Franciscan monastery
and a garrison. Cooke reported: "The Town of *Angra Dos
Reys* is on the Main, about three Leagues distant from the
Island, very small . . . They have a Guardhouse where, at
our Landing, we were received by the Governor, who is
Captain of about 20 Men there in Arms, with a Lieutenant
and Ensign and the Priests."

This was a special occasion, and Rogers described it
more explicitly: ". . . it being the Day kept for the Con-
ception of the Virgin *Mary*, and a high Day of Procession
amongst these people. The Governor Signior *Raphael de
Silva Lagos*, a *Portuguese*, receiv'd us very handsomely.
He ask'd us if we would see the Convent and Procession:
we told him our Religion differ'd very much from his. He
answer'd we were welcome to see it, without partaking in
the Ceremony. We waited on him in a Body, being ten of
us, with two Trumpets and a Hautboy, which he desired
might play us to Church, where our Musick did the Office
of an Organ, but separate from the Singing, which was
by the Fathers well perform'd. Our Music play'd, *Hey
Boys up go we!* and all manner of noisy paltry tunes . . ."

It was well intended, at any rate, and well received.
The faults were the faults of a limited repertoire and,
fortunately, nobody had to sing or disclose the lyrics. "Hey

Boys up go we!", for example, was an old cavalier song
satirizing the tastes and manners of the Puritans. As published in D'Urfey's *Pills to Purge Melancholy*, part of it
ran:

> ". . . Good manners has a bad repute,
> And tends to Pride we see;
> We'll therefore cry all Breeding down,
> Then hey boys up go we.

> "Thus having peel'd and plunder'd all,
> And levell'd each degree,
> We'll make their plump young Daughters fall
> And hey boys up go we."

Everyone behaved with admirable decorum. Following Mass, Protestant English and Catholic Portuguese
joined in the procession around the church and monastery.
". . . after Service our Musicians, who were by that time
half drunk, march'd at the head of the Company, next to
them an old Father and his two Fryars, carrying Lamps of
Incense with the Host, next came the Virgin *Mary* on a
Bier carry'd on four Mens shoulders, and dress'd with
Flowers and Wax-Candles, *etc.* After her came the Padre
Guardian of the Convent, and then about forty Priests,
Fryars, etc. Next was the Governor of the Town, myself
and Captain Courtney, with each of us a long Wax-Candle
lighted: Next follow'd the rest of our Officers, the chief
Inhabitants, and junior Priests, with every one a lighted
Wax-Candle. The Ceremony held about two hours, after
which we were splendidly entertain'd by the Fathers of
the Convent, and then by the Governor. . . ."

They learned about gold mines inland worked by
slaves but not—hospitality has its limits—where the mines
were: ". . . the Portuguese say they lie several days Journy

up in the Country; and some will tell you 'tis ten or fifteen days, others a month's Travel . . . for they are cautious how they discover the Truth, but there is certainly abundance of Gold found in this Country."

Rogers asked about the giant anaconda of the Brazilian jungles, known to him as the Liboya or Roebuck-Serpent from the fact that it was said to be able to swallow a roebuck. He had been reading up on the subject aboard ship, in the journal of a seventeenth-century Dutch traveler, Jan Nieuhof, and found the report incredible. The governor confirmed that some anacondas were nearly thirty feet long, as big around as a barrel, and could swallow a roebuck without much difficulty. Rogers was stunned.

At Grande the men had fairly good shooting for the pot. On a visit to the island some years before, Dampier observed quantities of turtledoves and two kinds of wild pigeon in such numbers that—particularly in the months between May and September—"a Man may shoot 8 or 10 dozen in several Shots at one standing, in a close misty Morning, when they come to feed on Berries in the Woods."

Fish, flesh, fruit, fowl: there was an abundance of good food and rum and wine and, certainly, song. But of women there is no mention here and very little later. Presumably the ships' companies, by necessity if not inclination, remained true to the girls in Cork and Bristol and London for a long, long time. In any case, both Cooke and Rogers maintained a discreet silence that was common to almost all the accounts of voyages during the period and earlier. It was shared by the buccaneers.

Though there are some buccaneer records of wholesale raping—together with torture and murder, particularly on Morgan's sack of Panama—most buccaneer writers treat the subject of sex as if it didn't exist. Many of them may have been bloody monsters, but almost all of them seemed on the prudish side, contrary to the pictures of popular fiction. Any exposure was considered indecent. Swearing and bawdy talk had, as has been noted, appropriate punishments. One buccaneer became notorious for his total depravity because he had hired (incidentally, at tremendous expense) a whore to dance publicly before him in her shift.

Doxies and whores they had certainly, ports full of them, sometimes whole islands; but the candles were decently snuffed, couples retreated into a discreet privacy to emerge with proper, almost churchly faces next day, and around the whole thing a curtain was drawn, like the curtain of darkness, with only the many stars—*cum tacet nox, furtivos hominum vident amores. . . .*

They had been at Grande a week and a half. The *Duke's* mainmast and foremast had been rerigged. Everything had been properly stowed: water, food, firewood, liquor and other supplies; everything was shipshape and Bristol fashion.

It was time to be going. They could not count on what lay ahead or how long it would take them. The Horn would be bad and icy enough while it was still late spring or summer in those latitudes: they had to make it before the Antarctic winter closed down. If they failed, the least they would face would be a wait of nearly another six months, and that they could not ride out. They would have to give up and return home. And if, somehow, they could still ride it out, or get through, the delay would end any hope of taking the Manila Galleon. They had only so much time to carry out their basic plan of operations and then prepare and be off Cape San Lucas in the Pacific for their possible appointment. They could be a little early, but they could not be late. If they missed by so much as a day, that chance even now some eleven months off would be postponed for an additional year or, within the range of the possible, forever.

Meanwhile, to return the hospitality of the governor and the Franciscans, a yawl was sent to town, the day following the religious celebration, to pick up their former hosts for a farewell party on board the ships. The yawl also picked up, and by no means incidentally, an additional store of certain "neccesaries," principally one: "Because we were to run near 2,000 leagues before we could expect any Recruit of Liquors, unless by extraordinary good fortune."

By "good fortune" he must have meant the capture of some ship properly laden, because if they failed to do that, they would sail a great deal farther than 2,000 leagues —some 6,000 nautical miles—before they would get anything stronger than water. On the deserted Juan Fernández Islands in the Pacific there were no grog shops such as advertised in Bristol, Portsmouth and London: "Drunk for a penny; dead drunk for two pence; clean straw for nothing."

The party was a success. The fathers, friars, governors, officers and gentlemen of the town came on board in the afternoon and did not get back ashore until the next morning. Rogers said the guests had to spend the night because the weather turned bad, with a blow and heavy showers. At any rate, the weather provided a decent excuse for not breaking up.

"They were very merry, and in their cups propos'd the Pope's health to us." Everybody drank to that. The English, in return, then proposed the health of the Archbishop of Canterbury, and everybody drank to that. Rogers, "to keep up the Humour," next toasted William Penn; and "they lik'd the liquor so well," everybody drank William Penn's health also. There is no note of how many other healths were hoisted, but there must have been a lot before morning, when "the Governor and Company were carry'd ashore; at parting, we saluted 'em with a Huzza from each Ship, because we were not over-stocked with Pouder."

The guests bore away presents and letters to be forwarded to England, the last letters the crews would be able to send home for almost two years. Then the ships weighed anchor, after the council had been convened to censure Carleton Vanbrugh and confirm his transfer to the *Dutchess*, in due legal order.

A sudden calm, crosscurrents, and then contrary winds, forced them to come to anchor again on the opposite side of the island, where they were held for two days. During this time they sighted a small vessel and sent the *Duke's* boat after her. She proved to be a Portuguese brigantine they had already encountered and examined some days earlier. Rogers gave the captain a half-hour glass and other small presents, together with a long, final communication to be forwarded through Portugal to his owners. He felt he had now done everything possible to insure that some word of their passage reached home.

On the afternoon of December 2nd they got a brisk, favorable wind. The sails filled; by six o'clock that evening Grande, with all its fruits, flowers, monkeys, serpents and turtledoves, was falling far behind.

The wind held. They ran south under an overcast sky and frequent showers. The signs or portents of the Horn were already beginning. They sighted their first albatross. Rogers reported: ". . . a large Bird call'd *Alcatros*, who spread their Wings from eight to ten foot wide." R. C. Leslie, who, some seventy years ago, wrote and illustrated a fine, abbreviated account of this expedition, considers that Rogers may have been correct in his spelling, since the name—thought to be derived from the Latin "albus," white, or "alb," a priest's vestment—was more properly derived from the Spanish "alca," meaning "razorbill."

On the twelfth, with a southwest wind of gale force blowing, the *Duke* was forced to reef her mainsail, for the first time since leaving England. The *Dutchess* shipped several seas, which filled her main deck and carried away some of the rails of the head.

"We find it much colder in this Lat. which is 43° 30′ S. than in the like degree N. tho the Sun was in its furtherest Extent to the Southward: which may be ascrib'd partly to our coming newly out of warmer Climates, which made us more Sensible of the Cold; or 'tis probable the Winds blow over larger Tracts of Ice than in the same Degrees of N. Latitude."

On the seventeenth, one of the *Dutchess'* men fell from the mizzentop to the quarter-deck and fractured his skull. "They desir'd the advice of our Surgeon, and I went on board with our two where they examin'd the Wound, but found the Man irrecoverable; so that he died and was buried next day."

They sighted killer whales, or grampusses, and curving schools of porpoise and round-eyed seals. There were petrels—a bird, in Dampier's description: ". . . not much unlike a Swallow, and with a shorter Tail. 'Tis all over black, except a White Spot on the Rump. They fly sweeping like Swallows, and very near the Water. They are not so often seen in fair Weather, being Foul-Weather Birds, as our Seamen call them, and presaging a Storm when they come about a Ship; who for that reason don't love to see them. In a storm they will hover close under the Ship's Stern, in the Wake of the Ship (as 'tis called) or the Smoothness which the Ship's passing has made on the Sea; and there as they fly (gently then) they pat the Water alternately with their Feet, as if they walk'd upon it; tho' still upon the Wing. And from hence the Seamen give them the name of Petrels, in Allusion to St. Peter's walking upon the Lake of Gennesareth."

The men stood their watches around the twenty-four hours, each man alternating four hours on deck and four hours below. The first night watch began at 8:00 P.M. and lasted until midnight. During that period half the ship's company was free to get what sleep it could before stumbling back on deck to relieve the watch before it.

There were, therefore, only hammocks enough for half the crew—a measure instituted by Queen Elizabeth as an economy when she noted that only half the men could be below at any one time. Each man, coming off watch, went to what would be known in modern slang as a "hot bed," one that has just been vacated by a previous sleeper, and one, in this case, that was probably cold and soaking from the clothes of the previous occupant and the water continually pouring in.

They had no clocks. No clock had yet been made that would work at sea. It was not until 1735 that John Harrison produced the first effective marine chronometer. Time was kept by sandglasses and checked by the sun's noon position, visibility permitting.

Ship's boys tended the glasses, day and night, turning them when the sand had run through, every half-hour, and striking a bell, one bell for the first turning, two for the second, and so on through eight bells, which completed a watch. These apprentices, to shorten their dismal, shivering hours on deck, sometimes heated the glass against their bellies to expand the neck slightly and make the sand run through faster; or they turned the glass and struck the bell before all the sand had quite run through. For such offenses—which added, among other things, to the complications of navigation—apprentices were stripped, lashed to the capstan and beaten.

During the first dogwatch, the company went to evening devotions about the mainmast and then to supper: biscuit and pease porridge, or salt meat and doughboys, or lobscouse. In the morning the decks were swabbed before breakfast, which might consist of oatmeal with molasses, and always the work went on; sails to be trimmed, rigging to be mended, the tops to be manned by lookouts, cannon and powder to be checked; supplies to be brought up from the hold or shifted; the ship to be cleaned. Men took their turns at the helm, at the pumps, hoisted and lowered canvas, went aloft to reef sails or shake them out, to disentangle yards, blocks, tackle.

Sick call was held around seven in the morning and announced by a ship's boy, who went about the decks ringing a bell. Such heralds were known as "loblolly boys" from the slang term for a thin gruel often administered to the ailing. Held, in good weather, at the break of the quarter-deck, and in bad weather, below decks, sick call was supervised not only by the surgeons but by the captain, to discourage mere faking and malingering. On board the *Duke*, the presence of the renowned physician, Thomas Dover, with his obdurate eye and uneven temper, should have been enough.

In bad weather, or any other emergency, nobody was off watch, all hands being on deck until the emergency was passed, the work done, or the master dismissed them. *The Watch is changed,/The Glass is running:/We shall make a good voyage/As God may will. . . .*

On December 22nd they sighted the "Companions of the Horn," the Falkland Islands. "This is Falkland's Land, described in few Draughts, and none lay it down right, tho the Latitude agrees pretty well."

It is not surprising the charts were wrong. The best available charts misplaced islands, and sometimes the coastlines of whole continents, by errors in longitude ranging from one or two to ten or more degrees. Since navigators had no clocks and the sextant had not yet been invented—it was only developed in 1731—longitude at sea could not be determined with any real accuracy.

Latitude could be plotted quite well, within minutes of a degree. They had the quadrant, the astrolabe and the cross-staff for measuring the altitude of the sun or the Pole star. But calculations of longitude depended chiefly on observations of the moon's motion based on the Caroline tables of Halley and Street; and the tables themselves were off by as much as five minutes of arc, or nearly three degrees of longitude, and could lead to errors in position of more than 300 miles. Moreover, all available instruments for measuring angles at sea either involved the use of a plumb line—fairly hopeless on board a ship plunging and rolling—or required the observer to look in two directions at once.

As a navigational aid the *Duke* and the *Dutchess* relied on Seller's *Practical Navigation,* published in 1614, and for a standard instrument had "Davis's Quadrant," dating from the time of Elizabeth.

For directional guidance they had, of course, the compass, which had been in use for centuries. To correct the compass heading for the easterly and westerly variation between magnetic north and true north, they had variation charts. These charts were continually being changed and corrected by captains and navigators, Dampier notably included; and, indeed, would need to be, since the magnetic pole shifts from year to year.

To correct the compass, they had a broad brass circle, divided into graduated lines drawn from a raised pin or sight on its surface. This circle was fitted over the compass bowl and made an azimuth compass. By observing the sun's azimuth, the total error in the compass, variation and deviation, could be reasonably well established.

Deviation in the compass due to the proximity of iron

in the ship and to other factors was not much understood or compensated for. In spite of the admonition of Grenville Collins, in 1693, that mariners should "have a great Care no Iron be near the Compass," more than half a century later Captain James Cook was keeping an iron key in the binnacle with the compass and complaining of errors, other than variation, for which he could not account.

The instruments for computing speed to measure distance run at sea were the log line, the log chip, or log ship, and sandglass. The log line, about 150 fathoms in length, was divided into knots to represent nautical miles. One end was attached to the log chip, a carved block of wood weighted on its curved side to float upright. In heaving the log, which was generally done as a routine every hour, the log chip was hove overboard and the line paid out from a reel, as fast as the chip would carry it away. When some fifteen fathoms had been paid out, as marked on the line, an officer cried "Turn!" and an assistant turned a half-minute glass. As soon as the sand had run through, the assistant called back "Hold!" and the officer grabbed the line to note the length, as marked by the knots, that had gone out during the running of the glass. Figuring by simple arithmetic, the number of knots, timed by the glass, then gave the ship's speed in nautical miles per hour when the log was hove.

It only seemed simple. Errors were frequent and inevitable. They arose from mistakes in measuring the line and in timing the log glass, from paying out too much stray line when a ship was moving slowly and, when she was moving fast, not paying out enough line to insure against errors in counting. Mistakes arose from careless steering, from sudden variations in the wind, from tides, currents and wave action on the log chip.

Considering, therefore, the total state of navigational

aids, instruments and knowledge available to men of this time, the wonder is not how many ships were lost through failure to plot their position correctly but how many solved complicated navigational problems with success.

The ships remained off the Falklands a couple of days, beaten by contrary winds, wondering if the slopes and headlands and cold rocks of those islands were inhabited by anyone, estimating their longitude and extent, not daring to come in too close. Most captains, and all prudent ones, when nearing land always hove to at night to avoid running ashore in the darkness, though the best calculations might show land still one or two or three days' sail away.

Both ships were blown far out of sight of land again, riding out a gale with staysails reefed, bows to the north, not knowing where, or precisely where, they might be. The unknown, the always possible opened all around them. *If thou beest borne to strange sights,/Things invisible to see . . .*

On Christmas Eve, while it was still light in those latitudes, they sighted through the spyglass a strange great ship bearing southeast of them. They began to overtake her, then lost her in the darkness. They decided she was a French ship homeward bound from the Pacific, and concluded that if this were so, she would turn north again as soon as she lost sight of them.

Accordingly they headed north in the short night to intercept her. Christmas morning broke calm and misty in the early hours. Then the mist lifted, and there was the prey again, twelve to fifteen miles away. They put out boats and began rowing and towing in the calm, until afternoon, when they got a breeze and, having crowded on all possible sail, began once more to overhaul her.

The *Dutchess* brought out extra guns that she had stowed in the hold. Rogers and Courtney consulted to determine the best plan of attack. The pursuit continued the rest of the day and that night. And then in the darkness the phantom was lost again. They ran on northward. Nobody slept. At daybreak the rolling sea was covered by thick fog.

Duke and *Dutchess* waited. Then suddenly, silently, the gray fog lifted like a curtain to disclose the strange vessel for the last time: a mile or two away, as still as themselves. The wind began to blow. It blew harder. Unaccountably the great shape outran them. She diminished and was gone over the horizon.

Rogers noted that it was "strange" from first to last, strange that a vessel they had from the beginning outsailed, should suddenly leave them behind, "as strange as our first seeing her in this place, because all Ships that we have heard of bound out or home this way, kept within Falklands Island."

Mist, fog, blowing darkness: an omen of the Horn. They turned south to resume their course. Whatever it may have been, this phantom, this sort of Flying Dutchman, had vanished. Nothing was holding true; everything was shifting, swinging, changing; and there was a chill to it like the cold flowing steadily up from the Antarctic.

6

COLD EDGE
OF
NOWHERE

January, 1709. Cape Horn.

The seas are the most consistently violent in the world. The winds are the prevailing westerlies; in the days of sail, a ship making the westward passage beat against gales that, if she were not lying under bare poles, stripped off every shred of canvas. Hail, rain, sleet, snow, tempests; moments of sudden treacherous wind; calm and fog in which the rolling and crashing seas never subsided.

Drake in the *Pelican*, later rechristened the *Golden Hind*, got through the Strait of Magellan and reached a

latitude of approximately 51° south, was blown back toward the South Pole to latitude 57°, beat painfully back
north until he was again beyond the western exit of the
strait and then—the little *Pelican* batted around in the
storms for weeks like a badminton bird—was driven down
below 54°, climbed and gained a degree or so, and then
was once more tossed toward the Pole, back to 57° south.

For several centuries it was supposed and accepted
by many that the island he reached in the course of all
this, and named "Elizabeth Island," was the Horn. It was
not. Reisenberg has shown that its topography does not
agree in any detail with that of the Horn, and its position—even allowing for slight errors in determining
latitude—was several hundred miles south-southwest.
Whatever the mass was—this Elizabeth Island, where
Drake's men landed and got fresh water and berries—it
is now almost certainly some seventy fathoms sunk beneath the ocean, creating in those depths a shallows
where the giant icebergs bump and grind and collect.

The Dutchman, Willem Schouten, first to round the
Horn, discovered and named it in 1616, after his home
port of Hoorn in Holland, where his ships had been built
and outfitted—as, a few weeks earlier, he and Jakob Le
Maire had discovered the strait named for Jakob's father,
Isaac, their principal investor and benefactor.

In probably no other stretch of sea has there been
such a number of ships lost in proportion to the number
attempting it. With some sail the Cape has dealt almost
easily and lightly, by comparison with the rest; but all
have been punished, most to the limit, many beyond it.
For more than three centuries after Schouten the record
of loss steadily mounted: the wooden barks and frigates,
the fast clippers, the steel ships with wire cables and
radio and the latest navigational aids. They foundered
in the seas, they struck on the black basaltic rock and ice

of the islands of Diego Ramírez; they smashed into the enormous icebergs and went down without trace. At one point in the race to the gold fields and the Orient, four clippers vanished in as many months. Melville wrote: "At those ends of the earth are no chronicles."

When the *Duke* and the *Dutchess* headed for the Cape, only two English voyages in all history had ever made the westward rounding, and Dampier had been on both. On the first he sailed as navigator for the buccaneer captains, Davis and Edward Cook, in the *Batchelor's Delight,* in 1684. On the second, in 1704, he had his own ship, the twenty-six-gun *St. George,* with her consort, the smaller *Cinque Ports,* commanded by Stradling.

This time, to avoid beating directly into the gales and against the westerly current, Dampier as pilot was going to take Rogers and Courtney on a long tack south and dangerously close to the ice: a course plotted to avoid, also, the rocks of Diego Ramírez, whose precise location nobody yet knew—huge, lonely rocks glazed with ice and beaten by the combers, thrusting nearly six hundred feet above the sea, and lying some undetermined miles southwest of Cape Horn.

Dampier could, of course, have plotted the alternate route, through the Strait of Magellan, but Rogers and Courtney and he had long before decided against it. The strait, if less violent, was almost as dangerous and presented even greater problems for a westward passage. There were the same prevailing winds, but in the strait they beat and howled in furious cross-gusts from the mountains; there was the same westerly current, but complicated by rips and tides, a current that sometimes ran at eight to ten knots and drove a ship clear back out of the strait. In winding narrows, where the steep slopes of snow-capped, cloud-wrapped mountains dropped precipitously down into the depths, there was no bottom the anchor cables could reach; no way to anchor and ride until daylight before continuing to thread a poorly marked passage between the rock walls.

Finally, it might take weeks and could take months, depending on conditions, to negotiate the 370-mile strait. Beauchesne de Gouin, before them, had been nearly seven months getting through. And, again depending on conditions, they might find it impassable. If something like that happened, they would have to try the Horn anyway, and then perhaps in the Antarctic winter.

No matter what, they could not afford to risk the time. Considering the state of their provisions, the delay of an added two months or even a month in reaching Juan Fernández meant that scurvy would almost certainly finish off half their crews. Moreover, they had a program to carry out and a hoped-for appointment. To labor in the strait for any considerable period would end all their chances of keeping it.

So the *Duke* and the *Dutchess* went south through the racing seas: 54°—56°—57°, hoping that the spirit of the Cape would smile on them at least briefly. By December 27th they were encountering strong gales and squalls. The *Dutchess*, to trim ship, put back into the hold the guns she had previously taken out when preparing to engage the phantom off the Falklands. On board the *Duke* six tailors had been at work for weeks sewing warm clothing for the men ". . . and pretty well supply'd their Wants by the spare Blankets and red Clothes belonging to the Owners; and what every Officer could spare, was alter'd for the Mens Use. The like was done on board the *Dutchess*."

Liquor on board the *Duke* and *Dutchess* was, fortunately, still in good supply because of all the stocks that had been laid in, at Teneriffe, the Cape Verde Islands and Grande. On New Year's Day, Rogers broke out a large tub of hot punch on the quarter-deck "where every Man in the Ship had above a Pint to his share, and drank our Owners and Friends Healths in *Great Britain* to a happy New Year, a good Voyage, and a safe Return."

And then the Cape hit them. The ships staggered and heeled over in the blast; and as they rolled, the sea came green over the sides, a wall of water as if they were submerging, the gunwales already below the surface and the whole inconceivable ocean pouring across, as if it were in a hurry to finish this at once, before they ever had a chance to recover and fight back; as if it meant to split, smash and engulf them at the very first overwhelming onslaught and deliver them instantly to the depths.

Slowly the small ships righted and rose, hundreds of liquid tons pouring from the decks—decks belly-deep, chest-deep in swirling, ice-cold, pounding green salt water. Any man who then lost his hold was gone; no boat could have been lowered and if it could have been and could have lived, it would have been lost from the ship in the blindness of the storm and the tremendous seas that obliterated everything.

Between the planks, at the gunports and hatches, through seams and cracks and edges, the water poured in. For the rest of that day and all that night and intermittently for days following, the *Duke* and *Dutchess* fought for their lives.

Sleep shall neither night nor day/Hang upon his pent-house lid. No sleep for anyone except a stiff, upright, fitful doze, gripping a line, a yard or a rail, gripping the tag end of life, the limit of endurance in paralyzing cold, in perpetual noise as the seas drummed and crashed and the wind beat on the rigging like somebody slamming and plucking at a gigantic harp—ropes, yards, spars, masts—a shattering discord: a howling, booming, strumming, twanging that never let up.

Into this nightmare of noise the sailors ascended hand over hand to hang on a yardarm against the whirling overcast or the spinning stars, the deck like a splinter far below: to hang belly-over, grabbing canvas and lines that cut their hands, their only purchase in the wildly revolving night an ice-coated rope beneath their feet. And always against the sheer suck of the drop below, the blue-green polar waves surged, far above the ship, almost up to their own dizzying height.

A man could not speak, could scarcely shout; the wind tore the words from his mouth. And the violence of that roaring water beating on the crowded, leaking, sea-crazy wooden tubs was incredible; it was so violent that a man standing on deck was hurled down to crack his head or the cage of his ribs; so violent that often a sailor gripping a stanchion could not even sit upright.

The spray and the sleet beat on a man's hands when he slid down the ice-glazed rigging from a swinging perch in the sky; when soaked, frozen, bleeding, he had most need of hot food or drink, there was never any to be had; through all those days and nights, the galley fires were out. The men off watch, if any were off watch, descended into the darkness of a huge refrigerator to munch on cold salt meat and biscuit and try for a moment's chattering rest in a drenched hammock, while the bodies of drowned rats and roaches swirled and floated underneath. And then in the petrified interval of delirium—in the crystal of dead-end fatigue—before the glass shattered and the man was roused again to take his turn at the pumps: then, maybe for a moment, proverbial visions of sugarplums danced in his head, visions of a galleon out of Manila and her cargo.

On January 5th the *Dutchess*, running south before the storm's increasing violence, was in trouble. Cooke reported: "By five in the afternoon the Waste was filling with Water . . . we expecting the Ship would sink every Moment, got down our Foreyard as well as we could and loosed the Spritsail, to ware the Ship."

And now it was as if the spirit of the Horn, having failed in its first tremendous onslaught, was throwing at them an accumulation of reserves that had no limit, no end. A few hours later the *Dutchess* shipped a sea at her stern that almost finished her. The Horn might as well have been saying, now it's over and done with, this wave or the next; you dream of Spanish towns and Spanish plunder and a galleon bound toward Acapulco and a great name in the world; but the dream founders here; it goes down with all the will and courage and ambition you will ever have, leaving only a stray hatchcover or combing beating against the rocks or the ice to tell anyone who might ever come after, where you disappeared.

Cooke reported: "At nine shipped a Sea at the Poop, as we were in the Cabbin going to eat; it beat in all the Cabbin-Windows and Bulk-Head, and hove the First Lieutenant half-way between the decks, with several Muskets and Pistols that hung there, darting a Sword that was against the Bulk-Head of the Cabbin, through my man's Hammock and Rug, which hung against the Bulk-Head of the Steeridge, and had not the Bulk-Head of the great Cabbin given way, all we who were there must inevitably have been drowned. . . . Our Yard was stay'd on the Deck, and it was a Wonder that many were not killed with the Shutters, the Bulk-Head and the Arms, which were drove with a prodigious Force; but God in his Mercy deliver'd us. . . ."

The *Dutchess* kept running south before the storm, an ensign in her main-topmast shrouds as a signal of distress. The cold was intense. Rogers, not knowing what had happened, and afraid both ships would be driven on the ice in the darkness, fired a gun to signal the *Dutchess* to bring to; but she could not. Informed of the distress flag and concluding her mainmast had been sprung, he bore south with her.

The ice-encrusted ships ran through the night. Slanting, pyramidal mountains surged and lifted them to hang high on the crests in the howling air for one instant above a caving emptiness and then be dropped violently down into the troughs, rolling and plunging, while unbelievable avalanches foamed, slammed down and went over them. The only thought left was a bare hope to hang on, to survive.

In the early hours of January 6th the storm began to abate; the weather of the Horn let go of them for a moment. It had other tricks in store. That day, though huge seas continued beating from the northwest, there was haze and fog with occasional rain squalls. The men of the *Dutchess* hung out all their clothes—"the Ship and Rigging cover'd with them from the Deck to the Main-Top" —in a hopeless effort to dry them. Rogers had an observation of the sun: Lat. 60° 58′; they were surrounded by ice.

The icebergs, drifting slowly east and north in the current, were, like almost everything else about the Horn, immense, incredible, the largest known. Numbers have been sighted by other mariners whose peaks towered 1000 feet and 1200 feet above the surface.

At the latitude the *Duke* and *Dutchess* had now reached, the exploding cold was just about unbearable for men without heat or fires, wearing soaked, stiff clothes, sleepless, beaten to exhaustion by the sea and living on a cold, inadequate diet. One by one, the men began to sicken. "*John Veale* a Landsman died, having lain ill a Fortnight, and had a swelling in his Legs ever since he left *Grande* . . . this is the first that died by Sickness out of both Ships since we left *England*." There were many more to follow.

It may have been with them, as it was with Shelvocke

a few years later, that they saw at this point no life of any kind, no birds, no fish. It is almost certain—since there are no entries on the point for several days—that they were not able to take an observation to determine their position, because of fog, snow, mist and overcast. Dampier, when he made the rounding with Davis in 1684, reported that they did not see the sun at rising or setting from the time they left the Falklands (the "Sibbel de Wards") until they got into the South Sea.

Here you pitch on this immensity, rolling from horizon to horizon, and how do you know exactly where you are on the vast surface of the turning earth or how far you have come? If the sun is blotted out, there must still, at times, be the stars on which the turning earth looks out, and sighting up with the proper instruments, knowing where certain fixed stars should stand in the heavens at that time of night, a man could draw lines back and triangulate from their light and the position they occupy in the arc of the earth's sky. Where the lines intersect, that is the man's position, within an allowable mile or two, on the huge surface of the turning world. But if the man does not know what the actual time of night is, and cannot observe the fixed stars' position with any exactitude, then he is more or less sailing into unknown space.

And when not only the sun but the ambiguous stars are invisible for days on end, the man, reduced to a sandglass, log line and erratic compass, has crossed over for a period into a freezing nowhere.

Another storm struck them: again the humming, booming, howling, twanging. Again the toy figures high aloft on yardarms were swung back and forth on whipping poles, whose arc covered almost the whole arc of the black sky; again the wind-driven, shotgun pellets of ice and, at the helm, five or six men on the whipstaff, fighting to hold it. Then as the inundations thundered over them—the immeasurable volumes of an immeasurable ocean—if a plank started, or a hatch gave, she would tilt, fill and dive down; and against that they could only curse after a fashion and pray.

They were allowed to pass. This storm was briefer. That same day, January 10th, they had an observation of the sun: "We have no night here. Lat. 61° 53′ . . . being the furthest we run this way, and for aught we know, the furthest that any one has yet been to the Southward."

We were the first that ever burst/Into that silent sea. But it was not the furthest. In 1687 the buccaneer Captain Edward Davis had been to 63° south by "reckoning" and turned north at 62° 30′.

The wind veered, the *Duke* and the *Dutchess* were able to bear north-northwest: The temperature slowly climbed. On January 15th it was perhaps twenty degrees warmer, and they had another observation of the sun: "56° S. We now account ourselves in the *South Sea*, being got round *Cape Horne*."

They had broken through. They were now in the King of Spain's ocean. But, in fact, they were not through with the Cape yet. The violence and the ice let go, the rot took hold.

Part Two

ENCOUNTER

~~~~~~~~~~~~~~~~~~~~~~~

7

HOW TO
MAKE TROUBLE
FOR THE
KING OF SPAIN

Duke AND *Dutchess* plunged north in the cold swells of
the Peru Current. On January 16th Rogers observed:
"Fresh Gales of Wind with cloudy Weather. These 24
hours we had extraordinary smooth Water, as if we were
close under Land: Indifferent warm Weather. Wind from
W.S.W. to W. by N."

They were headed for the islands of Juan Fernández,
lying several hundred miles off the coast of Chile, and

they were in a hurry. After the long weeks at sea and the ordeal of rounding the Horn, the men were beginning to sicken and die, principally from scurvy. It was imperative that the ships reach Juan Fernández as quickly as possible, particularly the one island where they could put in to refit and recuperate. But finding it was another matter.

This ocean into which they had broken, and which they would eventually cross, comprises an area so vast that there is, or was, a working hypothesis in geophysics that it covers the hole left in the earth's surface when the moon was torn out.

It is by far the largest division of the earth's hydrosphere, with double the area of the next largest ocean, the Atlantic, and more than double the volume. It is big enough, though its full extent was not known then— 63,801,700 square miles in area, 169,650,000 cubic miles in volume—to accommodate the entire land surface of the earth, with enough space left over for another Africa.

The sole proprietor of this area—according to the terms and concepts of human affairs—was the King of Spain; at least his dominions, or part of his dominions, ringed it.

One pictures an emperor in black: thin-lipped, spindle-legged, implacable, pacing the polished corridors of the Escorial beneath the El Grecos and the portraits by Velázquez; at his back the enormous shadow of Torquemada; on the wall the painting of the grim cardinal in crimson; around, before, beside him, the terrible presence of the officers of the Holy Inquisition in their cowls, moving with a measured gait, righteous, pitiless. But the king himself, Philip V, formerly the Duke of Anjou, did not conform to the picture at all. Born a Bourbon and a Hapsburg and raised at the court of Versailles, he was young and not unamiable, had fairly handsome features and a sometimes vacuous expression. At sixteen he was catapulted onto the throne of Spain by his grandfather, Louis XIV, who intended by this measure to annex the Spanish Empire to the Kingdom of France. Fortunately, or unfortunately, Philip had never been trained to do anything in particular, much less to rule.

When he first came to Spain, barely beyond the age of puberty, he was miserable and homesick beyond belief for France. Then he was married to a thirteen-year-old princess, María Louisa of Savoy. His sexual education seems to have been as neglected as the rest; but he made up for that instantly, becoming an insatiable and compulsively faithful husband—so faithful that he never considered another woman as long as María Louisa lived and so insatiable that he had to be restrained from exercising his marital rights on the night she lay dying.

He suffered from a predisposition to melancholy, and his melancholia grew progressively worse with the years until he took to spendng weeks or even months at a time in bed.

This individual ruled a good part of the earth. His empire included Spain, the Low Countries, Milan, Naples, Sicily, all of South America except Brazil, all Mexico, Central America, most of the West Indies, numerous trading posts in Africa, parts of the American Southwest, and the major parts of the Philippines.

Only, of course, he did not exactly rule. ". . . *pourvu qu'il ait une femme dans son lit,*" wrote the Duchesse d'Orléans, "*il n'en demande pas d'avantage.*" Provided, always, that the woman was his wife. And, therefore, his child bride ruled; and her close confidante, her Camarera or Lady of the Bedchamber, the Princesse des Ursins, ruled; and, beyond them, all the higher and lower echelons of state and church.

Still, the empire belonged to him in name and by representation, as it had belonged to his predecessors;

and the officers of the *Duke* and *Dutchess*, as they bore
north by west in the race for Juan Fernández, knew almost all about those who had been before them on this
course to strike at the power of Spain.

A seventeenth-century Dutch account of the Nassau
fleet, which sailed for the west coasts of Spanish America
in 1624, begins: "It was observed very early, by the best
politicians in the *United Provinces,* that the most effec-
tual method of distressing his Catholic Majesty would be
the sending of a fleet to the *South Ses.*"

The first to distress His Catholic Majesty in the South
Sea had, of course, been Drake. The Spaniards felt so
safe that when he attacked them there, they could not
at first believe the *Golden Hind* was a foreign galleon,
but thought she must be a Spanish ship turned pirate.
And even after it was over and done, they still felt safe.
The oceans remained; time and distance and all the rest
of the odds remained.

The next, however, was Thomas Cavendish—then
called Candish—the slight, smiling young man, almost
a boy. He made out nearly as well as Drake. Off Cape
San Lucas, at the point of Baja California, he captured
the Manila Galleon. He paused at the Philippines long
enough to hang a few people who had offended him,
bearded and delicately insulted the Governor of Manila,
and then went around the Cape of Good Hope and on
home laughing, the second Englishman to circumnavigate
the globe.

After that the odds began to work again and despite
other attempts the King of Spain suffered thereafter no
further distress from Englishmen in his closed sea for
nearly another century. But, after the English, the Dutch
got busy. As early as 1595, an expedition under Cornelis
de Houtman went around the Cape of Good Hope to the
Indies—in flagrant violation of the ruling that this route,

according to the Pope, belonged to the Portuguese—and brought back a treaty with the Sultan of Bantam, in Java. This founded the Dutch East India Company.

Other expeditions followed the other way, going through the Strait of Magellan or around the Horn— raiders like Spilbergh and explorers like Schouten and Jakob Le Maire. The Nassau fleet, sailing from Texel in 1624, consisted of eleven ships, 1637 men, 294 iron and brass cannon. This was the one that set out to distress the King of Spain in the worst way, and, indeed, it must have caused him considerable harassment and distress.

The fleet put in at Juan Fernández; careened, laid in supplies, and then headed north. Spanish intelligence was ahead of it, and the coast of Peru had been alerted. This may have saved most of the towns, but it did not save the shipping. The Dutch took and burned thirty to forty ships at Callao, the port of Lima, blockaded the port, sent a detachment down to Puna and up to the town of Guayaquil, which was captured and burned.

After a few more operations, they sailed northwest by north to refit and provision at the Galápagos, missed the Galápagos—anybody could have missed the islands, all of them, considering the charts and the state of navigation at that time—and finally cruised off Acapulco to wait for the Manila Galleon.

But the eleven ships had only so much food and water. They could not find any place to get more in the amounts required, and time, as they rocked and waited, ran out on them. As the weeks passed, there was scurvy again and dysentery, the crews so depleted or weakened that the fleet could barely be manned. And then they were at the final point.

There was just enough left of their putrid supplies to get them across the Pacific to Guam and then to Batavia. To delay any longer for a galleon which, while real

4*

enough, existed for them only as a hope and an imagination, meant that they would never make it across the Pacific at all. The odds had caught up. What was left of the original eleven ships and 1637 men went west across the empty ocean.

The Dutch were convinced. They pulled back to their profitable business in the Indies, and did not again bother His Majesty in the Great South Sea, except for one inconclusive operation in 1642, when five ships went through the Strait of Le Maire, fomented and aided a rebellion in Chile, raised general hell and then returned the way they had come.

From that point on, the Spaniards could consider any threat against them in these waters as a joke. They were still laughing when the English returned in 1670. Sir John Narbrough, with a commission from Charles II, got through the Strait of Magellan and sailed north. Narbrough did little or no damage and sailed back through the Strait of Magellan.

The following year, however, Henry Morgan crossed the Isthmus of Panama with 1250 English and French buccaneers. This force took the rich city of Panama, which was burned to the ground either by Morgan's orders or by accident. After a few weeks among the ruins—murdering, torturing, raping and looting—the buccaneers returned to their ships in the Caribbean.

Morgan generously doled out ten pounds apiece to the men, and then one night, with a few followers and the bulk of the treasure, weighed anchor and slipped away, leaving his faithful followers beached and abandoned to the Spaniards, the Indians and their own devices.

Morgan, of course, never sailed on the South Sea itself. He bought a knighthood and, full of years and honor, went into semiretirement as deputy-governor of Jamaica. The buccaneers who came after—not blessed, like him, with plenty and all the rewards of the just life—were forced to hunt further.

The first to operate on the South Sea was a group of buccaneers, commanded by a Captain Sawkins, which in 1680 crossed the Isthmus on foot and embarked in canoes. Dampier was along and with him a literate friend named Basil Ringrose, who also published an account of the adventures.

The advance guard of this group, sixty-eight men in all, fought the notable battle of Perico, in a bay on an island of that same name off Panama. Armed only with muskets, pistols and cutlasses, and crammed into canoes and periaguas whose gunwales were barely awash, they performed the almost incredible feat of engaging and defeating three small Spanish warships.

It was a bloody battle, and the Spaniards fought bravely. The buccaneers won it by the accuracy of their musket fire, shooting down the helmsmen and sail trimmers so that the ships could not maneuver, shooting through the gunports and killing the gunners so that the cannon could not be brought to bear. The battle lasted for hours, and the buccaneers lost nearly a third of their force, but on the Spanish barks there was hardly a man left who was not dead, dying or badly wounded. The warships struck their colors, and Sawkins' men seized them, together with all the shipping in that bay, including a fairly large galleon.

Now in possession of something like a fleet, they blockaded the city of Panama. When the governor sent a message to ask why and by what right they were there, Sawkins answered that they had come to help King Golden Cap, the King of Darien, "who was the Lord of Panama and all the country thereabouts. And that since we were come so far, there was no reason but that we should have some Satisfaction. So that if he pleased to send us five hundred pieces of eight for each Man, and one thousand for each Commander, and not any further to annoy the Indians . . . that then we would desist from all further Hostilities, and go away peaceably; otherwise we would stay there and get what we could. . . ."

The distracted governor then wanted to know "from whom we had our commission, and to whom he ought to complain for the damages we had already done them." Sawkins informed him that as yet all the company had not yet regrouped "but that when they were come up, we would come and visit him at Panama, and bring our Commissions on the Muzzles of our Guns, at which time he should read them as plain as the Flame of Gunpowder could make them."

They never did mount an attack on Panama, but they raided up and down the Pacific coast, and in one action Captain Sawkins was killed. After that they regularly elected and deposed captains, some of whom were alternately put down in irons and then reinstated. At one point they sailed south to the Juan Fernández islands to refit. They left abruptly when three large Spanish warships hove into sight—so abruptly that one of their men, an Indian named William, was left behind in the rush. He was not the first nor the last nor the most famous man to be marooned there, but he had a good long stay.

After some additional forays and a disastrous attack on the town of Arica in Chile, the original force split up. One group, including Dampier, headed north, crossed the Isthmus again and returned to the West Indies; the others remained in the South Sea a little longer to continue raiding under a Captain Bartholomew Sharp, each man hoping to make enough to retire on. They took a couple of prizes, one of them fairly rich, but in the next, the richest by far they ever captured, they were unfortunate. This ship, the *San Rosario*, had several thousand pieces of eight on board and other good things, which were promptly appropriated. She was also loaded with "700 pigs of plate" —crude silver from the mines. The buccaneers thought it was tin. They took one pig of this "tin" to make bullets out of it and left the other 699 in the hold when they turned the ship back over to its Spanish crew. Then, brawling and drinking, they went down and around the Horn and up through the South Atlantic to the West Indies. Here they learned the word was out for them; and, with an eye to the inevitable rope, they cautiously scattered. Most of the one pig of silver they took had long since been melted down and blown out of gun barrels. What remained, about a third of it, was given to a "Bristol man" at Antigua. This gentleman sold the fraction back in England for seventy-five pounds sterling. The 699 pigs of crude silver they left in the hold of the *San Rosario* were worth at that time nearly $850,000; and considering all you could get then for a penny, this would have been enough to buy each of them a comfortable estate.

News of these exploits got about. Fresh groups of buccaneers, some English, some French, started slogging across the Isthmus and embarking in canoes. Remembering the battle of Perico and the tactics employed there, they counted on shortly having ships of their own, Spanish ships, and shortly they had them. Many, if not all, of these groups sometimes combined operations for a period, particularly when anything massive was planned, and then, because of feuds and jealousies and the continual differences between English and French, split up again.

Rogers and Courtney and Cooke and Dover knew almost all about them—where they went, what they did and, most importantly, the islands they found where they could more or less safely careen and lay in fresh supplies; the officers of the *Duke* and *Dutchess* had available the published accounts of such literate members of the brotherhood as Ringrose, Wafer, Cowley and, notably, Dampier, who was at hand, of course, to brief them in person and detail—Dampier, whose memories must have been refreshed, or maybe darkened, by the seas in which he now found himself for the fourth time, as the frigates with their sick and dying drove north by west searching for Juan Fernández.

Dampier had returned to the South Sea a couple of years after his first voyage; in the company were the surgeon Lionel Wafer, a pirate of some note named Edward Davis, and sixty-seven other old hands under the captaincy of a John Cooke. They sailed from Virginia in 1683 in a ship of eighteen guns, which Davis and Cooke had stolen. Dampier kept a journal, later published in his famous *Voyages,* and said, "I came into these seas this second time more to indulge my Curiosity than to get Wealth, though I must confess at that time I did think the Trade lawful."

These gentlemen sailed to the Guinea coast, where they surprised and took a much bigger and better ship, fully provisioned for a long voyage and carrying thirty-six guns. They transferred to this ship, prudently burned the other, and proceeded south and around the Horn, on up to familiar Juan Fernández. At Juan Fernández the first thing they did was to look for and pick up William, the Mosquito Indian, still there after all those years since his ship had sailed away. William was understandably glad to see them.

Another small ship, the *Nicholas,* out of London and also bent on nothing but piracy, put in at the island while they were there. From her captain they learned of a third English vessel that had recently come into the closed sea; but that one, the *Cygnet,* had been fitted out by reputable merchants and provided with a cargo, her only purpose being peaceful trading and an honest profit. They did not come up with this bedeviled vessel and her distracted captain for a good many weeks, and by that time captain and crew had also "gone on the account."

The thirty-six-gun ship, *Batchelor's Delight*, captured off the Guinea coast, sailed north from Juan Fernández with the *Nicholas,* took some prizes and then put in at the Galápagos. There they found one island which afforded good facilities to refit and had plenty of fresh water, or so they reported. This account was important to Rogers and his captains. There were very few safe watering places in that sea, and the Galápagos, remote and difficult, could prove an excellent place to hide.

John Cooke, ailing at the Galápagos, died shortly thereafter and Davis succeeded him as captain of the *Batchelor's Delight*. A little later, following one of the usual quarrels about division of plunder, the *Nicholas* parted company and sailed west across the Pacific.

Davis in his single ship, with Dampier as his navigator, continued to raid. The first new ally proved to be the unhappy *Cygnet* they had heard about, bent on peaceful trading. Her captain, Swan, had done his best to carry out the original intentions of the owners and investors; but at every place he tried to trade, the Spaniards either went into hiding or saluted him with solid shot. After having had several men killed and wounded and having drawn a complete blank everywhere, he arrived at the Gulf of Nicoya on the coast of Costa Rica, where his crew voted to hoist the red flag and break out the guns. Swan never felt happy about piracy, though he practiced hard at it for a while; he kept seeing the rope's end over his shoulder.

Ringrose, who was with him, may have felt the same way but in the sense of a man who has repeatedly risked his neck and feels that he has used up most of his chances, that he has a very small stock left. This was the

Ringrose who had crossed the Isthmus and fought with Sawkins at Perico, cruised with Sharp and the first buccaneers in the South Sea, and was one of the survivors of the fight at Arica.

After he finally reached England again, Ringrose published a journal of his experiences, perhaps thinking, like many writers, that the book would make his fortune but finding, like most writers, that it did not. He was, therefore, compelled to ship out again as cape merchant or supercargo aboard the peaceful *Cygnet*.

And now he found himself back in the same place and on the same business. He and his companions had, of course, no commission entitling them to any consideration either by their enemies or their countrymen. In fact, the commissions generally carried by the buccaneers were so obviously false or worthless that the Spaniards commonly hanged prisoners with their commissions around their necks. As for Swan, he decided that the only commission he needed was the fact of having been shot at when he tried to trade.

Davis with Dampier in the thirty-six-gun ship and Swan with Ringrose in the small sixteen-gun *Cygnet* captured Payta and the small garrisoned island of Puna, tried to take Guayaquil but failed and turned north again. In the waters off Panama they were presently joined by a new influx of buccaneers coming across the Isthmus. The first of these was a mixed French and English force under a Captain Grogniet; then 180 Englishmen under a Captain Townley; finally 264 more French *"filibustiers."* Townley and his men captured a couple of ships for themselves. The French were given ships from among the prizes taken by Davis and Swan. In return, the *"filibustiers"* offered to provide all those who wanted some legal status for their actions with commissions, a commodity which they had with them in considerable quantity. These "commissions," it finally turned out, consisted of nothing more than a license to hunt and fish on the Island of Hispaniola in the Caribbean.

There were now 960 buccaneers on ten vessels of various sizes, with Davis as the commander. This combined force made a disorganized attempt on the Lima plate fleet, transporting the treasure from Peruvian mines. Unfortunately they caught up with it—not on its way to Panama but on its return passage to Peru—empty. The Spaniards knew all about them. The treasure had been hastily unloaded and hidden.

There were other dismal considerations. Only two of the pirate ships had cannon. The plate fleet, on the other hand, consisted of fourteen ships, six of them men-of-war, manned by 2500 men.

Only Davis attacked. The other buccaneer vessels either stayed out of range or ran. They would have been hunted down and hammered to pieces if Davis had not fought a brilliant delaying action during which his single ship was at one point engaging the whole Spanish fleet. He himself finally disengaged and escaped under cover of darkness. After that the combined buccaneer force broke up.

The subsequent operations of its component parts seemed singularly aimless and haphazard. The French went off en masse under Grogniet to operate on their own. Davis, Swan and Townley, with the larger part of the force, for a while cruised together before they split up. Swan and Townley, with their separate commands, decided to patrol the Mexican coast north of Acapulco in the hopes of intercepting the Manila Galleon; after that, Swan planned to sail to the East Indies. Dampier, who had long wanted to see the East Indies, transferred to Swan's ship, as did Ringrose. Davis, in the *Batchelor's*

Delight, headed south to continue to work the Spanish coasts.

The attempt on the Manila Galleon was, as usual, a complete failure. Swan and Townley cruised off Cape Corrientes until their water and food had just about run out; then they had to put in to the nearest place where they could get fresh supplies. While they were at this, the Galleon passed safely on its way and into Acapulco harbor.

Townley gave up in disgust and sailed back toward the area where Davis and Grogniet were separately operating. Swan, for one last strike, attacked and took the town of Santa Pecaque. Swan was not a really competent commander and, like Dampier, had trouble handling his men. The attack, while successful, was badly managed, and the withdrawal a disaster.

On the way back to the boats with their plunder, the buccaneers stumbled into an ambush. Fifty of them died right there, and among the dead was Dampier's old companion, Basil Ringrose: "My Ingenious Friend, Mr. Ringrose . . . who wrote that part of the 'History of the Buccaneers' which relates to Captain Sharp. He was at this time Cape-Merchant or Super-Cargo of Captain Swan's ship. He had no mind to serve this Voyage; but was necessitated to engage in it or starve."

Swan and Dampier in the *Cygnet* sailed west across the Pacific to Guam. They very nearly didn't make it. Even with bad water and worse food rationed to a minimum, they had only three days' supply left when they reached the Ladrones.

"It was well for Captain Swan that we got sight of it [Guam] before our Provision was spent." Not only for him; for Dampier, too. The crew, it turned out, had agreed that as soon as the food was gone they would cut up the officers and pop them into the kettle, beginning with Swan—not so much because he was the fattest as because they held him primarily responsible—and continuing, one by one as needed, with everyone else who had advocated their making this voyage. Swan, when he learned of it, said to bony Dampier: "Ah! Dampier, you would have made them but a poor meal."

While they were at Guam, the Acapulco Galleon, bound toward Manila, struck her rudder on some nearby shoals and was hung up for three days. The buccaneers learned about this from some natives and were hot to go after her. But, impossible as it seems, "Captain Swan persuaded them out of that humor." The *Cygnet* then sailed to Mindanao and anchored a couple of miles up river at a hospitable town ruled by a courteous and conniving sultan named Raja Laut, who coveted their ship, their money and their cannon.

For those who could pay—and everybody could—the town offered numerous diversions, plenty of food and drink and accommodating women. Then some of the buccaneers, not content with the girls available, began contemptuously taking familiarities with native wives in front of their husbands. The remedy for that was slow poison, at which the Mindanayans were adept; sixteen pirates succumbed. This was bad; but what was worse, the number of men with any money left to spend steadily decreased as the months passed; a growing number were confined aboard ship by economic necessity. After six months of it the large majority insisted on sailing. Swan stalled. He still had plenty of money, and he had no intention of returning to piracy. The men aboard ship promptly mutinied and, with Dampier along, sailed away, marooning Swan and thirty-six others on Mindanao.

After various adventures, the *Cygnet*, which was now both cranky and crazy, finally got into the Indian Ocean. Dampier, by then desperate, asked to be marooned on one of the Nicobar Islands. He was accordingly put ashore, along with two others who asked to be allowed to go with him. After incredible adventures Dampier finally escaped aboard an English ship in the harbor, leaving everything he owned behind him and taking with him only a tattooed native chieftain he had inherited—"The Painted Prince Jeoly." He arrived back in England in 1691, after an absence of twelve years, flat broke.

On January 20th Rogers had an entry: "Yesterday at three in the afternoon we saw high land bearing E. by N. dist. about 10 Ls. being the land about Port St. *Stephens* on the Coast of *Patagonia* in the *South-Sea*, describ'd in the Draughts. S. Lat. 47."

From the decks of the pestilential *Duke* and *Dutchess* Dampier could look around: only he out of all those others had returned to this ocean again. There were, of course, a lot of important differences. This expedition was far better planned, much better organized, equipped and disciplined than any other he had been on. But he remembered the others and what had happened to them.

Most of his shipmates marooned on Mindanao finally got away and went home. Swan, however, was not permitted to leave, first because he still had too much money and second because he took to boasting in his drunken rages that he would obtain another ship and return and blow the town apart. When he and a companion finally tried to escape down river, the thoughtful sultan had them murdered and dumped in the estuary.

At about the same time, off the western coasts of South America, the redoubtable Captain Townley was killed in action. Before that, he and his men had been joined by a number of the French *"filibustiers"* in those waters and proceeded on various enterprises chiefly notable for blood and barbarism. In one case, during negotiations for the ransom of a place they had taken, they decapitated twenty of their Spanish hostages and forwarded the heads in a canoe, just as a kind of earnest of what they might do if they were really annoyed.

After Townley died, his men joined the main group of French buccaneers under Grogniet. This combined force took Guayaquil, looted the city and retired with their hostages down river to the island of Puná, to wait for the ransom. When it was not forthcoming, they began cutting off heads again and sending these reminders to the city fathers. They had reached the number of four when, fortunately for them and their remaining hostages, the long-missing Captain Davis, their former over-all commander, hove to in the *Batchelor's Delight*. Davis and his men, operating on their own, had considerably enriched themselves in the course of a couple of years and were homeward bound around the Horn when they fell in with another ship, to whose crew they gambled away everything they had won. They, therefore, turned back and made a fresh start, cruising for some months and capturing several vessels, until they learned of the capture of Guayaquil and put in at Puná.

Davis, by all accounts, did not put up with outright murder. Moreover, he brought news that a Spanish squadron was on its way to the relief of Guayaquil. The buccaneers ashore had no fighting ships of their own and only the *Batchelor's Delight* stood between them and the guns of this squadron.

The killing of hostages stopped; the Spanish squadron duly appeared and was beaten off by Davis in a running, intermittent engagement that lasted seven days. Since he had saved not only their loot but their necks, the buccaneers ashore gave him and his crew a fair share in the plunder of Guayaquil. With this, and the rest, gambling losses now to some extent recouped, the *Batchelor's Delight* returned to Juan Fernández, sailed around the Horn and to the West Indies, where Davis and everybody took the King's pardon and went no more a-roving by the light of the moon.

The combined French force in boats and canoes headed north for Panama, recrossed the Isthmus on foot the way it had come, and dispersed. No buccaneers ever again troubled the King of Spain along those coasts. Dampier, it is true, came back to raise hell as captain of his own ship, the *St. George,* some sixteen years later, accompanied for a few months by a consort, the *Cinque Ports* commanded by a Captain Stradling. Dampier took the small town of Puná, failed in an attempt on the city of Guayaquil, and then off the Mexican coast actually intercepted and attacked the Manila Galleon.

He was beaten off and barely escaped being sent to the bottom, eventually lost his ship and headed home in a captured vessel. By the time of that voyage, however, the War of the Spanish Succession had begun, and Dampier sailed as a privateer with proper Letters of Marque.

The last of the buccaneers had long since left the Great South Sea. Less than half of those who started out ever got back. The rest were dead of scurvy, fever, dysentery, lead, steel and an assortment of accidents, including snakebite. Raveneau de Lussan, the only one of the French to publish a journal, wrote: "I had so little hope of ever coming back that for more than fifteen days I could not take my return for anything but an illusion— and this obsessed me to such an extent that I avoided sleep for fear that on awakening I would find myself back in those countries from which I had escaped."

It was to these countries and these places that the *Duke* and *Dutchess* were now headed.

8

THE HERMIT
OF
JUAN FERNÁNDEZ

THE *Duke* AND *Dutchess* held north for Juan Fernández, and every day counted in the race to get fresh food and water for the men. The *Dutchess* had already buried on January 14, 1709, one man dead of scurvy. On January 21st another died on board the *Duke:* "George Cross, a Smith by Trade, an Armourer's mate." On January 22nd the *Dutchess* buried two more; she had then thirty men critically ill with scurvy and eight with severe respiratory diseases. Her crew was in worse condition than that of the *Duke,* the number of men suffering from the effects of the cold, wet and exhaustion being greater because of the shattering wave that went over her south of the Horn. "We spoke with our Consort this day, who complains their Men grow worse and worse, and want a Harbour to refresh 'em . . ."

On both ships the cases of scurvy steadily increased. Now not only days but even hours counted in reaching the island. The desperate problem was finding it. January 26th: "We are very uncertain of the Latitude and Longitude of *Juan Fernandez* the Books laying 'em down so differently, that not one Chart agrees with another; and being but a small Island we are in some doubts of striking it, so to design to hale in for the main land to direct us."

The pressure mounted. Every delay meant additional deaths, but to miss the island entirely—to head west thinking they were between it and the mainland only to discover finally that it had all along been east of them and they had been many days voyaging into the empty Pacific—meant disaster.

Early on the morning of January 31st—Latitude 34° 10′S—the *Duke* and *Dutchess* sighted the key island of the Juan Fernández group, the plentiful one: Más a Tierra.

There are three islands. Más a Tierra, the largest, lies some 365 miles west of Valparaíso. Near it is the small island of Santa Clara and a hundred miles farther west Más Afuera, a mountain with plenty of water but little else. The Spanish voyager Ulloa noted that one of the streams cascading from its summit fell into the ocean with such violence that the foam could be seen at a distance of three leagues. But Más Afuera was interdicted: no harbor for any ship, no bottom for anchorage, almost no place along its precipitous shore for even a boat to put in.

Más a Tierra also presented difficulties: the same high

cliffs of volcanic rock, turbulent currents and strong off-shore winds; but there were a few good beaches and at least two bays suitable for anchorage. Although the name Juan Fernández actually applied to a group of three islands, this was the island referred to by custom as Juan Fernández.

Staring in the summer-morning light at its peaks—still many miles away across the rolling swell—the men on the *Duke* and *Dutchess* could almost smell its ferns and forests wreathed in early fog, its grassy savannas and stands of pimiento trees and sandalwood, its cascading, medicinal streams.

On those distant, bluish slopes there were plenty of goats, fruits and berries and various greens; there were the high cabbage trees, or cabbage palms, which Dampier had told about: "It has no Limbs or Boughs, but at the head there are many Branches . . . not covered, but flat, with sharp edges; they are 12 to 14 feet long . . . The Cabbage Fruit shoots out in the midst of these Branches, from the top of the Tree . . . The Cabbage itself, when it is taken out of the Leaves, which it seems to be folded in, is as big as the small of a man's Leg; it is as white as Milk, and as sweet as a Nut, if eaten raw, and it is very sweet and wholesom if boiled."

In those waters there were huge spiny lobsters for boiling and broiling and so many fish that Ringrose had reported he caught numbers weighing up to twenty pounds each without even baiting his hook.

By noon the island was still nearly thirty miles away. Captain-Doctor Thomas Dover could not wait. He wanted to go ashore at once with a boat crew in the pinnace. It is probable that this time his customary impatience was not for himself, but for the sick and dying men under his care.

Rogers, though reluctant to let the pinnace put out while they were still so far from the island, finally gave in to oblige Dover and perhaps also to avoid precipitating at this point a conflict which was slowly and certainly shaping. At two in the afternoon the dauntless physician was on his way. The men on the *Dutchess* thought it crazy, or more politely: "Admir'd our Boat attempted going ashore at that distance from Land."

As darkness settled over the deserted island, when the boat was still three or four miles offshore, suddenly, unaccountably, a pinpoint of light appeared on the indistinct heights and then another, flaring rapidly larger and brighter.

The pinnace put about fast and headed back for the ships. Rogers broke out lights and had a quarter-deck gun and muskets fired to show the *Duke's* position as she plied in the lee of the island. Eventually, twelve hours after he set out, Dover and the boat crew were back on board, having first been picked up by the *Dutchess,* and just in time, for it began to blow strongly.

The captains concluded the lights were those of a landing party and that the large French squadron, of whose earlier departure for the South Sea they had heard at Oratava, was there before them and at anchor in one of the bays on the other side of the island.

During the rest of the night they prepared to engage, to hunt out the enemy and try to smash him. If the information they had received was correct, they would be facing a considerably superior force. Nevertheless, they had no choice. Water, food, repairs were essential. Being beaten in battle and sunk was a gamble; but what would happen if they didn't get ashore, if they turned away from Juan Fernández, was certain.

The next morning, February 1st, the two frigates were on a long tack, fighting winds and currents to round the southern end of the island and come up the eastern side to reconnoiter its bays. Strong offshore "flaws"—sudden bursts or squalls of wind—whipped and hammered them. They sighted the middle bay, the one that afforded the best harbor, and found it empty, found the other bay empty also. The French squadron, they supposed, had sailed and was standing somewhere off to sea.

The bay spread before them, its waters slanting briskly in the sunlight, open and inviting. But each time they tried to enter it, they were turned back. Gusts from the mountains drove down with force enough to strip their topsails, then abruptly died, then slammed them again.

It was, in fact, the very difficulty of reaching into this bay and of tacking off a shore on which several ships had been wrecked—and more were to be in the years to come—that prevented the Spaniards from visiting the island more often or patrolling it effectively.

Across the decks of the *Duke* and the *Dutchess* blew the freshness of woods and streams, mixed with the sting of the spray and the rottenness of the ships. They were near enough now to hear the sea lions barking on the rocks.

In desperation, Rogers sent the yawl ashore to pick up whatever fresh food could be found. Dover, again in command, was accompanied by seven armed men, in case the enemy might have left a garrison. By noon of that day the offshore gusts were so violent that on the *Duke*, "We were forc'd to let fly our Topsail-Sheet, keeping all Hands to stand by our Sails, for fear of the Wind's carrying 'em away . . ."

When the yawl did not return, Rogers dispatched the pinnace with more armed men to find out what had happened. A few hours passed; there was no sign of either boat. He broke out a signal, and the pinnace immediately returned, carrying a load of fresh crawfish for the sick, and one passenger: ". . . a Man cloth'd in Goats-Skins, who look'd wilder than the first Owners of them." It was **this** man who had lit the fires the night before and who had been for more than four years the solitary inhabitant of Más a Tierra.

His name was Alexander Selkirk or "Selcraig" and he was to serve, though he may never have known it, as the model for Defoe's classic, *Robinson Crusoe*. He had been born and raised in Largo, Scotland. He was a seaman for many years, and Dampier knew him from a previous voyage, though not what happened to him. Selkirk had been a mate on the *Cinque Ports*, the ship that, under the difficult Captain Stradling, had for a period accompanied the *St. George*, during Dampier's privateering foray in 1704.

Dampier and Stradling, after stopping at Juan Fernández as usual for essential supplies and to make repairs, had been abruptly driven off by the appearance of a strong enemy squadron. They left all their boats behind, and the *Cinque Ports* inadvertently stranded five men. Later, when Dampier and Stradling parted company, the *Cinque Ports* returned to pick up her boats, and any of the five orphans who remained. It turned out that boats and men were gone: long lost, and for good, to the visiting Spaniards. But Selkirk, having had all he could stand of Stradling and the *Cinque Ports*, which he considered ready to sink (as it finally did), took the occasion of this return to demand that he be marooned. Stradling accommodated him at once and sailed away.

For the next four years and two months Selkirk had, except for one brief interruption, the island to himself. "At his first coming on board us," Rogers said, "he had so much forgot his Language for want of Use, that we could scarce understand him, for he seemed to speak his words by halves. We offer'd him a Dram, but he would not touch it, having drank nothing but Water since his being there, and 'twas some time before he could relish our Victuals."

Later he regained a taste for these victuals and the dram, too, and for all the other things which the ships brought back to him and which were to prove for him more or less fatal.

The *Duke* and the *Dutchess* came to anchor in the middle bay on the night of February 2nd. Clearing and unloading of the frigates began. Sails were stripped and carried ashore to be mended and to provide tents for the sick. The *Duke* had twenty-one men in serious condition, and the *Dutchess* even more. Able men were assigned to catch fish, which they hooked in quantities. Watering parties filled buckets and casks. As the Spaniard Ulloa later wrote: "The water, of which several streams fall from the eminences into the sea, is very light, creates an appetite, and among other medicinal qualities, is excellent against indigestions."

A smith's forge was set up. Near it the coopers were put to work. Sailmakers stitched canvas to make a tent city. The captains had their own pavilion. " 'Twas very pleasant ashore among the green Piemento Trees, which cast a refreshing Smell. Our House was made by putting up a Sail round four of 'em, and covering it a-top with another Sail; so that Capt. *Dover* and I both thought it a very agreeable seat, the Weather being neither too hot nor too cold."

On the first day ashore Selkirk "The Gouvernour," as Rogers called him, "tho we might as well have named him the Absolute Monarch of the Island," caught a couple of wild goats barehanded, an art he had been forced to learn for survival when his powder and shot ran out. He boiled the meat with turnip tops, from a turnip crop Dampier's crew had planted five years before, and made an excellent broth for those suffering from scurvy. During the rest of their stay on Juan Fernández, Selkirk never failed to provide a number of goats daily, as well as herbs, fruits, vegetables and a general fund of information concerning an island about which he knew, had been forced to learn, more than anyone else.

When first put ashore by Stradling, Selkirk had with him his clothes, bedding, musket, a pound of powder, bullets, tobacco, a hatchet, knife, kettle, Bible, his books and mathematical instruments. He was comfortable enough and secure, with the freedom of an enormous privacy.

But as he watched the last visible sign of the *Cinque Ports'* hull down on the horizon, he must have felt something like a boy who has chosen to camp out for the night—his cooking fire laid, tent all cozy and snug, his axe and pocket knife handy, everything a bubbling anticipation for the boy, until the sun sets and the night comes on to disclose to him his utter aloneness: an unanswering silence split now and then by the noise of an insect like the report of a gun; a night of eyes and stone watchers and unbearable menace: a night strung to the scream of terror, saturated with the terrors in himself and of himself projected in patches on the huge, impassive, inscrutable face bending everywhere over him.

But for Selkirk, it was not just one night. Another ship, a friendly ship, might not come for years, might never come. During the first eight months, the terror of his solitude steadily increased and he suffered long periods of suicidal depression.

He tried to keep busy. He built two small huts of pimiento wood; in the larger one he slept and in the other dressed and stored his food. But at first he never ate unless driven to it by hunger pangs—partly because he could not relish his food without bread and salt but chiefly because of his profound depression and melancholy. And he never slept until complete exhaustion set in and he could watch by his signal fires no longer. The fire, at the very least, was cheerful and promsing; the pimiento wood burned with a fine fragrance, and the light reached out into the darkness and the sea as a kind of assertion of his existence—to inform anyone who might cross the edge of this nothingness that here, among these lost rocks, was Alexander Selkirk, still alive and not yet mad.

But no one came. Like almost every other individual in enforced solitude, he was compelled from time to time to confront all those buried conflicts and evaded issues in himself, all those unanswered questions, that men in civilization or among their fellows escape by work and ambition and diversions, by drugs or drink or sex or entertainment or just by talking. He was compelled to stare into the abyss from time to time as it opened, with all the horrible vertigo of height and depth, of the vertical inner being.

He nearly lost his reason. He read and wept and raved, sang psalms and prayed. And gradually he began to be well and whole again, more truly whole than he had ever been, to achieve balance and serenity.

A few ships passed, but only two ever came to anchor. When he approached the shore to determine their nationality, he stumbled on a landing party. He had decided that if the ships were French he would surrender but not if they were Spanish—preferring, in that case, to risk dying alone on the island, since he was convinced the Spaniards would either kill him outright or send him as a slave to the mines for life, because he knew too much about their interdicted ocean.

Discovering these were Spaniards, he ran, and they shot at him. Selkirk made for the woods, where he climbed to the top of a tall tree and lay hidden among the leaves.

After a while a number of men searching for him passed near, beat around, killed a few goats, urinated at the base of the tree and went away. Selkirk was left with the silence.

His cure continued. After the first, worst eight months, recovery not only from his immediate condition but from what might be called a lifelong condition had been fairly rapid and steady, with only a few, rare remissions.

He was calm, he was at peace; he had come to terms, or so it seemed, with his island and himself, "so that he said he was a better Christian while in this Solitude than he ever was before, or than, he was afraid, he should ever be again." And Selkirk's Christianity during this period had, it is safe to say, little to do with convention or evangelism. It was at something of a remove from the emotionalism of the revival meeting and from the solidarity of the church social, from the obsession with terms and symbols, the belaboring of texts, the insistence on arbitrary and often contradictory assumptions. It did not even much concern good works for his fellow men; he had no fellow men to do good to—equally, there could be no question of bringing them to the light and saving them.

Whatever he found during those years was almost certainly free from all the customary preoccupations with sin and rigid spiritual predestination and determinism, free from intellectual fixations on points of dogma as a kind of defensive drawing-together—creed by creed, concrete wall by wall—in protection against the unanswered, the unresolved, the face of the night. Selkirk had been too far for that; he had looked over the edge; he had been forced, at least for once, to the face; and instead of destroying him—though it nearly did so—it gave him back a little less Selkirk and commensurately, at least for a period, something more whole.

As a sort of corollary to this, his physical condition steadily improved, until his general health, strength, reflexes, and coördination were incomparably better than they had ever been in his life.

When his gunpowder was exhausted, he had to depend for meat on catching goats barehanded, and barefooted as well, because his shoes had also long since given out. His feet soon hardened and toughened, and he became so fast and agile that he could outrace a goat in the open and outclimb it on the cliffs and rocks. He kept a tally: by the time Rogers arrived, he had taken over 500 goats this way for the pot and caught and set free, after earmarking them, 500 more. Some of these goats marked by Selkirk were still around when Anson put in at the island thirty years later.

Rogers and his officers and the crews were stunned by Selkirk's speed and endurance and general physical condition. They may have seen stronger or more powerful men but none, considering the diet of the times at sea and ashore, with such a combination of reflexes, energy and all-around good health. "We had a Bull-Dog," (the *soi-disant* Lord Harry, who had sailed with them from Cork) "which we sent with several of our nimblest Runners, to help him in catching Goats; but he distanc'd and tired both the Dog and the Men, catch'd the Goats and brought 'em to us on his back. He told us that his Agility in pursuing a Goat had once like to have cost him his Life; he pursue'd it with so much Eagerness that he catch'd hold of it on the brink of a Precipice, of which he was not aware, the Bushes having hid it from him; so that he fell with the Goat down the said Precipice a great height . . ." Luckily, when he crashed over the cliff, the goat was under him and he landed on top of it, breaking his fall. He came to, after a considerable period, with the dead goat beneath him; he was conscious but couldn't move and remained where he had fallen during a night and a day, until he finally took hold of enough strength to start crawling back, inch by inch, toward his hut, over a mile away. When he finally reached the hut, he collapsed and lay there for ten days.

Goat meat, during his years on the island, was both a staple and a necessity; it provided almost his only source of protein. Fish teemed, of course, in the shallows, but he found that without salt they gave him a kind of dysentery. Shellfish, however, were another matter, and on spiny lobsters, either boiled or broiled, he dined well.

He had turnips, when the crop came up, and the hearts of cabbage palms and water cress from the streams and small wild plums which grew in more or less inaccessible places and were very sweet. For seasoning he had pimientos and "found there also a black Pepper call'd *Malagita*, which was very good to expel Wind, and against Griping of the Guts."

He came to relish his diet, came to relish everything. The climate was mild, winter lasting only through June and July, with very rare frosts and occasional hail but frequent and heavy rainstorms. The rest of the year there were few storms, the days sunny and clear, and even at the height of summer no severe heat, thanks to the fact that Juan Fernández lies in the cold Peru Current.

When his clothes were gone, Selkirk made himself a coat and cap of goatskins "which he stitched together with little Thongs of the same, that he cut with his Knife. He had no Needle but a Nail; and when his Knife was wore to the back, he made others as well as he could of some Iron Hoops that were left ashore, which he beat thin and ground upon Stones. Having some Linen Cloth by him, he sow'd himself Shirts with a Nail, and stitch'd 'em with the Worsted of his old Stockings, which he pull'd out on purpose. He had his last shirt on when we found him in the Island."

During those first terrible months—the months that nearly finished him—part of Selkirk's ordeal had been the rats: thousands upon thousands of rats, prolific descendants of prolific ancestors from ships which had from time to time put in or been wrecked here. The rats swarmed over him in the fitful intervals of his tortured sleep—*Oh the mind, mind has mountains; cliffs of fall/ Frightful, sheer, no-man-fathomed.* . . . They gnawed his clothes; they bit and gnawed his hands and feet.

Fortunately, from the same pestilential hulks that disgorged the rats there had come, now and then, a few cats. And the cat population, reluctant as always to do anything but expand to the ecologically permissible limit, had enjoyed a correspondingly swift and satisfactory rise.

Selkirk, when he began to emerge from his terror and depression, set out to solve the rat problem by taming the cats, which had reverted and become completely wild. He coaxed them. He enticed them. He bribed them with banquets of goat meat. Soon, when he lay down to sleep, he had literally hundreds of cats curled up to sleep about him, in his hut, around his hut, on its roof. No rat ever came that way again.

Sometimes, as a kind of diversion, he carved his name on trees with the date of his being put ashore and the length of his stay up to that point, in case he did not survive to tell the tale. He also tamed a few kids. By day, and at night by firelight, he would sing and dance with them and his cats. Other of his cats sat in a circle around him— some curled up and watching, some dozing, some sitting and staring and some joining in. He was merry and content and no longer alone: until the ships came.

He had dreamed of rescue so long in the nightmares and frightful anxiety and then more or less forgotten or dismissed it, in the ease of that solitude which was no longer a solitude but everywhere informed and alive. But when he saw the ships and the lights in the rigging and heard the booming of the quarter-deck gun, the dream was back and he ran, almost automatically, as a reflex, to light his signal fires—not knowing what he was igniting, what, for him, was burning.

Rogers, trained in action and command for which he had a kind of genius, a man of wit and warmth, born to the world and its affairs with little or nothing of the recluse about him, very much admired Selkirk, not only for the way he had survived the ordeal but for his character and everything he showed then and thereafter. He wrote of him at length with a good deal of praise and very little moralizing.

And Dampier, that always curious observer, must have studied Selkirk carefully. As for Dover, it might be presumed that he was interested but impatient; this was a tale told among the rocks, lived out among the rocks, with just about zero significance in matters of any importance; it advanced no designs; it cured no one of anything; it built nobody a town house or country house, provided no carriages, filled no libraries, contributed nothing to anyone's professional reputation. Even as an individual the man offered little—there were plenty of ship's mates in the world, castaways were also not uncommon— and this one was not even a patient. He needed no treatment or dosages, exhibited no pathological symptoms of anything, unless it might be of some mental condition in the failure to care about things that counted. He was too damned healthy for any professional notice—though, of course, given a civilized diet and a civilized way of life, that would be changed.

Oh, yes, it was interesting; yes, it was odd—like a

visit to the zoo at the Tower of London, or to Bedlam—
but not interesting enough to sit up talking about it all
night; so circulate the port, or the Madeira, and let's get
on with plans.

But while Dover was called "Dr. Quicksilver"—because later in life he prescribed mercury in massive doses
for just about everything—it was Dampier who had the
quicksilver mind. And across that rolling, restless intelligence, inquisitive and acquisitive, something must have
flashed and flickered briefly as Dampier studied Selkirk
and listened to him, comparing this Selkirk with that other
Selkirk he had known years before.

He cannot have been unduly impressed by the mere
fact that the man had been marooned for so long and had
shown such ingenuity in coping with the physical problems. Dampier had been marooned himself, if much more
briefly, and had marooned others. Furthermore, he knew
at first hand of a very similar case on this same island—
that of the Indian named William—previously mentioned.

"This Indian," Dampier had written in the first volume of his *Voyages,* "lived here alone above three years,
and altho' he was several Times sought after by the *Spaniards,* who knew he was left on the island, yet they could
never find him. He was in the Woods, hunting for Goats,
when Captain *Watlin* drew off his men, and the Ship was
under sail before he came back to shore. He had with him
his Gun and Knife, with a small Horn of Powder, and a
few shot; which being spent, he contrived a way by notch-
ing his knife, to saw the Barrel of his Gun into small
Pieces. Wherewith he made Harpoons, Lances, Hooks and
a long Knife; heating the pieces in the Fire, which he
struck with his Gun-flint, and a piece of the Barrel of his
Gun, which he hardned; having learnt to do that among
the *English.* The hot pieces of Iron he would hammer out
and bend as he pleased with Stones, and saw them with

his jagged Knife; or grind them to an edge by long labour and harden them to a good Temper as there was occasion. All this may seem strange to those that are not acquainted with the Sagacity of the Indian: but it is no more than these *Moskito* Men are accustomed to in their own country, where they make their own Fishing and Striking instruments, without either Forge or Anvil; tho' they spend a great deal of Time about them."

But William—the extent of whose rough time could be gauged by the unstoical celebration he indulged when the first of his rescuers, a fellow Mosquito Indian, came ashore—apparently emerged from his ordeal unchanged *. . . and heard great argument/ About it and about: but evermore/ Came out by the same door where in I went.*

Selkirk, however, very definitely was changed, as Dampier could observe, definitely was not the same person that in he went. He had gained or found something, even if he might be on the verge of losing it again. There was about him at times a sudden stillness, a kind of silence that spread out and almost touched them—as if there were a little pool of it in him and around him, from all those years, almost something communicable—and together with this at times a kind of withdrawn concentration as if he were attending to some other voice or other insight, even partial, which had escaped them all.

Dampier must have wondered. In a sense, both he and Selkirk were misfits, unlucky, almost cranks, though in very different ways. The thought must have occurred that Selkirk in the terrible and unremitting solitude of his island might have touched, might have almost grasped, an indefinable, indeterminable something that Dampier—like a man chasing his hat in the wind—had been pursuing in the form of fame, fortune and intellectual curiosity all over the wide world.

But, of course, it was not his nature to be otherwise.

Dampier was born for that restlessness, born to make and to leave all those tables and maps and records and observations of four oceans and several continents that other men would follow and profit by. The question, the temporary misgiving about Selkirk, almost certainly crossed his mind—that was in his nature and the nature of his intelligence, too. But it may have been with him a little like the busy and successful man who talks about going off for a while by himself, of getting clear of all this for a month or so, living the simple life on plain, nourishing food, fishing and dozing, maybe meditating ten minutes a day and discovering who he really is. Or like someone, driven and tired, who reads a book about monastic life and dreams of a glorious escape as a monk or a nun or maybe of going to India or Tibet. But the next minute there is the drink to be drunk, the play to be seen, letters to be dictated, affairs to be arranged, bills to be paid, friends to be met, a breast to be kissed, the accelerator slammed to the floor—all suddenly equally glorious and a damn sight more substantial and "Hey Boys up go we!"

In any case, even if Dampier had been suited by temperament to undergo what Selkirk had undergone, it was too late. He was fifty-six. His fame was secure, but in respect to fortune or any provision at all for his old age, this voyage was his now or never. And there was a lot of work to be done.

In the tent city two more men died, Edward Wilts and Christopher Williams, for whom rest and warmth and a good diet came too late. All the other sick men recuperated rapidly.

Fish were hooked as easily and in the same tremendous quantities as earlier explorers had reported; snappers, bonitos, sea bass, yellowtail, weakfish, cavallas, oldwives. The huge spiny lobsters or crawfish caught among the rocks often ran to two and a half feet in length and weighed over ten pounds.

Herbs and plants were also available in great abundance: Rogers notes, among others, parsley, purslane, sithes and one "not much unlike Feverfew, of a very grateful Smell like Balm, but of a stronger and more cordial Scent . . ."

There are, as a matter of fact, some 142 species of indigenous plants on Juan Fernández, and two-thirds of these plants have not been found anywhere else. The rich vegetation on the high slopes includes huge ferns and plants with leaves measuring six to ten feet across, and in that day there were, but are no longer, fragrant sandalwood trees.

Seals swarmed ashore by the thousands, as Dampier had previously observed. Since this was now the Southern Hemisphere's autumn, they were not quite as plentiful, and not at all as savage, as in the mating season, when a man could not take a step without beating them aside with a stick; but they lined the shore of the bay to a considerable distance inland. Sea lions also frequented the place in incredible numbers, and many of these animals were huge. Rogers reports seeing one some sixteen feet long and weighing, at a guess, a ton. It might be concluded that he had seen something like a sea elephant, but his description is fairly exact and it is that of a sea lion.

The only land birds they found on the island were a kind of black bird, with red breast, and the hummingbird —the latter being abundant and of various colors, so abundant that a couple of hundred years later one of the principal exports of the Juan Fernández group was hummingbirds, hideously stuffed and mounted. But this bastard traffic did not, of course, exist then, and the bird could be observed as it still is seen in many places of the world today. Dampier described it: "The Humming-Bird is a pretty little feather'd Creature, no bigger than a great over-grown Wasp, with a black Bill no bigger than a small Needle, and his Legs and Feet in proportion to his body. This creature does not wave his Wings like other birds when it flies, but keeps them in a continued quick Motion like Bees or other Insects, and like them makes a continual humming Noise as it flies. It is very quick in Motion, and haunts about Flowers and Fruit, and like a Bee gathering Honey, making many near Addresses to its delightful Objects, by visiting them on all Sides, and yet still keeps in Motion, sometimes on one Side, sometimes on the other; as often rebounding a Foot or two back on a sudden, and as quickly returns again . . ."

The overhauling and refitting continued. Foul, contaminated casks were cleaned and filled with fresh water. Quantities of fish and goat meat were salted for future rations. A few sea lions were rendered to produce eighty gallons of oil for use in lamps, to save candles. Many of the men, lacking butter, also used such oil for frying meat, and some of them ate young sea lions; they insisted these were just as tasty and as good as English lamb, "tho' for my own part," Rogers remarked, "I should have been glad of such an Exchange."

Cargo and ship's stores were unloaded or shifted so that the frigates could be careened. And Selkirk, the Governor, was Rogers' adviser on everything about the island —how far out it was safe to anchor, the prevailing winds at that time of year, the location of springs and streams, where best to find herbs and greens and fruit, where to fish and to hunt.

These were some of the things they had brought with them, things he had not tasted or smelled in nearly half a decade: bread, salt, sugar, molasses, oatmeal, mustard, onions, vinegar; marmalade and tobacco; pipes and butts of wine; kegs of brandy (though he still could not relish the liquors); coffee, and chocolate.

Here in storehouse quantities were all the things he

had so long been without and seemed at one point so desperately to need: matches, knives, axes, clothing, chests of needles and thread; hammers, nails, chisels, squares, planes, awls, braces and bits, grindstones, ropes, blocks, pulleys and hoists; caldrons, kettles, pans, pots, bowls, porringers and cups; barrels of powder and shot; an arsenal of muskets, pistols and cutlasses; spades and shovels; canvas, baskets and mats; blankets and candles.

There were thousands of fish hooks, lines, nets, fish spears and harpoons. There were chests full of medicines, boxes of surgical instruments, pills, powders, tonics, elixirs, purgatives, stimulants, sedatives and painkillers, soap.

And all the other useful or essential things: pens, paper and ink; calipers and compasses; quadrants, astrolabes, telescopes, maps, mathematical tables, eyeglasses, forges and bellows and anvils; all the tools of the blacksmith, those of the carpenter, sailmaker and armorer; pumice stone, brimstone, turpentine, paint, rolled sheets of leather and lanthorns and padlocks; scales, weights, measures, sandglasses, calendars.

The check lists, the itemizations ran on in a fever. Everything paraded before him: sails, cannon, flags, ensigns, drums, trumpets, flutes, fifes, stringed instruments; the brave music and the merry, the nostalgically sad.

The personal possessions and perquisites of the captains, too, were spread out in a sense: the silver punch bowls and ladles and goblets; the packed finery for important occasions, coats of scarlet and cobalt blue with gold or silver buttons and silver and gold thread; stockings and shoes with bows and two-inch heels; soft leather boots; linen and broadcloth and velvet and lace; fine swords and pistols whose barrels and butts were inlaid with silver; books by the hundred, leather-bound, gilt, new books he had never yet seen, old books he had never yet read.

For Selkirk, all of it must have been, as the first sight

of the ships and the first sound of English voices had been, like a wave rolling over him, with all the combined impressions and associations of the past, the conditioning of a lifetime, in which the four years he had spent on this island were smashed and sunk.

It was not merely the things but what they and his rescuers represented—the cities with their smokes and shops, crowds and noise and industry; churches and hedges and gardens and palaces; women and bells and shouts and stinks and savors and, best of all, the freedom to spread, to communicate, to cross and recross that world at will, with the seas and the lands open to you, in the company of men, serving some use, not pinned to a deserted island misplaced on the maps, in a hostile ocean, confronting yourself.

Here, here—all of this might as well have been saying, with irrefutable logic—is the reality. What contentment you had, or seemed to have on the island, what Providence you seemed to discover in the quiet, that was an imagination, a fantasy, as hermits in their caves heard the wind speaking or conversed with animals—did not you in your extremity dance with kids and sing to cats? The whole of it, everything, was only an imagination projected out of your loneliness, forced on you by the solitude as your last defense, the way children alone in an extremity of terror imagine a guardian angel, and maybe it is a saving defense, as even an aberration can sometimes be saving, as long as it is temporary—but now the reality is back, the aberration is over, you're awake. This and everything it represents is the only world there is. That other world you had is no world at all; it is a simulacrum, a delusion, a nothing.

And with that, almost everything he had found or gained, or thought he had gained, on Juan Fernández was in doubt; it was gone. All that time looked to have been simply four years lost in a life.

Work on the ships went forward fast and efficiently. Rogers and Courtney pressed it. Every added day was a danger, compounding the chances of being caught here helpless—ships heeled over, half their cargoes and armament on the beach. By February 13th, careening was completed, cargo and supplies stowed, and the *Duke* and the *Dutchess* were ready to put to sea again. When they weighed anchor, Selkirk sailed with them as mate on the *Duke,* a position for which Dampier had recommended him at the beginning. The goatskins, of course, were long since discarded; Selkirk now wore good woolen stockings and pantaloons and a linen shirt and sturdy English shoes, though shoes of any kind, for a considerable period, cramped and distorted his feet and made them swell painfully.

He had, with all the other compensations of this return to reality, the comfort of being a man much marked and admired by almost every one—from Rogers, who respected and valued him for his qualities, and Dampier, who considered him as a kind of explorer and discoverer of a different order, to the most apparently unimaginative and insensitive hand, who knew something about the facts of marooning and could think of those four long years and shudder.

Rogers, noting reports of other men who had been marooned on the island, said: "But whatever there is in these Stories, this of Mr. *Selkirk* I know to be true; and his Behavior afterwards gives me reason to believe the Account he gave me how he spent his time, and bore up under such an Affliction, in which nothing but the Divine Providence could have supported any Man. By this one may see that Solitude and Retirement from the World is not such an insufferable State of Life as most Men imagine, especially when People are fairly call'd or thrown into it unavoidably, as this Man was . . . It may likewise instruct us, how a plain and temperate way of living conduces to the Health of the Body and the Vigour of the Mind, both which we are apt to destroy by Excess and Plenty, especially of strong Liquor, and the Variety as well as the Nature of our Meat and Drink: for this Man, when he came to our ordinary Method of Diet and Life, tho he was sober enough, lost much of his Strength and Agility. But I must quit these Reflections, which are more proper for a Philosopher and Divine than a Mariner, and return to my own Subject."

The bows dipped and plunged and sparkled as they headed North, everything again shipshape and Bristol fashion—cleaned, repaired, fumigated, aired, with plenty of fresh supplies of food and water. The ocean proffered itself, rising, pressing, cushioning them on the long swells, and the light on the vast, secret sea as the sun rose and set might have been like a path east and west to all the treasure houses of the King of Spain, now standing wide open.

They headed toward the island of Lobos off the coast of Peru to begin operations—a thousand miles away. The great guns were ready behind the closed gunports. All canvas was crowded on, and the ensigns and Union Jack snapped bravely. Between-decks were freshly painted red —a fine and convenient color that would cover the color of blood.

On Juan Fernández, now truly deserted, the waves still slapped and crashed and beat at the base of the cliffs, and the wind went emptily through the trees. Seals and sea lions coughed and barked; goats capered but to no music; the cats slipped back into wildness, and Selkirk's signal fires were long cold ash.

9

PERU
CURRENT

Duke AND *Dutchess*, as they continued north from Juan Fernández for their first appointments, had almost uninterruptedly fine weather. They were in the cold Peru Current: the immense ocean river that flows north from the Antarctic up the South American coast past the islands of Lobos, turns westward at Cabo Blanco, near the Gulf of Guayaquil, to wash the Galápagos, and so on out into the Pacific. Its temperature near the surface is fifteen to twenty degrees lower than that of adjacent waters; and the chill—as well as the incredible richness and variety of sea life the current supports—is continually renewed by upswellings from the great depths.

This current, also called the Humboldt, is perhaps the richest area of all the world's oceans in marine life, ranging from the microscopic to the immense. Cold water can absorb and hold more oxygen than warm. The Peru Current, having a high oxygen and mineral content, maintains a superabundance of those microscopic plants and animals on which the schools of small fish feed—schools which, in turn, support the other predators ranging in an ascending scale of size, the busy eaters busily eaten.

For the men on the decks of the two frigates, the first indication of the incredible abundance of life in this current would have been the birds. The ships kept some leagues safely out to sea to avoid being spotted from the coast; but even there, even that far out, in the early morning light the flocks would come from their invisible offshore islands—first the scouts hovering, banking in vertical turns, going up on the tip of a wing and on over and down, diving into the cold green water with a solid plop, to rise again gobbling their catch. And then after the scouts had located the schools of surface-swimming fish, the enormous flocks would arrive—white-breasted cormorants, big gray pelicans, white-headed gannets—flocks that overcast the sky, their cries and the booming of their wings creating such a compression and concussion of the air that a man had to swallow again and again to clear his ears.

They landed in masses, settling on the long swells in gigantic rafts, measureless acres of birds, falling, feeding, rising in overlapping vans to dive and gorge again, and in the late afternoon, having feasted to the limit, they headed home: sometimes in strange, unsymmetrical streaks or in patterns against the sky that ancient people read as a communication from the gods; sometimes in a straight formation so long that it has been observed one column requires four or five hours to fly past a single point. The islands they inhabit are rocky, barren and white with their guano—an accumulation so great that over the centuries it has covered whole islands to depths of more than a hundred feet.

Once Rogers mistook the whiteness of a couple of islands for the sails of possible prizes and sent the boats to investigate. He was now off the coasts they had come to harry and nearing the sea lanes where anything sighted was their lawful prey. They were also overanxious and a little like sharks in the current striking at casks or bottles or cloth or anything floating. "Our Men begin to repine, that tho come so far, we have met with no Prize in these Seas."

They put the two pinnaces into the water on February 27th to try them under sail. These were large boats equipped with oars, and lug- or schooner-rigged. They had each been armed with a swivel gun and could be useful in attacking small merchant vessels when there was too little wind for the big ships to maneuver.

Small arms and the great guns were exercised regularly: the marines to their stations, sharpshooters to the tops, the surgeons with their blades and saws to the orlop deck; the ships' boys running cartridges and canvas bags of powder up from the magazines to the gun decks hung with wet blankets; the gunners, spongers, rammers, standing to the artillery run out at the ports, lieutenants and mates at their stations with pistols to shoot anyone who deserted his post; carpenters, mechanics, sail handlers, everyone to his assignment so that the confusion of battle, when it came, might be reduced to a minimum.

In gunnery practice, privateers often threw empty beefcasks overboard as targets both for small arms and for the cannon loaded with reduced charges of powder. The cannon were fired in sequence in a broadside. Under actual battle conditions when full loads were used, few if

any ships could have withstood the combined recoil of all
the heavy artillery firing simultaneously.

Practice had its own hazards. The big guns were substantially the same as those of the sixteenth and seventeenth centuries. Some were of cast iron, others of brass,
others of wrought iron. Because of inevitable and unde-
tectable flaws in their manufacture, they might blow up
the first time they were fired, or the fiftieth or the two
hundredth; and each or any or every time the gunner put
the flaming linstock to the touchhole, no one knew what
would happen.

All the guns jumped and bucked violently when hot,
sometimes snapping their breaching and slamming back
into a bulkhead, sometimes overturning, sometimes leaping up against the beams overhead. And in any extended
action, if they were not allowed to cool off for a couple of
hours—no matter how much sluicing and bathing and
washing they got and how much sponging with cold water
and vinegar between shots—any or all of them would
burst.

The powder they had, "corned" or "grained," was a
considerable improvement over the earlier "serpentine"
variety, whose behavior was always unpredictable and
often dismal; and, still, no one knew much about its exact
properties and potentialities or even, with any exactitude,
the right loads to use. Nobody knew anything about the
actual velocity of projectiles, because the ballistic pendu-
lum had not yet been developed.

As for the loads, these had varied from a weight of
powder equal to that of the shot, to two-thirds the weight
of the shot, to one-half. The guns could not be aimed with
any great accuracy; they had to be traversed or elevated or
depressed by hand; moreover, the iron round shot generally did not closely fit the barrels. Therefore, although
cannon balls might travel several miles, effective seafights

were carried on at a range of no more than a quarter-mile and, at the optimum, the point-blank range for flintlock muskets.

The *Duke* and the *Dutchess* continued, from time to time, blowing casks out of the water. They had to keep the men in practice, but they also had to conserve their powder. And not only powder. On March 4th, Rogers cut the water ration to three pints a day per man. "My reason for it was, that we might keep at Sea some time and take some Prizes, and not be forc'd to discover ourselves by wat'ring, before we attempted anything ashore; because an Enemy being once discover'd, there's nothing of Value, as I'm informed, puts to Sea from one end of the Coast to the other."

They still had a good reserve of water aboard, from the stock laid in at Juan Fernández. However, it would be more than a month before they could safely renew the supply; at their next strategic base, the island of Lobos de Afuera, there would be none.

In the further interests of secrecy, an order was issued strictly prohibiting any conversation with prisoners except publicly, in the presence and with the consent of the captains and officers—"for fear," Cooke noted, "of making any Discovery of our Strength and Design, the punishment for such as transgress'd to lose all their Shares, and be kept in Irons during the Commander's Pleasure, or turn'd ashore where they should think fit—" *i.e.*, marooned.

Additional rules and agreements were drawn for methods of attack and the proper division of plunder, two representatives from each ship being exchanged as observers to keep everything fair and decent, and guard against one crew holding out on the other. "God be thank'd we have a good Concord between each Ships Company hitherto."

All gambling at cards and dice was now prohibited;

men had been betting and losing just about everything they owned. And probably few of the officers needed to be told of the sad case of the buccaneer Captain Davis' crew who, a quarter of a century before, homeward bound after a year's hard labor and fighting in the South Sea, had put in at Juan Fernández, gambled away everything they'd won to the crew of their consort, and had to turn back and begin again.

Rogers and Courtney decided to cruise forty or fifty miles northwest of Lima to pick up some prizes which would provide them with the latest intelligence on the coast and its shipping.

The usual routine, accidents, discipline continued. On the *Dutchess* a boy fell from the mizzen-top to the deck and was badly injured. Three men were thrown into irons for cutting meat from the steep-tub and hiding it; a large bowlful was found stashed away in one man's sea chest. Courtney ordered two of them "to be whipp'd and pickled; but before the third had suffer'd, we begged them off."

By day the current was cold green or blue-green, its surface cut by the fins of shark, marlin, broadbill, porpoise, and heaving with the enormous rafts of birds. Beneath the surface wide layers, moving platforms of little silvery fish, slanted down into the depths to escape the birds, flashed upward again from the jaws they encountered below.

By night there were strange, cold lights rising from the depths as the layers of life that had sunk at daylight down through the fathoms filtering out the spectrum— down through green, blue, violet, indigo, midnight black —ascended from the abyss.

East of them spread the Spanish Empire. They knew what to expect from it if they were beaten and taken alive; for if the old tortures and barbarities were no longer practiced, at least on quite so large a scale, the administrative machinery functioned just as ruthlessly as before and perhaps somewhat more efficiently. From the standpoint of Madrid, human beings—particularly those in the vast areas overseas—tended to become mere ciphers, numerical figures in statistical reports, to be weighed and utilized against profits and potential profits. It had been debated, for example, whether Indians had souls or were animals. If animals, then by the terms of dogmatic theology, like those of Marxism, they had no souls and could be treated just about any way one liked—with the sensible reservations of reasonable men, not mere maniacs, that the treatment prove advantageous to the colonial administrations and the state.

In any case, Indians were enslaved, when they weren't being exterminated, and extermination had many devices, from conventional fire and bullets and steel, to the charitable distribution of free blankets in which victims of smallpox had died. And Negroes and mulattoes and sambos and prisoners of war were enslaved, to labor their lifetimes in the mines.

The English, like the bloody Dutch who had thoroughly earned the adjective, were horrified by these conditions, though the Dutch held their own private millions in servitude and the English had long been busy transporting totally involuntary labor from Africa and elsewhere to their colonies.

What really galled the English was that there was no free trade, which they had reason to believe many Spanish merchants in those territories would welcome. Rogers had been rereading M. Beauchesne de Gouin: "Besides what I said from my own Observation, to prove how extensive a Trade we might have in those Seas, I shall add the following Observations from M. *de Beauchesne;* who says, that tho he was look'd upon as a Free-Booter, and that the then *Spanish* Governours on those Coasts were forbid to trade or suffer the People to trade with any but their own Subjects in those Seas, and that at *Valdivia* and other places they fir'd at him when he approach'd their Harbours, and deny'd so much as to sell him any Provisions, or to suffer him to wood or water; yet at *Rica* some Particular Persons traded with him to the value of 50,000 Crowns, and told him, That that place was not so proper for them to act so manifestly contrary to Law, but if he went to a place more retir'd they would buy all he had, tho both his Ships were full of Goods." So Spaniards themselves suffered under their government's monopoly, which was vast and formidable.

The ore from the mines of Mexico and Peru, during the first century of their operation, more than quadrupled the amount of silver and gold in circulation throughout Europe. Mexico might be said to be surfaced with these metals, particularly along the Pacific highlands. Peru, of course, was fabulous from the start. Potosí, in what is now Bolivia but was then upper part of the Viceroyalty of Peru, became the richest mining center in the world; the total output of the mines over the full period of high productivity has been conservatively estimated at more than two billion dollars, and Potosí was only one center, though the largest.

Moreover, if gold and silver mining provided the chief and most spectacular part of the wealth of the King's American dominions, there were other resources; mountains of iron in Mexico, zinc, tin, bismuth, quicksilver, copper, sulphur, fine marble, onyx, precious stones. There was the trade of most of a hemisphere, enormous ranches and plantations, prosperous cities extending from El Paso to Buenos Aires.

To Panama went the King's share of the wealth of Peru to be transported across the Isthmus and shipped to Spain. After the city was sacked and burned in the course of Morgan's raid, the Spaniards built a new Panama, a few miles from the site of the old one. Its defenses were so high and cost so much that the King of Spain, when he stared at the bill, asked his ministers if the walls couldn't be seen from his palace windows in Madrid.

Mexico City was the only real metropolis in North America, until well after the American Revolution. Thomas Gage visited it in the seventeenth century: "It is a byword that at Mexico there are four things fair: that is to say, the Women, the Apparel, the Horses and the Streets. But to this I may add the beauty of some of the Coaches of the Gentry, which do exceed in Cost the best of the Court of Madrid and other parts of Christendom, for there they spare no silver, nor Gold . . . nor the best Silks from China to enrich them."

On the other side of the ocean lay Manila, even richer, the entrepôt of Asia, the "Treasure House of the East," termed the most precious jewel in the King of Spain's crown. Through Manila funneled the riches of China, Japan, India, Siam, the Spice Islands. Harris in his *Voyages* stated: ". . . it may be justly considered as the best situated place for Trade in the East Indies, or perhaps in the Universe." Philip IV called it, "the best and most honored city in the overseas dominions of my monarchy."

The two great staples of trade were silks from the north and spices from the south for shipment to Europe and the Americas; and this trade could be handled at Manila, centrally located and with an excellent harbor, more easily than at any other port in the Far East. But, of course, there were more than silks and spices, though these constituted the bulk of the cargoes. There were fine cottons from India, pearls, rubies, diamonds, jade and porcelain, gold work and silver work from China; lacquered boxes and cabinets and writing desks, bronzes and armor and delicately painted screens from Japan, drugs from the

Indies, such as camphor, borax, musk, indigo, tobacco and teak; ivory combs and fans, sandalwood boxes, jasper, figurines; crucifixes, rosaries and reliquaries carved by Buddhists, Taoists and Shintoists for the commerce; necklaces, earrings, bracelets, pendants, uncut gems.

And the finest, the best of all this trade, went east across the Pacific to Acapulco once a year in one big bottom, the Manila Galleon. On the return trip she or a sister ship sailed west from Acapulco with a cargo consisting partly of such staples as cochineal from Mexico and chocolate from Guayaquil, but mostly of bullion: Mexican and Peruvian gold and silver to buy at a discount what the Manila Galleon brought back to sell for a profit—so many million in silver each year that the Mexican dollar became for a couple of centuries the standard medium of exchange throughout the Far East.

The trade, of course, had its hazards. Galleons foundered on reefs, burned and blew up in mid-ocean, were swallowed in the storms of the North Pacific, or simply ran out of time; one of them, delayed too long in crossing, was finally found drifting southwest of Panama, everyone on board dead of starvation and thirst.

Compared to the hazards of the crossing itself, the danger of a galleon being captured could be practically dismissed. Though these were the richest ships on all oceans and therefore the ultimate dream of pirates and privateers and enemy men-of-war, only one in the century-and-a-half the line had been operating, up till this time, had ever been taken, and that was in the early days: the *Santa Ana*, taken by Cavendish in 1587.

The galleon, in fact, had become over the years an argosy so wrapped in mystery as to her actual route and probable time of arrival at any point, so strongly built and so capable, even with a reduced armament, of overwhelming any single attacker, that by this time it looked as if only a whole fleet fanning out on patrol could hope to capture her; and the Dutch had long ago bitterly learned that the logistics of maintaining and supplying a fleet in those waters were insuperable.

The *Duke* and the *Dutchess* set sails, trimmed ship, headed slowly up the coasts of Chile and Peru. They had not come this far and endured so much for mere wishful optimism and some vague conviction of the power of positive thinking. They were not in sufficient force, they had not the slightest chance to attack the centers of power and wealth in the Viceroyalties of Mexico and Peru, any more than they had the slightest chance of taking Manila. But they could hit the Central and South American coasts for their own handsome profit. And if, just conceivably, between the thin edge of logic and reason and the depth of self-confidence and faith, they could manage the galleon, then they might seize at one stroke a year's accumulation of the treasures of the Orient; they might put a sizeable dent into the means to make war of His Majesty Louis XIV and of his grandson, Philip V, from whom all control of the Spanish empire was slipping or had slipped into the hands of the Queen, the clergy and the administrative officers.

At night in the cold current the process of eating and being eaten continued below the surface in explosions of pale fire, in streaks shooting through the water with meteor trails. Sometimes the sea was filled with milky clouds, and sometimes in the darkness huge luminous shapes some fathoms down, indistinct and at the limits of vision, appeared for a moment and vanished. No one knew what was down there or how deep it went or where the bottom was, if there were a bottom. No one knew really what it was that rose in great bands and areas of phosphorescence, in whirling and darting forms, mostly the size of pinpoints, often as large as a man's hand, as his arm, as the length of an oar, and now and then as big as a longboat and much bigger, shining, moving, gorging, and again disappearing downward at the first signs of dawn. No one knew, and perhaps it did not pay to think about it too much.

Often by day they sighted the Andes to the east, snow-capped, sometimes cloud-capped, presenting another mystery. "Within the Country there's a vast high Ridge of Mountains, named *Cordilleras*, all along this Course; some parts I believe are full as high, if not higher, than the *Pico-Teneriff*, with Snow on the top." Dampier judged their size a good deal better: "The Land . . . lies generally in Ridges parallel to the Shore, and 3 or 4 Ridges, one with another, each surpassing the other in heights . . . These are the highest Mountains that I ever saw, far surpassing I believe any Mountains in the World."

No one really knew what civilization they had sheltered or what lost, roofless cities still remained standing on ridges or in valleys higher than the Alps. All that had been learned from the Spanish Conquest was learned from the Incas, and the Incas, relative latecomers, had systematically suppressed or obliterated almost all history of the peoples they had themselves conquered—peoples whose greater achievements they appropriated for themselves.

A thousand years before Khufu built his great pyramid in Egypt, there was agriculture and weaving on these coasts. When Europe was still barbaric, the city of Chan-Chan was standing on the coastal plain: eight miles square and surrounded by walls forty feet high, inhabited by a quarter of a million people, with palaces, temples, forts and giant-step-pyramids, with walled compounds and irrigated gardens and stone-lined reservoirs.

The people on their mountain heights brought agriculture to a peak of development that had never been surpassed, or even equaled, anywhere. They diverted the courses of rivers; they dug enormous channels and erected towering aqueducts many miles in length. And for fertilizer they brought guano from the offshore islands—that residue of the Peru Current the birds harvested, guano whose use and value was not understood by any Europeans when Rogers and Courtney and Dampier and Dover cruised off this coast.

The Inca Empire, which suppressed and absorbed its predecessors, was in turn smashed, a few years after it had reached its fullest extent, by a company of Spanish adventurers in armor. The Conquistadors did not, of course, care about agriculture. When the Inca Atahualpa duly paid his ransom on Pizarro's solemn promise to set him free, a room was filled to the height a man could reach with gold and then again with silver: seventy cubic yards of gold alone— a greater amount of gold than any European monarch had ever seen. For having kept his part of the bargain, and allied crimes, chiefly being considered too dangerous to live, Atahualpa was thereupon sentenced to be burned alive.

Other Indians died by the countless thousands, murdered and burned. Then, with the empire conquered, conquerors turned and tore each other to pieces like cannibal fish.

One of the first to go was the Conquistador Orgoñez, murdered by his compatriots from Estremadura; then Diego de Almagro, Francisco Pizarro's best friend, if he had any. Almagro was captured, garrotted, and the corpse beheaded. Hernando Pizarro went next—into a Spanish prison where he eventually succumbed at the age of nearly a hundred. And then the conqueror himself, Francisco Pizarro, was ambushed in his palace at Lima and his throat cut. Carvajal, "the demon of the Andes," was quartered alive by having his arms and legs tied to four strong horses which were whipped and beaten until they pulled him apart.

Order, issuing or leaking from the Escorial, began to return. Very few of the original Conquistadors remained. One of these, the last survivor, Mancio Sierra Lejesma, on his deathbed in Cuzco addressed a confession and apology to the then Emperor, Philip II, neither blaming anyone in particular nor attempting to set right things so long gone wrong, but simply in the interest of truth.

With order established, the successors grew fat. Everything, as at Manila, was profits; money meant more than lives. When new killers cruised these coasts and took prisoners, the solid Spanish citizens often abandoned these hostages to their fate rather than part with the assets needed to ransom them.

On March 8th *Duke* and *Dutchess* were off Callao, the port of Lima, and stood well out to sea to avoid being sighted. They were now completely committed—alone without friends, on the greatest expanse of ocean in the world, facing the full power of these enemy coasts. There was no way back. The Horn they had rounded was now closed to them; there could be no returning to Juan Fernández. The only way lay north and, ultimately, west. And the first prize they sighted, if they failed to seize and silence her, if they struck and she got away, would alert all the coast, would bring down the full power of French and Spanish squadrons to smash them.

"March 9. Fair Weather, a moderate Gale at S. E. We go under an easy Sail, in hopes of seeing rich Ships, either going or coming out of *Lima*, being now near it. We keep about 7 Ls. from Shore, to prevent our being discover'd."

There was indeed life in this current, and continual blood. The ships may well on their long course through it have come on a group of the orca gladiator, or killer whales, twenty to thirty-five feet long, circling a school of porpoise or a herd of seals to panic their victims and

bunch them together, then racing to tear great chunks
and pieces from the live flesh while the water darkened
and the sharks waited for the cripples and remains. If
Selkirk saw this slaughter, with the men, he must have
grown thoughtful.

He was back now with a way of life he had always
known, almost as if there had been no interruption. He
was reaccustomed to shoes and the diet and visits to the
surgeons for purges and pills and bleeding, reaccustomed
to bedbugs and lice and constant wet and jammed decks
and perpetual work. As a mate he was driven and compelled to drive, and he had his own duties and stations
during battle practice, when musket balls spattered the
water and the big guns jumped.

And certainly, eager and impatient as everyone was
by now, it could not have been only Selkirk who grew
sometimes thoughtful—particularly at night, when the
water chilled the air, though they were nearly at the
equator, and when anyone on watch might see the millions of things that wheeled and darted and shimmered in
the sea around them, the eruptions of cold, hostile flame.
Neither captains, officers nor men knew actually anything
of the inhabitants of the depths or of the existence of the
deep-sounding layer. They did not, certainly, know of an
ancient text in the Hindu *Puranas* which describes one of
the lowest planes of existence as "A Place of Darkness
where monster serpents crowned with dim light, live in
perpetual anger."

But in that sea, in that place, the very jamming of
men together in the packed hammocks between-decks
and the smoky glow of the dim lanterns must have been a
reassurance. And for the men on deck, on watch, it was
better to attend to the work and not stare very long over
the side and down. Because every one knew or sensed
that under these few calked timbers that for a period

shielded them, under their steadying keels, lay the depths that knocked and rapped, so to speak, on the wood, resounding through the hulls in the ear of the sleeping man: bottomless, omnipresent, altogether unknown.

On March 15th they sighted and seized a small ship. They hit her quickly, almost before she could even run. This little craft they converted to an auxiliary fighting vessel, and they happily and ominously rechristened her the *Beginning*.

10

ARCHITEUTHIS PRINCEPS

IN THE CAPTURE of the *Beginning,* there were no casualties on either side. She surrendered after one shot was fired across her bow. The captain, a mestizo, had with him one Spaniard, a Negro and six Indians. From these prisoners Rogers and Courtney obtained some useful information. They learned that all the French ships previously in those waters—there had been seven—had sailed for home six months earlier, following a series of quarrels and fights with the Spaniards in which a number of men had been killed and after which shore leave was canceled for all French sailors.

That, obviously, reduced the number of enemy warships Rogers and Courtney would have to worry about.

But there was still the threat of the strong French squadron to which they had been alerted at Oratava and which
apparently had been sent to hunt them down. And there
still remained the certainty of avenging Spanish squadrons
which would be putting out of Valparaíso and Callao, once
their presence had been discovered.

The prisoners also informed Rogers and Courtney that
the entire South Sea had been empty of any enemy since
Dampier cruised it in the *St. George,* four years earlier,
and that Dampier's consort, the *Cinque Ports,* under the
same Captain Stradling from whom Selkirk so earnestly
wished to be separated that he asked to be marooned, had
foundered. Stradling and six or seven others got ashore in
a boat, were captured and "had been four years Prisoner
at Lima, where," Rogers adds, in a further reflection on
the hermit's fortunes, "they fared much worse than our
Governour *Selkirk,* whom they left on the Island of *Juan
Fernández.*"

The day after capturing this vessel, the *Duke* and the
Dutchess sighted Lobos de Afuera, the outermost island
which lies some thirty-five miles from the mainland, and
dropped anchor a cable's length from shore in twenty
fathoms of clear water. They had scarcely come to anchor
when mettlesome Carleton Vanbrugh again distinguished
himself.

He spotted a flock of what he took to be turkeys and
"bless'd himself at the sight," being so eager to sink his
teeth into some of these succulent fowl that he could not
wait until the landing boat touched shore but jumped
overboard into waist-deep water, let fly with his musket
and brought down what proved to be a couple of vultures:
"When he came to take up his Game, it stunk insufferably
and made us merry at his Mistake."

Vanbrugh was not so merry. He ordered a sailor to
pick up his brace of vultures, "*alias* Carrion-Crows" and

when the sailor flatly refused, threatened to shoot him. For this and for having "lately abus'd" the eminent physician, Captain-Doctor Thomas Dover, Vanbrugh was once more hauled up before the council, of which he was a member. The overwhelming majority voted to dismiss him and appoint in his place Dover's nephew, Samuel Hopkins, the prayerful apothecary. Carleton Vanbrugh, agent of the owners, man of accounts, who succeeded in spite of everyone in having himself clapped into jail at Teneriffe, who murdered an Indian at Grande, and who had now taken to shooting vultures for turkeys and threatening to shoot sailors, at last came apart. It would be a long time before he again enjoyed any status at all.

A number of men had scurvy again, and tents for the sick were put up ashore, as they had been at Juan Fernández. Two died, a Dutchman and a Spaniard, and were buried by night on Lobos.

And again the ships needed to be careened and cleaned, though it was little more than a month since this had been done. "This Morning we began to scrub our Ship, and clear'd abundance of Barnacles off her Bottom, almost as large as Muscles (*sic*). A Ship grows foul very fast in these seas." Frequent careening was important not only for general seaworthiness and ease of handling but for speed. In any engagement between two ships, the one that had been most recently cleaned and scraped enjoyed, other things being equal, a distinct advantage.

Work was completed first on the *Dutchess*, and she put out to sea on March 20th, to cruise for prizes. She was followed the next day by one of the pinnaces and the captured bark, the *Beginning*. The *Beginning* had now been converted to a privateer, fitted with a new deck, new masts, four swivel guns, and was manned by a crew of thirty-two men: "I saw her out of the Harbour with our Pinnace, she looks very pretty and I believe will sail well in smooth Water, having all Masts, Sails, Rigging, and Materials, like one of the Half-Galley's fitted out for her Majesty's Service in *England*."

There was no fresh water on Lobos; but the men got plenty of fish (Lobos lies in the current), and shot numbers of birds which resembled teal and proved very good eating. Seals and sea lions abounded, though not in the same enormous herds as on Juan Fernández—larger in individual size but with poorer fur. They bit, and they smelled. "A large one seiz'd a stout *Dutchman,* had like to have pull'd him into the Water, and bit him to the bone in several places, in one of his Arms and Legs."

Some of the crew killed a few of them for their livers, but gave that up when one man, after eating a piece, suddenly died. "Our Prisoners told us, they accounted those old Seals very unwholesom. The Wind always blowing fresh over the Land, brought an ugly noisom Smell aboard from the Seals ashore; which gave me a violent Head-Ach, and every body else complain'd of this nauseous Smell; we found nothing so offensive on *Juan Fernandez.*"

Nobody, as usual, was idle, except the very sick; and time, as always, bore down. The carpenters worked almost around the clock to build a large landing boat for a scheduled attack on the city of Guayaquil—the building of this craft being, in fact, one of the principal reasons for the ships' stay at Lobos.

Guayaquil was prosperous and its defenses supposedly weak, in spite of the fact that it had twice been captured, during the previous century, by the Dutch and the buccaneers, and had several times been threatened— by Davis and Swan and Dampier, among others, and by Dampier again when he was in command of the *St. George.*

The chief export was chocolate, a lot of which went to Manila in exchange for goods from the Orient. Dampier had written: "This town makes a very fine prospect, it being beautifi'd with several Churches and other good Buildings. Here lives a Governor, who, as I have been informed, hath his patent from the King of Spain. . . . Guiaquil may be reckoned one of the chiefest Sea-Ports in the South Seas; the Commodities which are exported from hence are Cacao, Hides, Tallow, Sarsaparilla and other Drugs, and Woolen-Cloth, commonly called 'Cloth of Quito.' "

The English were in sufficient strength for a successful attack and counted on the advantage of surprise—not only to facilitate the storm and reduce casualities but to prevent the inhabitants taking off into the woods to bury their cash and valuables, a practice to which these citizens obstinately reverted whenever the place was threatened. "This Morning we came to a full Resolution to land and attempt *Guiaquil*. In order thereunto we fix'd two Barks, put Ammunition and Arms on board them, with our four Quarter-Deck Guns and Field-Carriages." There were other resolutions, among them a new definition of legitimate plunder for the men and strict prohibitions against drinking ashore and any familiarities with the women.

Meanwhile, the killing in the current continued. On March 26th the *Dutchess* came in with a prize, another small vessel of about fifty tons burden bound from Guayaquil for Trujillo and carrying a not very valuable cargo of cocoa, coconuts, timber and tobacco, plus about 100 pounds in plate and money. This vessel was also careened and cleaned and promisingly christened the *Increase*. All the sick were put aboard her, and the long-rehabilitated hermit, Alexander Selkirk, was appointed her master.

They had by this time a number of prisoners, from whom they obtained a lot more information: some of it wild, some vague, some conflicting. They heard that the widow of the late Viceroy of Peru would be shortly embarking for Acapulco in a King's ship of thirty-six brass guns, carrying all her family and treasures. They heard that a big merchant galleon, commanded by a Captain Morrel, was recruiting at Paita, en route to Lima. They heard that a French-built and Spanish-owned frigate, the *Havre de Grace*, had recently sailed from Panama for Callao richly laden and conveying a bishop who had with him 200,000 pieces of eight and a good quantity of plate. "Resolved," Cooke laconically reported, "to cruise for said Ship."

On March 29 they sailed from Lobos with their two prizes, and the *Duke* towed at her stern the new landing boat for the attempt on Guayaquil. They could taste an excitement like the excited water. On April 1st the sea turned red for miles, a phenomenon observed by everyone and reported by both Rogers and Cooke. They concluded it was due to the spawn of fish; but actually this red sea —often occurring here and in other parts of the world— is caused by countless numbers of a marine protozoan.

The following day across the discolored water they sighted a big set of sails. Rogers sent the *Duke's* pinnace to discover what ship she might be and, if possible, to capture her. The pinnace had no trouble, though this was the large merchant vessel of which they had heard—a galleon, the *Ascension*, of about 450 tons, commanded by two brothers named Morel and laden with dry goods and timber. She carried, in addition to her crew, a number of passengers and fifty Negro slaves, and she surrendered to the little pinnace without firing a gun. The fact was, she seemed so safe on the King's private ocean that no gun had ever been put aboard her to fire. Cooke, who examined her, said: "This was one of the largest Merchant-Ships in those seas . . . but for Arms, I saw not so much as a Pistol in her."

The galleon was immediately manned by a prize crew.

Some of the Spaniards aboard her were transferred to other ships and Robert Frye, chief lieutenant of the *Duke*, put in command. That same evening, the little *Beginning* scored again, capturing a bark from Guayaquil with a cargo mostly of timber and a crew of eleven white men and one Negro. They joined the other prisoners. Silence was essential.

The cruise for the French-built frigate and the bishop continued. Stations were settled: the big merchant galleon and the new hospital ship, *Increase*, to ply some twenty-five miles off shore, within sight of the humps of land called the Saddle of Paita, and keep clear of any action; *Beginning* to patrol close in to Paita, with *Dutchess* and *Duke* standing farther out to sea on separate courses.

They were still in the current and would be until they rounded Cabo Blanco for the Gulf of Guayaquil. The endless schools of silvery, finger-long fish still shot up toward the surface and dived down again, racing from the pursuers below, the pursuers above. Now and then a giant jellyfish, trailing poisonous filaments twenty to thirty feet long, drifted by. There were still the killer whales, sharks, friendly and harmless porpoises. Cooke noted: ". . . saw many large Sword-Fishes but could take none." And Rogers, after the meeting of the captains on board the *Dutchess* to settle cruising stations, wrote: "Just as the sun set I left them; they fancy'd they saw a Sail, and chas'd in great haste: we saw nothing except the blowing of a Whale, of which there are abundance on this Coast. Wind from SE by S to the ESE."

And so darkness and the lights below again, shooting and darting: streaks of green-white fire that erupted suddenly through the water and trailed off in the blackness and then flared again; still deeper, the big, indistinct, luminous shapes that appeared now and then and hung there, fathoms down, for a moment and were gone: perhaps meaningless, certainly unanswerable.

But at least they must have by this time known the meaning and answer to some of it, because they were now in an area which had been noted as a particular hunting-ground for squid, ranging from the tiny to the terrible. *Yea, slimy things did crawl with legs* . . . Only, these things did not crawl; they shot through the water in swift streaks of phosphorescence while showerlike sparks trailed off in the abyss. Sometimes little ones, escaping from their bigger cannibal brothers, may have come clear onto the decks of the pinnaces; small squid have often been known to propel themselves more than six feet into the air.

The lookouts, the men in the shrouds, or Rogers or Courtney or Dampier or Dover or Cooke pacing a deck, could look downward and watch. They would be watching something that came up from the depths at night to feed, and moved by propulsion backward, trailing its tentacles in bursts of speed, ejecting powerful jets of water from a siphon in the mantle of its body—ejecting also, against anything big enough to attack it, its protective sepia ink to cloud the water with a phantasmal form at which the enemy might strike, and sometimes squirting the same ink in a stinking stream high up onto the decks of boats.

They would be watching something with a cylindrical, elongated body ending in two flat caudal fins and about a fourth as long as the longest tentacles: something with a pair of huge, luminous, unblinking eyes, highly organized, having transparent lenses and circular irises—cold, intelligent eyes to serve its ferocity and appetite.

The things moved through the water in soundless explosions of light or lay like ghosts near the surface, their great eyes baleful and observant. Anything that was thrown or fell overboard they would attack, and if one of them were hurt or disabled, another would eat it.

The seaman on a yard, or in the shrouds, the man on deck looking down, must have suspected an alien and hostile intelligence; and, in fact, these creatures, with their relative the octopus, are—second only to the air-breathing mammals like whales and porpoises—the most intelligent of all the inhabitants of the sea.

Far out in the darkness of the current winked the signals and lights of the ships on patrol for the French-built frigate. And alongside, everywhere, this, with the old stories and superstitions always recurrent, like the legend of the giant remora which attached itself to vessels and dragged them back; not a kind of oversized sucking fish on the order of the remora which attach themselves to sharks but something with ten tentacles like these things, only much larger. The giant remora—meaning "delay" —may well have been an attempt to account for errors due to unknown, contrary currents and other factors in computing speed and distance covered, just as the Dutch hypothesized a Land of Indraught when ships consistently ran on a coast which the charts said lay much farther away.

But it may have been also, mixed up with all this, that earlier sailors had now and then sighted something really gigantic—something compared with which these squid they had around them now were the merest baby brothers —something the sperm whale long ago learned about and still knows far more about than any human being.

Rogers had noted the abundance of whales in this area. Many of them, the huge, toothless species, were feeding on plankton; but the great sperm whales with their enormous jaws had come to devour the squid, little and large, as a boy gobbles gumdrops. Because Moby Dick and his brothers and sisters and ancestors and their descendants long ago learned that the real meal, the full one and the one for which a price has to be paid, lies deep in the night-black depths. In that cold hell—about which no one in this time knew anything—there exists the actual giant squid: the literal nightmare, sixty-five feet long, almost certainly longer in some cases, the principal of all those dominions, *architeuthis princeps;* and if one were somehow to be hoisted into the air it would just about equal, from its caudal fins to the tip of its two longest tentacles, the height of a seven-story building.

Nobody yet knows how big they grow, how long they live, to what depths they descend. Now and then they rise; and it may be much more frequently than has yet been established, because *architeuthis* would rise on the blackest night, to sink again at the first indications of light in the sky.

But several, through some accident or submarine upheaval, have been seen long after cockcrow. They have sometimes been sighted by whalers when a whale surfaced battling with one. Some have attacked boats and men, and a few have been harpooned. Among the creatures of the sea, only the sperm whale, as far as is known—and nearly nothing is known—goes deep enough and is big enough and well enough equipped to cope with them.

The whale is equipped. He has a body maybe sixty feet long, weighing seventy tons, so powerful that when driving up from the abyss he can explode clean out of the water into the air, falling back with a whack and the crash of a cannon. He has a body that is built to withstand a racing ascent from incredible pressures to no pressure at all; a lung capacity that enables him to stay submerged for tremendous periods; a quick intelligence that the small eyes hardly indicate; a lower jaw twelve to fifteen feet in length lined with twenty-odd teeth on each side, each tooth several inches in circumference and eight or twelve inches high. With that jaw and these teeth working like shears—*Engine of beauty, volted with delight*—the whale below in the motionless black goes through *architeuthis* and the tentacles like so much soap. But even the whale does not come off scot-free. If in his belly are found gigantic black beaks and the fragments of enormous tentacles, his hide also bears the permanent scars of huge sucker rings. And it must also be that the whale himself— the unripe, the unready, the not-yet-grown and too-eager —sometimes loses, to drown in the blackness below and be chopped and sliced by the beak.

In a sixty-five-foot specimen of *architeuthis* the two longest tentacles would measure some forty-eight feet; tremendous, slender whips without suckers except at the paddlelike ends; each sucker armed, like the big discs all along the other eight tentacles, with a ring of horny teeth to hold the victim even more tightly until the other eight tentacles bring it to the hooked mouth, a steel-hard chopper, retracted or protruded from a puckered sphincter muscle resembling a gigantic anus. But the beak, of course, cannot taste; the tongue tastes, or the brain, and the tongue is a long flexible file equipped with hundreds of little hooks that rasp and shred into fragments what the beak chops up.

Architeuthis' gleaming, unwavering and intelligent eyes are the size of dinner plates. Unlike his enemy the whale, he has no place in his existence for nourishing or defending or protecting anything; he is only himself at the center of his huge tentacles, ready to attack and devour whatever appears, including his own if the chance comes. When excited, he changes color; when angry, he blushes to the point of apoplexy, the color of battle and blood.

One of them may have been sighted, rising by night. They live, after all, in the depths of most oceans and seas —Pliny long ago described one caught in the Mediterranean—and in this area off Peru squid of all sizes were to be seen and observed as nowhere else. And if somebody or everybody on the *Duke,* perhaps, or the *Dutchess* or one of the other vessels ever did get a brief look at *architeuthis* himself, the principal of the dominions of darkness—even a momentary glimpse of two enormous eyes and an abrupt, violent eruption out of the foaming sea of wheeling, multiple arms as the thing went, maybe, through a school of big tuna—then it would be better not to mention it, better never to have seen it.

Because behind this *architeuthis* there is always a larger and even vaster *architeuthis*. Without drawing parallels or conclusions about particular men who have left on this point no record, it is nevertheless a truism that out of the horror sighted, the horror merely heard of, something much bigger and much worse, from the depths of anxiety and imagination, always rises.

The current was empty. The frigates, their boats and prizes, had been cruising off Paita since the beginning of April, and now, having earlier captured four vessels in a few days, there had been for almost two weeks no sign of a sail.

And this emptiness, this failure of anything at all to appear in more or less busy shipping lanes, provided a wide range for speculation. It might have been that they had somehow been sighted, in spite of their best efforts, and the coast alerted—in which case, as Rogers had foreseen, nothing would put to sea until they were gone or had been destroyed.

It might have been, in the eye of superstition, that the prey had vanished—warned by some sixth sense, by a smell on the wind, an alteration in the sky, by a bubbling from the depths—had run not from any fear of them but from some possible disaster into which they themselves were blindly heading.

Rogers' privateers had come a long way from home into a strange sea where they were without friends or allies. They had come through a great deal of hell and a great deal of dying into a hostile ocean where things happened and things were sighted which it was more sensible not even to mention, much less report. And in the superstitious eye of the common seaman the first sign of anything even partially unaccountable brought in all the possibilities lying just outside of, but encroaching on, reason and common sense. It may well have been to many like the nightmare in which the green, clear waters of a bay slowly begin to rise and fill with high tide but also with the weight of something else, and all the lazy, graceful fish in the green, clear water slowly rising are suddenly gone—running, running, warned by a kind of foreknowing from the behavior of the sea that something frightful is coming slowly up from the depths.

Rogers may have sometimes at night and in dreams suffered such alarms. No man, obviously, whatever the pretense, is wholly rational, and there always comes a point where the man wise enough to know knows that reason itself gives out and Socrates pays his debt to the gods and his demon. But that, of course, is different from mere headlong panic, which Rogers could not and would not indulge at any point—above all at this one, where nothing had happened at all, no threat appeared. Actually, from the point of view of command, the problem reduced itself to very simple terms. Whatever the reason for the disappearance of all Spanish shipping, they had waited as long as they could; time was again, and as usual, pressing them.

When daybreak of April 14th still showed the sea empty, he decided to break off the search and sail into the Gulf of Guayaquil for the assault on the city. The barks and the landing boat were manned and guns, ammunition and provisions stowed aboard. The *Duke* and the *Dutchess*, according to plan, would stand out to sea—both to prevent discovery and to intercept any Guayaquil-bound ship that might interfere with the operation.

On April 15th they entered the gulf. Suddenly, at daybreak, the lookouts shouted and there was a big sail "between us and land." The pinnaces went to investigate, in such a hurry that they could not wait to mount their swivel guns. The boat from the *Dutchess* did not even carry enough small-arms for her complement of men.

Here again, because of divided counsels and because of the strange apparatus of authority which the owners had set up to safeguard the corporate investment, there seems to have been a breakdown in command. Rogers was against the pinnaces going off so precipitately and so poorly equipped. He strongly opposed the determination of his younger brother, John Rogers, a second lieutenant on the sister ship, to join the attack in the *Duke's* pinnace, "My brother *John Rogers* being unfortunately aboard our Ship, to assist me in getting ready, because he was to be Lieutenant of my Company ashore, he stept into our Boat. I had before this oppos'd his landing, which he resented as a Slight; and this hinder'd me stopping him now, tho it was not his business, he being second Lieutenant of our Consort, and we having Officers enough of our own for that Service; but Mr. *Frye*, who commanded the Boat, being related to us, was the occasion of my Brother's Willingness to go as a Volunteer with him."

So Woodes Rogers, not much older in years but a lot older in almost every other way, consented against discipline, order and better judgment. He loved his brother and was proud of him; and he must have considered what such a twenty-year-old would always suffer and resent if kept out of danger, presumably by the privileged fact of being the brother of the squadron's commander.

At nine that morning the pinnaces closed with the stranger, the *Duke's* boat coming up first. She proved to be the French-built frigate, supposedly carrying the bishop and his silver and 200,000 pieces of eight. But this was no easy prey such as they had previously taken in the current. The two boats were attacking, in fact, a frigate bigger than the *Dutchess*. The strange ship opened up at once with what guns she had mounted. The pinnaces were forced to fall back. Frye, John Rogers and Cooke decided to try the old buccaneer tactic of crossing her bow and stern and raking her decks with small-arms fire. She had, however, a gun mounted astern and with this forced them abaft, where she blasted them with five cannon loaded with partridge-shot, a kind of shrapnel. John Rogers, who could not wait, who had to come to it as fast as he could, this young victorious John Rogers was hit in the head and instantly killed, together with a sailor who apparently was not trying to prove anything. Three other sailors were wounded, two of them fatally.

Early that afternoon both the *Duke* and *Dutchess*, having been more or less becalmed during the previous hours, finally made sail and came up into action. Their big guns began firing and the French-built ship, having run out of hope and luck, after fighting as bravely and well as she could, surrendered. She had no hope in the long run, it is true; but if all her guns had been mounted, many more would have died. Cooke wrote: "The Men begg'd for good Quarter and we promis'd them all Civility imaginable. This Ship came from *Panama* and was bound for *Lima*, to be fitted out for a Man of War . . . There were 70 Blacks and many Passengers with a considerable quantity of Pearls aboard . . . we found several Guns in the Hold, for the Ship would carry 24 but only had six mounted. Many of the Passengers were considerable Merchants at *Lima*, and the briskest Spaniards I ever saw."

They missed the bishop. He was gone for good, having disembarked with his attendants, silver plate, valuables and 200,000 pieces of eight at Point St. Helena, ten days before. John Rogers was dead and another, and two more among the casualties were to die shortly. After the cold and the scurvy and the lung diseases and the men falling from the rigging into the sea or onto the bone-cracking deck, now this and many more to come.

"At this Attack my unfortunate Brother was shot thro the Head and instantly died, to my unspeakable Sorrow: but as I began this Voyage with a Resolution to go thro it, and the greatest Misfortune or Obstacle shall not deter me, I'll as much as possible avoid being thoughtful and afflicting my self for what can't be recall'd, but inde-fatigably pursue the Concerns of the Voyage . . ."

The dead were sewed in their canvas shrouds with lead weights put to them and, after the reading of the service for the burial of the dead and the firing of several volleys, were tipped gently overboard to plunge far down below into the levels devoid of all color and light.

Well, Master, the day is spent, the Night draws on, let us consult. Chirugion, look to the wounded, and winde up the Slain, with each a Weight or Bullet at their Heades and Feet to make them sinke, and give them three Gunnes, for their Funerals. Swabber, make clean the Ship (sprinkle it with hot Vinegar to avoid the smell of Blood); Purser, record their Names; Watch, be vigiliant to keep your Berth to windeward that we lose him not in the Night; Gunners, spunge your Ordnance; Sowldiers, scowre your Pieces; Carpenters, about your Leakes; Boat-swaine and the rest, repair your Sails and Shrouds; and Cooke, your directions against the Morning Watch; Boy, Holla, Master, Holla, is the Kettle boiled? Yea, yea, Boat-swaine, call up the Men to Prayer.

Architeuthis had surfaced.

11

GUAYAQUIL
UNDONE

ON APRIL 16TH, at sea, the *Beginning* captured another
small bark. On April 17th final preparations were completed for the attack on Guayaquil. Rogers assigned 111
men to the frigates and the various prizes. There were
now more than 300 prisoners—the majority Spaniards
and Indians, the rest Negroes—and these, since they
would considerably outnumber the men left to guard
them, were now put in irons as a regrettable but reasonable precaution, until the main force returned.

This force, consisting of 201 men, left the ships at
midnight on the seventeenth of April and headed up the
gulf in two barks, the pinnaces and the landing craft. For
the actual fighting there were 180 men divided into three

companies of sixty men each, one company commanded
by Rogers, the second by Courtney and the third by
Dover.

"Captain *Courtney* and I being willing to compli-
ment our President Captain *Dover,* agreed that he should
have the Preference in Command at our Landing: being
a considerable Owner in our Ship . . ."

The remainder of those going ashore, twenty-one
men under the command of Dampier and Thomas Glendall, were detailed to take care of the guns, ammunition
and provisions.

Dampier, of course, knew something about land-
fighting, but not many of the others did, certainly not
Dover and certainly not most of the sailors. "To prevent
their stragling when we Landed," Rogers said, "we gave
each Man a Ticket that he might remember what Company he belong'd to; and appointed the best and soberest
Man we could pick to command every ten Men under
the Captains . . ." Altogether, if Guayaquil were able to
mount any kind of effective resistance at all, it did not
look too promising.

Rogers' first objective was Puná, an island in the gulf
about forty miles from Guayaquil. On Puná there was a
small settlement and a garrison, which had to be silenced.

They reached this objective on the evening of the
nineteenth and attacked at daybreak of the twentieth.
Puná capitulated without any casualties on either side.
Some of the inhabitants took off into the woods, but Rogers made sure they were immobilized by destroying all
the boats, bark logs and canoes on the island.

There might be said to have been, after a fashion, a
couple of casualties. "The Day was hot, and two of our
Men finding Liquors in the Houses, got drunk betimes."
For this lapse they were publicly whipped . . . "as a
Terror to the rest."

Puná produced some surprises. They learned that Spanish intelligence had for upwards of a year known a great deal about them, even if much of it was inaccurate. The lieutenant in charge of the garrison had a copy of orders from the Viceroy of Peru to the lieutenant-general in command of Guayaquil. Rogers gives an English translation, part of which is as follows:

"In the Packet with Letters from *Spain,* which I have received, there are Orders from his Majesty, giving an account of a squadron of 7 Sail, getting ready at *London* by several Lords, from 44 to 74 Guns each, to sail to the *South Sea,* under the conduct of an *Englishman* nam'd *Dampier:* That they are first to sail for *Ireland* in *April* to victual there, and afterwards to possess themselves of an Island and Harbour in these Seas, and particularly the Island of *Juan Fernandez.* You are to give an account to all those Provinces where 'tis necessary, that they may take proper Measures to guard the Coasts and Harbours. Order *Don Hierononino,* as soon as he receives this, to give notice of it to the People on all the Coasts under his Jurisdiction to withdraw their Cattle and Provisions . . . that so the Enemies finding no Provision, may be oblig'd to retire from these Seas, whither they can't bring Provision enough to maintain them for so long a Voyage . . ."

The Spaniards, of course, were counting on the old logistical problems; but they had also spread a net. Rogers now learned that the information he had received at Oratava seven months earlier was accurate: as soon as Spanish intelligence reported that the ships had sailed from England, a strong French squadron had started after them.

So the pursuing squadron was back on, or just over, the horizon. However, now Rogers knew its strength and how and where it was distributed. There were five great ships, frigates, faster and better-built than the English, each mounting forty-four to fifty or more guns. Two were at Callao, one at Pisco in Peru, two at Concepción in Chile. As soon as the English disclosed themselves by a strike along the coast, this force would be about its business.

Rogers counted on the fact that the actual location of his own squadron was, as of this date, still unknown and that he had time and distance in his favor. Once they hit Guayaquil, of course, the report would be out. But it would take days for the news to reach Lima, days for the French to arm out and arrive in sufficient force at his present position—a minimum, he was confident, of twenty-four days in all—"by which time," he noted, "we hope to finish and be gone where they cannot find us."

It was time to finish. Guayaquil is situated on the right bank of the Guayas River, thirty-three miles up river from the Gulf of Guayaquil. Puná secured, they started at once. "It blow'd fresh, was very dark, with a small rolling Sea, and the Boat being deep laden and cram'd with Men, I had rather be in a Storm at Sea than here; but in regard we are about a charming Undertaking, we think no Fatigue too hard."

A few hours later they were at the river mouth. The "charming Undertaking," with fieldpieces, guns, cutlasses, pistols and tickets, moved slowly and quietly up the Guayas.

By noon they were about halfway to the city, the boats carrying 110 men in the lead, the barks some distance down river. The advance party, discovering just above them a plantation which might alert Guayaquil, pulled in among some mangrove trees to hide until dark and "were pester'd and stung grievously by the Muskitoes . . ." After the scurvy and typhus and lung diseases at sea, they were now to encounter the diseases of the swamps.

Guayaquil has two seasons: a wet and a dry. The dry one (from May to January) is considered fine and salubrious. During the wet season, hot days are followed by nights of drenching downpour. Malaria, bilious fevers and yellow fever were in that era endemic, and the plague walked abroad. They had come in the wrong season.

Aside from this, which could not be planned, everything had been most carefully planned and had proceeded on schedule. As they waited in the boats among the mangroves, the landing party might have reviewed the new, encouraging rules about plunder that had been drawn up and promulgated by the Council a week before. Plunder was what the men might take for themselves, share and share alike, with none of it to be set aside or preëmpted by the owners and investors . . . "all manner of Bedding and Clothes without stripping, all manner of Necessaries, Gold Rings, Buckles, Buttons, Liquors, and Provisions for our own expending and use, with all sorts of Arms and Ammunition, except great Guns for Ships, is Plunder, and shall be divided equally amongst the Men of each Ship . . . whither aboard or ashore, according to the whole Shares.

"It is also agreed, that any sort of wrought Silver or Gold Crucifixes, Gold and Silver Watches, or any other Movables found about the Prisoners, or Wearing Apparel of any kind, shall likewise be Plunder."

But while it was necessary—in spite of what had earlier been decided by bankers and investors in Bristol— to encourage and fortify the men by broadening the definitions, the Council knew that it would also have to face, if it ever got back, the shark-cold eyes of the shareholders. The "Resolves" therefore sensibly added: "Provided always we make this Reserve, that Mony and Women's Ear-Rings, with loose Diamonds, Pearls and precious Stones be excepted. And if anything is short and omitted in this Publication, we do hereby declare, that when this Expedition is over, every particular Man shall have a Hearing." A long time later the survivors duly, and according to the promise, got that hearing, for whatever good it did them.

Anyway, and for the moment, the directions about plunder were extremely heartening, even if the same order contained some solemn warnings and sobering occasions for thought. "And to prevent all manner of pernicious and michievous Ill-Conduct that may accrue by Disorders on shore, we pressingly remind you, that any Officer or other that shall be so brutish as to be drunk ashore in an Enemy's Country, shall not only be severely punish'd, but lose share of whatever is taken in this Expedition. The same Punishment shall be inflicted on any that disobeys Command, or runs from his Post, discourages our Men, or is cowardly in any Action, or presumes to burn or destroy anything in the Town without Order, or for mischief sake; or that shall be so sneakingly barbarous to debauch themselves with any Prisoners on shore, where we have more generous things to do, both for our own Benefit and the future Reputations of ourselves and our Country."

By midnight the boats, still moving quietly, oars muffled, were in sight of Guayaquil. The men could make out a few lights there and a big fire blazing on a neighboring hill. Half an hour later they were abreast of the town and preparing to land. And then everything so carefully prepared and so well carried out up to this point fell apart—as many other even better and more brilliantly conceived battle plans have collapsed when confronted with developments not only unforeseen but apparently beyond prediction.

The beginning, in this case, was small; the end, compounded by panic, indecision and divided counsels, came close to being catastrophic. It began, as they were preparing to attack, with a sudden breaking-out of lights in the town and lights running, like messengers with torches, down the hill where the big fire flared.

The captains hopefully asked their Indian guides if the celebration of some saint's day or other religious occasion or even some national holiday were in progress. The guides disabused them; this could not be anything but an alarm. To confirm it, everyone who understood Spanish could hear someone shouting that Puná had been taken and the enemy were coming up the river.

All the bells began to ring. There was a volley of small-arms fire from the shore. Two big guns somewhere inland began firing. Guayaquil, for certain, was alarmed and awake.

Rogers wanted to land at once, before the city could organize any really effective resistance. Courtney and Dover would not listen to him. They were only listening to the bells and the guns and the bullets, all wide misses, splashing somewhere off in the darkness. "I asked Capt. Dampier how the Buccaneers behav'd themselves in such Cases, and he told me they never attack'd any large Place after it was alarm'd". An hour was spent in futile argument over how to proceed.

Rogers continued to insist on the only measure that offered any hope of taking Guayaquil with the maximum profit at the minimum cost; but he had now only one voice in a three-way divided command. The dispute, as Cooke wrote, grew so loud and so hot that the Spaniards heard it, even over all the uproar, and summoned a prisoner they had been holding for some years, an Englishman named Boyce, to interpret what was being said. By the time Boyce was brought up, however, the great debate had suddenly and abruptly ended, at a point where it seemed to be barely getting its second wind. The formidable and wholly indifferent ebb tide ended it. Dampier had earlier recorded that the tides at Guayaquil are among the highest in the world, the difference between high and low being often as much as sixteen feet. Therefore, when the ebb set in, there was no longer any question of boats staying abreast of the city, much less of attacking it. The yelling and the shouting were swept downstream.

Actually, the argument was not settled by being irresistibly floated away; downstream it began again. The English had now some hours to wait before they could move with the flood back to Guayaquil. These hours Dover, Dampier and Courtney employed in compounding the previous errors of delay, vacillation and plain bad judgment.

All the carefully prepared strategy of surprise had collapsed. And by now they had apparently lost the last chance of attempting the city when it was still confused and disorganized. Rogers reasonably demanded that they either proceed with the operation or abandon it. He pointed out that, if they had lost many advantages, nevertheless every hour they delayed multiplied the odds against them, that minutes still counted and that as soon as the tide returned they ought to attack.

He must have felt himself suddenly in the company of unaccountable, panic-stricken fools. Dampier's frequent hesitation and indecision at moments of crisis had long since been established and may well have been congenital. Courtney's behavior is less easy to understand. As for Dover, he had suffered for months under the nominal title of a sea captain who was no captain at all; he had presided impressively as president and biggest shareholder at meetings of the council, as he might equally well have presided at a board of directors meeting in Bristol. He supervised the care of the sick and injured.

But he did not know much more about navigation than a
boy who spits on his finger and holds it up to test the
wind, and he knew even less about the command of a
ship at sea. This Dover, then, after all that eclipse, now
had come into his own and on him descended an epis-
copal mantle of infallibility—like the one that has retro-
actively settled on the shoulders of every Pope and the
ones that continue to settle on a large number of properly
qualified physicians.

It was suddenly given Dover to know that any attack
on Guayaquil had become impossible. He therefore called
for a meeting of the chief officers (they were now into
the morning of April 22nd) so that they could have another debate. They had it.

An attempted landing, Dover proclaimed, would be
merely a waste of lives; even if eventually successful, it
would cripple them for any further operations and make
impossible the pursuit of their major objective: the Manila
Galleon. He added, as Rogers recorded, that "tho' the
Spaniards in these Parts had no extraordinary fighting
Character, yet if they arm'd the Mulatto's, as they generally did on the like Occasions, we might find the Attempt
very desperate . . ."

The same flash of light that revealed all this to Dover
also revealed to him the solution: send a trumpeter ashore
with proposals for the city to ransom the prisoners and
the ships and to buy, at prices arranged in an orderly
meeting, the slaves and cargoes. Guayaquil would then
give hostages for its good conduct, and the English, in
return for all of this, would pledge themselves not to attempt an attack which, according to Dover's other argu-
ments, should have been as obviously hopeless to the
Spaniards as it was to himself.

Rogers patiently pointed out certain flaws. He fore-
bore quoting, if he knew them, the words of John Selden:

"If you say you have had a revelation, then I must have one, too, to know you had one." He did not forbear repeating what he had previously said: that every added delay made their position worse, that the citizens of Guayaquil would jump at any chance to prolong the delay by dickering, not only in order to gain time to increase their forces but to send away and bury in obscure parts of the hinterland every bit of cash and treasure they possessed.

Rogers' reasoning won. Or almost won. No sooner had the majority voted to launch the attack than Dover insisted that Rogers be held personally, financially and criminally responsible for whatever happened. This motion was about to be carried. Rogers, understandably, refused to go along with it. He was not only reluctant to accept such an outrageous proposition but he saw that with a command so divided, so many officers either hesitant, opposed or plainly mixed up, no chance of concerted and properly organized action was at this point possible.

Dover's solution was accordingly, and by default, adopted. The more often he was proved wrong the more strongly he believed that he had been essentially right. Some glimmer of reason did, however, assert itself in the meeting, and instead of a trumpeter the captain of the French-built frigate and the lieutenant captured at Puná were sent ashore, under a flag of truce, to negotiate. Cooke reported: "When the Captain . . . of the French-built ship came to the *Corregidor,* or the Mayor of the Town, he asked him our Number, which the Captain magnify'd, the *Corregidor* answered they were Boys, and not Men, and the Captain reply'd, he would find they were Men; for they had fought him bravely in their open boats, tho' he had killed one of the Commander's Brothers, and wounded and killed others; and therefore advised him to agree for the Ransom of the Town; for tho' he had 3,000 Men, he would not be able to withstand them. To which the *Corregidor* reply'd: 'My horse is ready.'" This, as it turned out, was a considerable overstatement concerning the condition of his cavalry, but no one, least of all the *Corregidor*, knew it then.

While that interchange proceeded, four barks put out from Guayaquil and tried to escape up river. Rogers dispatched the pinnaces and promptly captured them. He also took possession of the big, newly launched ships that were at harbor. Meanwhile, the *Duke*'s yawl, cruising in the gulf, had come up with an empty bark, abandoned by its crew off Punta Arenas. The total bag of Peruvian shipping, over a period of little more than a month, was now fairly impressive.

The haggling and bargaining at Guayaquil did not go so well, as Rogers had foreseen. It went according to plan, the Spanish plan, continuing all that day, throughout the night, and during most of the following day, and the young Spanish *Corregidor* was very good at it.

He appeared at a meeting, verbally agreed to buy their goods at a hundred and forty pieces of eight per bale and was gone. He agreed to a later meeting, failed to appear. People came and went. Around midnight of the twenty-second, the *Corregidor* sent a gentleman with a present of two bags of flour, two sheep and two hogs, two jars of wine and two of brandy. The night wore on.

In addition to the purchase price of the slaves and cargoes, the English demanded 50,000 pieces of eight as ransom from the town, in return for which they would hand over the two big new ships and the six barks they had captured, sufficient hostages to be given them to guarantee payment within nine days.

Guayaquil countered with an offer of 40,000 pieces of eight. It may seem astounding to those not accustomed to the uses of trade that people could bargain and beat the price down, with the muzzles of so many guns jammed up against them; or that, if this was just a delaying tactic to gain time, resistance should not have been more effectively organized for the attack when it was finally launched. But if divided counsels prevailed afloat, they prevailed just as certainly ashore.

Moreover, the merchants of Guayaquil—like those in Mexico and at Manila and even elsewhere, like those in France and Holland and Germany and England and, in fact, around the world—had long been noted for putting a considerable premium on their goods and chattels, in the balance of which the mere lives of their neighbors were weighed and found wanting. And Guayaquil was inured. When the French buccaneers took the place twenty-two years earlier and retired to Puna with a number of important hostages to await the faithfully promised ransom, the good citizens began to slash offers and underrate the value of the collateral. When the buccaneers, definitely barbarous and obviously not fooling, replied by cutting off the heads of hostages, one by one, and dispatching these coupons up river, still the citizens, divided between conscience, good repute and sound business practice, refused to redeem them. The buccaneers, who had nothing at all to go on but an almost complete lack of conscience, wound up defeated.

Rogers and his captains knew the story. When, therefore, the demand for 50,000 pieces of eight was countered by an offer of 40,000 pieces of eight, they accepted. More delays: more close scrutiny of possible savings; more clouds of ink. In the early afternoon of the twenty-third, at signs of hostile preparations on shore, some of Rogers' officers advised him to attack at once, but he would not break his word of honor which he had given to the *Corregidor*. An hour or so later, after the time allotted for a final answer had expired, a messenger arrived to say that

30,000 pieces of eight were all the citizens could or would raise. Rogers sent back word to send three additional hostages within half an hour to guarantee payment of 40,000 pieces of eight, or he would blow Guayaquil apart. Before this ultimatum expired, emissaries returned with their absolutely flat, final, rock-bottom offer: 32,000 pieces of eight. Rogers ordered Guayaquil to prepare. He hauled down his flag of truce and hoisted the English and field colors. The attack began.

It had waited incredibly, thanks to Dover and his faction, through the night of April 21st-22nd, through the following day, the following night and well into the afternoon of the twenty-third. By that time Guayaquil must have decided that, with the bulk of its treasure buried and secreted, it had nothing of much importance to lose except the lives of its citizens.

Under covering bombardment from the guns of a bark, the first English wave went ashore in three boats; there were about seventy men and two cannon mounted on field carriages. They landed at the river-end of a street lined with houses in which enemy infantry was strongly posted. At the far end of this street, which opened onto a square, several hundred horsemen were drawn up.

The first wave disembarked quickly, each man falling to one knee, shooting, reloading and moving on. Their fire was fast and accurate. The Spaniards got off only one volley before breaking and retreating to the square. At the square they formed around four cannon emplaced in front of a church. The barrage from the bark was lifted, and the groups under Rogers, Courtney and Dover moved forward.

Black powder makes a lot of smoke. Often a man must wait until the air clears to learn whether or not he has hit what he is shooting at. With so many hundreds of muskets and pistols and so many cannon crashing, the smoke choked the street; it piled up in a front like miniature thunderheads split with continual flashes. Bullets whanged and hummed and splatted against buildings. Men began falling and some of the horses went down. For the second time the Spanish cavalry broke and scattered. "My horse is ready," the *Corregidor* had said; but give him credit—he was only twenty-four.

The cannon in front of the church kept pounding and failed, unbelievably, to hit anyone—even though the pieces were charged both with solid ball and with partridge shot, loads of scrap iron and stones. Leading the advance, Rogers with eight or ten men stormed these guns, cutting down gunners and the troops massed around them.

Courtney and Dover with their own companies came after him. The Spanish troops ran. The gunners abandoned their guns. All except one, an Irishman. This man, fighting in a cause not his, except by wrongs of his own nation and for his faith, in an obscure corner of history, abandoned by everyone and with nothing to gain or save except his courage and his duty as conscience directed, stood alone by his piece and continued to serve it. He was fatally hit in four places and pitched over the wheels of his cannon. Dead in a dirty square of a small colonial town, he joined all those who throughout time have been awarded no posthumous medals, received mention in no communiqués, whose names never appear in history even as footnotes, who simply did what they had to do as they conceived it, and went down, leaving—if only briefly—*the vivid air signed with their honour.*

This was his, it belonged to him. And his enemies, Cooke and Rogers, paid him a short honest tribute in a couple of sentences. And that is all. The Irishman disappears; he is dead; he is gone.

With the Spanish cavalry scattered, the troops running, the guns abandoned, Rogers secured the church and took some twelve prisoners, while Dover and Courtney proceeded on a mopping-up operation. Rogers' own field-pieces, plus the captured guns, were put under Dampier's command and trained on the enemy, "who run clear out of town."

In the space of little more than half an hour from their first landing, they had taken Guayaquil and at the astonishing price of only two casualties: Yerrick Derrickson, an implausible Dutchman belonging to Rogers' company, was shot through the shoulder and lower part of his neck; John Martin, a Portuguese gunner aboard the bark, was killed by the premature explosion of a mortar shell.

They had the city. The problem now was holding it long enough to collect. The enemy, though at the moment scattered and disorganized, still greatly outnumbered them, was relatively intact and would soon regroup. And, with all the bargaining and delays, messages had long since been dispatched to the Viceroy at Lima to inform His Excellency that the English were at Guayaquil.

The captains disposed their forces as follows: Rogers held the church where the guns had been planted, Courtney a church in the middle of the town, and Dover a church at the far end. Thomas Dover's position was the most exposed and hazardous and definitely the most unpleasant. From a hill overlooking the jungle close by, "the Enemy were almost continually popping at him all Night." He had some adjacent houses set on fire to provide light against surprise and to give clear shooting during the various sporadic attacks which were launched against him. Nevertheless, as Rogers notes, if the Spaniards had

combined on a real assault, they would have overrun
Dover's position before Courtney and Rogers could have
come to his relief.

As it was, he and his men were forced by the sniping
fire to spend the night mewed up in a place permeated
with an overpowering stink of decomposition from the
numerous corpses recently buried there: victims of one
of Guayaquil's then recurrent plagues who filled the floor
of that church as they filled the floors of all the others.

Guayaquil appeared to be dismally empty of plunder. As Rogers prophesied, the inhabitants had taken advantage of the long delay to pack most of their coin and
valuables off into the hinterland. On the night of the
town's capture, an Indian prisoner informed them of a
lot of money hidden in houses and "Bark-logs" up the
river. A boat with twenty-one men was dispatched to
look for it.

On the following morning, April 24th, the companies
in Guayaquil set out with iron crowbars and mauls to
break open buildings. They found very little. What they
did find was more on the order of Dampier's sad capture
of the ship loaded with marmalade; it amounted to some
flour, peas, beans and jars of wine and brandy. The
weather was wet, hot and enervating. A number of the
men wanted to pry up the floorboards of the churches on
the theory that money might be hidden in the graves, but
Rogers and Dover refused to permit it for fear of the
plague.

Work parties began to carry stocks of supplies to
the water front. Rogers sent off the lieutenant captured
at Puna and another prisoner to deal with the Spaniards
hidden in the brush. These envoys returned some hours
later with an ambiguous answer. If the town had changed
a little, the inhabitants obviously had not. Rogers said
something about the possibility of burning Guayaquil to

the ground, and the lieutenant at once departed to resume negotiations.

The search party sent up river the previous night returned. It had been having itself quite a time, including several active skirmishes with the enemy—during which one man received a superficial neck wound—and a chaste skirmish with some of the best-looking ladies of Guayaquil, during which no one got hurt or harmed or even ruffled. "The Houses up the River were full of Women, and particularly at one place there were above a Dozen handsom, genteel Young Women well dress'd, where our Men got several Gold Chains and Earrings, but were otherwise so civil to them, that the Ladies offered to dress 'em Victuals, and brought 'em a Cask of good Liquor. Some of their largest Gold Chains were conceal'd, and wound about their Middles, Legs and Thighs, etc. but the Gentlewomen in these hot countries being very thin clad with Silk and fine Linnen, and their Hair dressed with Ribbons very neatly, our Men by pressing felt the Chains, etc. with their Hands on the Out-side of the Lady's Apparel, and by their Linguist modestly desired the Gentlewomen to take 'em off and surrender 'em. This I mention as a proof of our Sailors Modesty, and in respect to Mr. Connely and Mr. Selkirk the late Governour of *Juan Fernandoes*, who commanded this Party; For being young Men, I was willing to do 'em this Justice, hoping the Fair Sex will make 'em a grateful return when we arrive in *Great Britain*, on account of their civil Behavior to these charming Prisoners."

The boat brought back about a thousand pounds' worth of gold chain, earrings and plate and would have brought back more if it hadn't been for the fact that as fast as the search party ransacked one of the up-river houses, all the people hiding in adjacent places lit out for the opposite shore in bark logs and canoes with every-thing they could carry.

The search party also brought back word that it had spotted a patrol of upward of three hundred foot and horse. Rogers decided that the Spaniards would continue to delay until they had mobilized enough strength to re-capture the town. He and his captains sat down to sweat out the night.

The next day one of the envoys returned with an offer of 30,000 pieces of eight for the town and the cap-tured shipping, to be paid within twelve days. They were right back at the maximum, rock-bottom offer. The situa-tion, it turned out, was further complicated by the fact that many of the Negroes and Indians whom the citizens in their haste packed off into hiding with considerable money and valuables had simply bagged the stuff for themselves and kept on going.

Rogers accepted the offer but not the delay of twelve days, a delay he could not afford for twice the price: partly because it would give the resistance more time to reorganize but principally because it would narrow by so much more the lead he now had on Lima and the big ships that would be coming up to attack him.

There were continual skirmishes. That afternoon, April 25th, nine men and an officer engaged a party of the enemy at the north end of town, chased them too far into the woods and were counterattacked. One man was shot in the middle, but the bullet flattened itself against the blade of a poleaxe he had strapped to his belt. An-other man was shot through the calf of the leg, and "by his Irregularity and hard drinking fell into a Fever that carried him off." Not, presumably, on the spot.

At the same time, Courtney's chief lieutenant, an officer named Mr. Stratton, was going gingerly about his duties when one of the pistols with which he was festooned suddenly discharged itself and put a slug in his thigh. He was carried back to the bark, disabled and perhaps babbling but in no danger.

That night not many slept. The Spaniards ringed them and were pressing. They knew what could happen if they were taken. "The Inquisition," Rogers observed, "rages worse here than in Old *Spain*; their Chief Court is at *Lima*, but 4 officers from that Court were settl'd at *Guiaquil*, besides 24 Clergy belonging to the Town, who inform against any Person that they suspect of Opinions contrary to the *Roman* Church, and with a violent Zeal prosecute 'em almost without any Formality. The Offenders are speedily sent to the Court at *Lima*, where nothing but a great deal of Money can save 'em, if found guilty in the least degree." When the Spanish inhabitants themselves might be treated like this, what kind of treatment would be reserved for those who were at one and the same time enemies, Protestants and privateers?

At Courtney's headquarters there was a strict order to shoot anyone who did not answer when challenged. Accordingly, a Frenchman detached to duty there as a sentinel from Rogers' company shot and killed one of Courtney's men, a sailor named Tidcomb. It turned out that neither the sentinel nor Tidcomb knew how to ask or answer a watchword. After this, Courtney moved his company in with Rogers.

On the morning of the 26th, Rogers sent the Spanish an ultimatum: sufficient hostages to guarantee payment of 30,000 pieces of eight at Puna within six days or he would burn Guayaquil to the ground at three that afternoon.

The Spaniards beat the deadline by an hour. The hostages were delivered. There was now a cease-fire, but the legal mind had yet to work. An agreement being duly drawn up and signed and sent to the Spanish camp, the instrument was returned in a few hours with the objection that it omitted, by an essential "whereas," to establish once and for all that the town had been taken by force.

The change was duly made, attested and initialed by the party of the first part and party of the second part, in both the Spanish and English documents and all copies. By the time this had been accomplished—such things take time—the occupying force had been compelled to spend another less restless but still hot and drenching night ashore. Early on the morning of the twenty-seventh, they received the Spanish agreement all properly signed and in order and returned the English one.

It ran as follows: "Whereas the City of Guiaquil, lately in subjection to Philip V. King of Spain, is now taken by Storm, and in the possession of the Captains *Thomas Dover, Woodes Rogers,* and *Stephen Courtney,* commanding a Body of Her Majesty of Great Britain's Subjects: We the underwritten are content to become Hostages for the said City and to continue in the Custody of the said Capts. *Thos. Dover, Woodes Rogers,* and *Stephen Courtney,* till 30,000 Pieces of Eight shall be paid to them for the Ransom of the said City, 2 new ships, and 6 Barks; during which time no Hostility is to be committed on either Side between this and Puna. The said Sum to be paid at Puna in six Days from the Date hereof, and then the Hostages to be discharg'd and all the Prisoners to be deliver'd immediately, otherwise the said Hostages do agree to remain Prisoners till the said Sum is discharg'd in any other Part of the World. . . ."

Anything missing or ambiguous, or open to interpretation in this could be left—as the legal mind must have inevitably hoped it would be left—to later litigation and the courts.

The Spaniards returned to their homes. The English companies were drawn up and marched to the barks with colors flying. They made a brave display, only little

7

marred by the fact that a lot of the men, weak and weary of playing soldier, had discarded their pistols, cutlasses and poleaxes on the way. Rogers, like a good nurse or parent, followed along behind with a few helpers picking things up. One man was A.W.O.L., another Dutchman, named Gabriel.

They spent the afternoon disposing the crews and plunder aboard the barks. The immediate haul was not exactly impressive. It included some 230 bags of flour, peas, beans and rice, some jars of oil, "about 160 Jars of other Liquors," ironware, small nails, powder, a ton of pitch, 150 bales of dry goods, a parcel of clothing, a ton of sugar loaf and about 1200 pounds' worth of plate, earrings and other jewelry. Of course, the ransom was still to be paid, but they could reflect, as Rogers and Cooke definitely did reflect, on what they might have got if it hadn't been for the infallible Thomas Dover's obstinacy and William Dampier's contagious irresolution.

Later that afternoon "our *Dutch*man that was missing rose out of his Brand-wine Fit, and came aboard: he was disturbed by the honest Man of the House where he lay, who first called in his Neighbours, and cautiously seized his Arms, then gently rais'd him, and when his Eyes were open, told him there was his Arms again, and bade him hasten aboard to us."

They weighed anchor and sailed down river the following morning, "and at parting made what Shew and Noise we could with our Drums, Trumpets, and Guns, and thus took our Leave of the *Spaniards* very cheerfully, but not half so well pleased as we should have been, had we taken 'em by Surprise."

Rogers, on the available evidence and his information from prisoners and hostages, says they might have got some 200,000 pieces of eight, plus gold, silver and jewelry. Cooke says that if the attack had been launched at once, the booty might have been prodigious because they later learned there were 80,000 pounds of the King's money in the town, in addition to all the money and plate belonging to the merchants, which had been packed away in the woods.

Rogers and his captains still had to conclude the business of the ransom to be paid at Puna, the release of most of the prisoners, and the general winding-up of affairs in those waters as fast as possible. On the afternoon of April 29th, the *Duke's* pinnace captured a thirty-ton bark bound for Guayaquil with a cargo of groceries.

The crew of this bark, having been at sea for seven days, knew nothing about the sacking of the town but confirmed the fact that there were two large French warships at Lima, one at Pisco and others in harbors of Chile. Rogers and his officers already knew that the first dispatches from Guayaquil had been started down the coast a week before. The hunting of the hunters was about to begin.

On the day set for the final payment, the authorities at Guayaquil, true to form, sent Rogers 20,000 pieces of eight—10,000 pieces short of the sum agreed upon. Rogers informed them that if they didn't remit the balance at once, he would sail and take the hostages with him.

A number of prisoners were released, among them the lieutenant of Puna to whom, "being a Man we had some Respect for," they gave four old, sick slaves and a bale of damaged goods. "We also parted very friendly with several of our Prisoners we took at Sea, particularly an old Padre that I had treated civilly at my own table, ever since we took him, for which he was extremely grateful."

They gave the latest prize taken, the ship loaded with comfits and groceries, to the prisoners. They released the *Increase* and various other prizes, sold the *Beginning*.

By now it was May 6th. They cleared the channel but came to anchor again a short distance down the gulf off Punta Arenas, where they discharged most of the remaining prisoners, giving them back their wearing apparel. They handed over three Negros to the captain of the French-built ship and one Negro apiece to the two officers of the other ships.

Cooke noted that during the period of operations which began off Lobos they had captured a total of fourteen vessels. All but four had now been disposed of. These four—the big merchant galleon, the French-built frigate, and two barks—were to go with them, carrying the remaining prisoners and hostages.

They were in a hurry to go—particularly Courtney and Dover. Rogers objected. He wanted to take on more water; their last supply had been laid in at Juan Fernández, months earlier, and what they had so far obtained at Guayaquil was not very good and far from sufficient in quantity. The other chief officers, with the exception of Cooke, refused to listen. They kept seeing the topsails of the avenging French squadron coming over the rim of the gulf. Rogers had estimated a period of twenty-four days' grace from the time they first hit any town on the coast. But nearly eighteen of those days had already elapsed, and so many imponderables were involved that it was reasonable to suppose Rogers' minimum estimate might be far wrong.

The enemy warships reportedly scattered from Callao to Pisco to Concepción might long since have been assembled at Callao; the messages from Guayaquil to the Viceroy might have reached their destination much more quickly than anyone had calculated. In that case, it would be a matter, not of a few more days, but of just a few more hours before the guns of five big ships would be ranging on them.

Besides, at the Galápagos—only a few days' sail
away—they could get plenty of water, according to many
reports. Hurry up, it's time. Hurry up, please; it's time to
be going.

At the last moment, emissaries from Guayaquil arrived in a small boat with 3,500 additional pieces of
eight, still 6,500 short. The ships weighed and set sail,
taking with them the rest of the prisoners and the hostages, among them the son of the Governor of Panama.

Dutchess and some of the prizes went first, not pausing for any more water, not pausing for Rogers' orders.
She was promptly becalmed and wasted a day. Then, as a
favorable wind rose, *Duke* finally caught up with her and
the squadrons set course for the replenishing streams of
the reputedly rich, abundant and wholly isolated Galápagos, where no one would look for them, where no one
could.

They had completed the operation in spite of everything, in spite of themselves, at the price of some men
dead on both sides, many men hurt. Guayaquil, in spite of
everything, had been surprised, thrown down, undone.
But Guayaquil was no maiden city. As they sailed west,
they carried with them, together with the loot, hostages,
prisoners and their self-congratulations, something invisible and fatal.

12

CIRCE'S
ISLANDS

THE SHIPS stood out to sea at 2:00 A.M. on May 8th. Within twenty-four hours the first men began to sicken. By May 11th there were twenty men critically ill on the *Duke*, and fifty on the *Dutchess*, one of them Captain Courtney, and it was just beginning. Guayaquil had bequeathed them its plague.

Woodes Rogers, finding that a regimen of well-laced punch seemed to preserve his own health, prescribed it in more or less massive doses as preventive therapy. Captain-Doctor Dover administered to the sick and dying the same treatment that Sydenham had once successfully prescribed for him—abundant fluids and copious bleeding. He describes the epidemic, "They all had spots which in

the Great Plague they called Tokens, few or none of the
Spanish escaped death who had them but my people had
them and Buboes, too," and says: "I ordered the Surgeon
to bleed them in both arms and to go round to them all
with the command to leave them bleeding till they were
all blooded, and then come and tie them up in their turns.
Thus they lay bleeding and fainting, so long, that I could
not conceive they could lose less than a hundred ounces
each man." That would be about half of each man's total
blood volume.

Captain Courtney finally recovered, but Dover's
brother-in-law, Samuel Hopkins, died on the fourteenth
and was committed to the sea with regret. Rogers had an
entry: "At 6 last night *Mr. Samuel Hopkins,* Dr. Dover's
Kinsman and Assistant, died; he read Prayers once a Day
ever since we pass'd the Equinox in the North Sea: He
was a very good temper'd sober Man, and very well beloved by the whole Ship's Company."

Two days later, as they neared the Galápagos, 140
men were down with the plague and more were still
dropping. They lay in the pitch and heave of the creaking
ships, sick and delirious in the stinking darkness where
the rats ran, thick with lice. They lay chattering and
drenched in the continual wet as the seas worked or
splashed in, buckets of excrement around them, and
below them the beat and slop of the putrid water in the
bilge; and they might be said to have lived, if they did
live, on a diet of rot.

On May 17th another man died. The number of sick
continued to mount until it reached 180. By now the race
for the Galápagos was even more desperate than their
earlier race for Juan Fernández after rounding the Horn.

They had to have water, of course. They needed a
place where they could lose themselves for a period after
what had been done at Guayaquil—*Past reason hunted;*

and no sooner had,/Past reason hated, as a swallow'd bait,/On purpose laid to make the taker mad. And that was the crux of it, the poisoned bait, because beyond everything else they needed an island where the sick could be put ashore to rest and recuperate.

These considerations were largely, but not solely, humanitarian. They were also the plain, practical considerations of survival. No one needed any complicated, mathematical tables to figure that if the plague killed the men in the same proportion it had killed the people at Guayaquil, there would not be enough crews left to man the ships, much less to attempt any further enterprise. They would all leave their bones on these coasts, or in Spanish prisons, or on various gibbets in various public squares, or in and around the mines of Peru.

The Galápagos, however, were at this point very near, not more than another day's sail away. The Spaniards called them "Las Encantadas"—the enchanted islands—because of the mysterious currents which alternately drew in and drove back ships. The name Galápagos came, of course, from the Spanish for tortoise; and on these islands giant tortoises and sea and land turtles were to be found, of a size and variety and abundance observed nowhere else. The islands, however, were an antediluvian, fire-cracked world.

Rogers, who had read the accounts, was aware of the grimmer aspects. And Dampier knew them at first hand. But Dampier, along with other writers, was reassuring. He had set down, from the account of his old commander, Davis: "There he found such plenty of Land-Turtle that he and his men eat nothing else for Three Months that he staid there. They were so fat that he saved sixty Jars of Oil out of those that he spent: This Oil served instead of Butter, to eat with Doughboys or Dumplings on his return out of these Seas. He found

very convenient Places to careen, and good Channels be-
tween the Islands: and very good anchoring in many
Places. There he found also plenty of Brooks of good
Fresh-water, and Firewood enough . . ."

In his manuscript journal Dampier wrote that when
he went to the Galápagos with Davis and Cowley, the
first island off which they anchored was rocky and barren,
without wood or water. However, the next island, according to the account Cowley himself later published, had
"excellent sweet Water." Dampier inserted a note: "At the
north end of the Island we saw Water running down the
Rocks."

Finally, Dampier referred to a second visit to the
Galápagos by Davis. "Part of what I saw of these Islands
I had from Captain Davis, who was there afterwards, and
careened his Ship at neither of the Islands that we were at
in 1684, but went to the other Islands more to the westward, which he found to be good, habitable Islands, having a deep fat Soil capable of producing anything that
grows in these Climates; they are well-watered, and have
plenty of good Timber." He related that another buccaneer captain, Harris, "found some Islands that had
plenty of Mamee trees, and pretty large Rivers," and concluded, "so that take the Galapagos by and large, they are
extraordinary good Places for Ships in distress to seek
Relief at."

Altogether, to Rogers' desperate squadron, the Galápagos represented a haven that was, if not precisely in the
words of the old hymn, *Jerusalem the golden, with milk
and honey blest*, still something very like it.

They had now been at sea nearly ten days, not very
long at all compared with previous stretches of their voyage but too long for the condition they were in. And sick
men, particularly nearly two hundred very sick men, might
well dream of that landfall so long delayed . . . *The isle is*

7*

full of noises,/Sounds and sweet airs, that give delight, and hurt not./Sometimes a thousand twangling instruments/ Will hum about mine ears; and sometimes voices,/That, if I then had wak'd after long sleep,/Will make me sleep again; and then, in dreaming,/The clouds methought would open and show riches/Ready to drop upon me, that, when I wak'd,/I cried to dream again.

On May 18th, the mist, or the dream, lifted when they sighted two large islands and the reality began slowly to disclose itself. A boat went ashore and returned "with a melancholy account that no Water was to be found."

But that was only part of it. These and all the rest of the islands the squadron subsequently searched were merely cinders, slag heaps, where the lava rock was so sharp it cut through a leather boot. And the Encantadas, true to their name, were not only continually shifting and changing position on the undependable charts of the period but many of them actually kept changing shape from year to year because of volcanic activity. Darwin, when he visited them in the *Beagle,* was reminded of "the iron furnaces of Wolverhampton."

Melville, who went to the Galápagos on a whaler, wrote: "There toil the demons of fire, who at intervals irradiate the night with a strange, spectral illumination for miles and miles around, but unaccompanied by any further demonstration; or else, suddenly announce themselves by terrific concussions, and the full drama of a volcanic eruption. The blacker that cloud by day, the more you may look for light by night . . ."

This then was their haven, their landfall—volcanic heaps not only heaved up obviously from the bottom of the Pacific but apparently from the bottom of time. The chief, the overwhelming forms of life on these mountainous clinkers were reptiles: turtles, tortoises, snakes, lizards, immense iguanas. Instead of the "Sounds and sweet airs," the "thousand twangling instruments," there was, as Melville noted: "No voice, no low, no howl . . . the chief sound of life here is a hiss."

Two boats again went ashore and returned: no trees, no water; nothing on these islands but some green scrub and crumbling cinderlike rock, and soil so dry it broke under the men's feet. Nothing but that and immense numbers of lumbering, crawling, or poised and then racing creatures—forms with expressionless eyes hooded by nictitating membranes and with skins pebbled like dragons. *Here is no water but only rock/Rock and no water . . .*

The frigates, barks, boats and prizes fanned out. Somewhere in this swirling, primeval expanse with its unpredictable currents there was an island with good timber and clear running water. Not only had Dampier reported it and Davis and Cowley and other buccaneers, but its existence was confirmed by all the available Spanish records.

The fact that they could not find the one or ones with water did not prove Dampier or the others wrong. Dampier had been here before in a season of brief rains, but they were here, as they had been at Guayaquil, in a bad season.

The English squadron was merely trying to locate in an archipelago extending over more than 3,000 square miles of ocean, and comprising twelve large and several hundred small islands, the one or two islands which were said to have year-round sources of water, when all the islands were hopelessly misplaced and misidentified on the maps.

More men died. A bark commanded by Simon Hatley, with several sailors and some prisoners and slaves aboard, simply vanished. The enchantment had begun. Fires flared by night, and the breakers surged and spouted among the caves and potholes, and by day above the slag heaps and the curtains of falling spray wheeled flocks of screaming birds.

They no longer believed in any haven of tall timber and cascading streams and fruit and flowers. Rogers wrote about Davis: ". . . these sort of Men, and others I've conversed with, or whose Books I have read, have given very blind or false Relations of their Navigation and Actions in these Parts, for supposing the Places too remote to have their Stories disprov'd, they imposed on the Credulous, amongst whom I was one, till now I too plainly see, that we cannot find any of their Relations to be relied on . . ."

The ships were short of food now. They were short of medicines for the sick, which dumbfounded Rogers when he considered the quantities of drugs that had originally been put on board. Day after day, island after island, the search went on. More men died, among them a George Underhill: "a good Proficient in most parts of the Mathematicks and other learning, tho' not much above 21 years old: He was of a very courteous Temper and brave . . ."

They replenished their food supplies with turtle and tortoise, and quantities of fish: grouper, mackerel, mullet, snook and tuna. Still there was no water, no place where the sick could be put ashore. *If there were water/And no rock/If there were rock/And also water . . ./If there were the sound of water only . . .*

The heat, fortunately, was not excessive because the islands, though lying in the equator, are washed by the cold Peru Current. At the Galápagos its temperature is from fifteen to twenty degrees colder than the surrounding tropical waters. But the shifting, the shape-changing, the mirages and visual delusions continued and grew worse.

Cowley, strange enough in himself, timid and predatory and unpredictable, who seemed to find something ludicrous in everybody's misfortunes but his own, had mapped and named some of these up-thrusting slag heaps, and wrote about one of them: "My fancy led me to call it Cowley's *Enchanted Isle*, for we having had a Sight of it upon several points of the Compass, it appeared always in so many different Forms; sometimes like a ruined Fortification; upon another point like a great City . . ."

Melville much later noted that a ship might spend almost a month going from one island to another, though there were only thirty miles between them. Nowhere else, he said, was the wind so light and unreliable, the currents so unpredictable.

The *Duke* and the *Dutchess* and their escort vessels were floating sick bays, warped and rotten asylums filled with an unbearable stench. To join Samuel Hopkins, the "very good temper'd sober Man . . . very well beloved by the whole Ship's Company," and George Underhill, "of a very courteous Temper and brave . . ." there had now gone numbers of others: among these one Edward Downe, and James Daniel, ship's carpenter, and *"Law" Carney* of a malignant fever and *"Jacob Scronder a Dutch*man and a very good Sailor."

The ships and the boats continued their search on a last gamble, and occasionally they broke out signals and fired guns in the hope of retrieving the bark commanded by Hatley that had simply vanished.

The echoes disturbed the screaming birds, hawks, finches, frigate birds, pelicans, blue herons, the flightless cormorants, and penguins; disturbed the reptile populations, land and sea turtles, iguanas, lava lizards, snakes, miniature dinosaurs. Some of this life at the sea's edge slid into it, while some disappeared into the security of the rocks and huge cacti. Giant tortoises, capable of carrying two or three men on their backs, tortoises weighing from five hundred to seven hundred pounds each, who live longer, it is said, than anything that walks, or swims or crawls—these docile monsters at the rolling concussion drew in their heads with a hiss of alarm. The big marine iguanas, the only marine lizards anywhere, formidable-looking but timid, butting each other in bloodless battles over food and mates, paused suddenly motionless and alert.

Day after day was the same: burials, the slap of sails, the creaking of oars, shouts, signals, the occasional booming of a gun whose echo was lost among black, basaltic mountains and smoking craters, while the useless hunt went on and the ageless, unthirsting eyes of the things crowded on the rocks watched them. This was the place they had come to: a world in which man did not belong; a planet on which he had not yet arrived.

Any one of them, officer or hand, must sometimes have paused and thought incredulously that in another world, in Bristol perhaps, unbelievably remote, at that very moment the coffee houses were already full; merchants, lawyers, physicians, powdered and bewigged, sat at ease with their long clay pipes over cups of mocha, reading the latest papers from London and turning a neat piece of business. One who had shares in some ship at sea might be driving with his sprinkled and glittering wife in one of their ornate, upholstered carriages out to view the latest estate he had bought: a noble, Augustan house with a wide prospect of trees and lawns and streams and sheltered gardens—*Annihilating all that's made/To a green thought in a green shade.*

Men would remember the ways and the harbor, thicker with tall masts, as Pope observed, than the Thames between London and Deptford. They would remember the shops and industries, the weavers and joiners and coopers, the smiths and dyers and chandlers, the bake shops and taverns. Men sick with the miasmas of their tortured ships might picture the prosperous gentlemen walking those streets. At that moment, off the Galápagos, Woodes Rogers was writing: "This Day *Thos. Hughes,* a very good Sailor died . . . About the same time another young Man call'd John English, died aboard the *Havre de Grace,* and we have still many sick."

But there must have been water. How did the lizards and snakes, tortoises and birds survive? The reptiles, of course, were adapted: they got moisture from leaves, such as the acacia, and from the giant prickly pear. The birds, most of them, could fly to hidden sources, maybe far inland on various islands. Many did not even need to do that. Captain Colnet, when at the Galápagos was puzzled as to how the small birds which seemed to remain in one spot could exist without water, until he was informed by some of his men that "as they were reposing beneath a prickly-pear tree they observed an old bird in the act of supplying three young ones with drink by squeezing the berry of a tree into their mouths. It was about the size of a pea, and contained a water juice of an acid and not unpleasant taste. The bark of the tree yields moisture, and, being eaten, allays the thirst. The land tortoise gnaw and suck it."

There was no water for men. The Encantadas were cursed, as they always have been held to be from the time they were first discovered in 1535 by Frey Tomas de Berlanger, third Bishop of Panama, drifting helplessly onto them in the current. Sailors believed that all wrecked sea officers were turned at death into the tortoises of the Galápagos, to crawl and hiss for centuries in their enormous shells. They bred superstition; they were a kind of superstition in themselves. If these were the damned, or the transformed, out of what craters or caldrons or vortices in time did the rest of that company come, and equipped for what?

These islands were a blank—worse than a blank, worse than a mere suspension, a sort of emptiness. They were recognizably something but something lost, ancient, fathomless. It can be said that a secret was always there to be discovered. The Encantadas always posed a question beyond the questions to which they may now and then have suggested an answer. They assaulted immediately and directly by denial, by desperate thirst—as in the case of Roger's squadron.

They also assaulted men's reason, and will presumably continue to assault it in one form or another in time and space; if not as an archipelago lying in the Pacific at about Latitude 0° Longitude 90° West, then as a symbol of some archipelago at the rim of this galaxy.

Boats, barks, prizes and frigates had now been searching among these islands for nearly nine days, and everything got steadily worse, all problems compounded. The longer they pushed the search for water, the lower went the level of what they had in their casks, until they were approaching a sort of point-of-no-return.

They were sucked in, turned around, beaten back, with the hands of the sorceress moving in a blur of presto-chango. There were more burials. There was never a sign of the bark commanded by Hatley with four sailors, two prisoners and three Negroes; the bark, seaworthy and well-handled, had done nothing more than sail around a nearby point or headland; but that was a headland in the Galá-pagos.

The sense, if it made any sense, might well have been that of Faust, Mephistopheles and Irrlicht on the Brocken:

*In die Traum-und Zaubersphäre/sind wir, scheint es
eingegangen/. . . in den weiten, öden Räumen . . .*

As an indication of that sense, of one aspect of this
sphere of dream and magic, a hermit came to the Encantadas—a hundred years almost exactly to the month after
Rogers and company had suffered there. This was a very
different hermit from Alexander Selkirk. This one was an
opposite side of the coin: a hermit with face reversed and
upside down, like a face pictured in a work on demonol-
ogy.

His name was Patrick Watkins, and he was a living
proof that solitude and silence by themselves are not nec-
essarily conducive to either improvement or understanding, but may well, given most men, work for the worst.

Watkins luckily landed on one of the islands with
fresh water. He has been called the first resident of the
Galápagos, and he seems to have had an affinity for them
from the first—a misplaced affinity, however, because
what was natural for the birds and reptiles was for him
unnatural. Where they were mild, he was savage; while
they remained more or less static, neither advancing nor
deteriorating much, for Watkins it was all steps going
down, from the moment he first set foot ashore. He
started calling himself "Oberlus" and then "Fatherless
Oberlus," by some wild freak of association in his dis-
oriented mind as the Encantadas worked on him. He was
literate and could write a smooth and very neat letter—
as several captains knew who either lost or nearly lost
men to him.

Everyone who visited his island—shipwrecked men
or boat crews in search of water and food—he tried to
capture and enslave or kill. He was Fatherless Oberlus,
the abominable hermit, wolfish and mad; and for possible
subjects he kept careful watch with a gun. *Hail, mildly
pleasing Solitude,/Companion of the Wise and Good.*

Long after he was dead, his swine shape or wolf shape presumably continued to haunt the cinders and the garden patch he had cultivated. While he was there, ship captains came to consider the island a kind of plague area— or maybe more like one of those holes or pockets in the earth whose fatal concentrations of carbon dioxide or other gases are indicated by the bones of small birds and animals lying all about. In any case, that was a place where no sailors who went ashore could be sure of ever being seen again. And long after the abominable hermit had gone, skippers continued to avoid those shores.

He was an example of what Circe, what the Galápagos, could do, had done before, have done since, given the right material. And, in fact, he was described as "the victim of some malignant sorceress; from having sipped at Circe's cup."

That cup, that caldron, steamed also visibly in the sea, where the cold Humboldt and the warm equatorial currents met, an area in which the air temperature might vary by fifteen degrees within the distance of a few hundred yards, a seething, turbulent edge where the surface was striped and rippled and, to the accompaniment of a continual hissing and rumbling and a sound like surf, millions of incredible forms and shapes, forced up from the depths, devouring and being devoured, boiled to the surface.

The light, by now, for the searching ships was no more than that of a dim, waning moon. Circe had done enough to them; a little longer here, another day or two spent looking for the island they had heard about, like a gambler pushing for everything on the last card, might well finish them. They had just enough water left to enable them to reach the nearest place where it was certain fresh supplies could be found. Rogers noted that the men available to work the ships were by this time so weak that they could hardly hoist out the daily boat.

The only hope left was to turn and head for Gorgona, an island off the coast of what is now Colombia. Gorgona had plenty of water and vegetation and tall trees. However, it was some ten days' sail away, and the voyage might prove longer at this time of year when, their Spanish prisoners informed them, there was the possibility of running into calms. Gorgona was also a roundabout for them and their plans for the galleon. Worse, they might be caught either in the crossing or at the island by the French and Spanish squadrons. They had no choice.

Rogers might justifiably have felt bitter about his captains and council: about brilliant Dampier, pacing the deck, who had been so confident; about suggestible Courtney, and unmanageable Dover, who had been in such a panic haste to get away from the work at Guayaquil that they would not wait to take on enough water. "Had we," he observed, "supplied ourselves well at Point *Arena* we should, no doubt, have had time enough to find the Island S. *Maria del Aguada* reported to be one of the *Gallapagos*, where there is Plenty of good Water, Timber, Land and Sea Turtle, and a safe Road for Ships. This was the Place we intended for, and would have been very suitable for our Purpose, which was to lie some Time concealed."

Now they were being driven out into the open and on a course which, at the best, even if everything went well, they would have to retrace.

Orders were given to sail. Rogers, even then, was reluctant to abandon among these nightmare islands the bark with Hatley and the others aboard—particularly since her stock of water had been no more than enough to last a couple of days. Although everything possible had already been done, he made one more attempt to locate her. The squadron spent a final night searching, keeping lights out and firing guns. It was useless. Hatley, with his four sailors, two prisoners and three Negroes, had simply winked and gone out like a phosphorescence in the waves, or as if he had vanished over the horizon into space, removed with one sweep of the conjurer's cloak from the surface of the seas. He was seen no more. But that vacancy into which he disappeared gave him back many years later, and then, nearly a century after it had swallowed him for good, once more disgorged him in an unfathomable shape, armed with a crossbow, an albatross around his neck.

They ran from the black Encantadas for green Gorgona.

13

GORGONA
TO THE
THREE MARYS

THE EVENING that the last of the Galápagos dropped behind, "*Paunceford Wall*, a Land-Man," died; he was followed within the next few days by two more, Thomas Morgan and George Bishop.

On board one of the prizes, the *Ascension* galleon, Indian and Negro prisoners were discovered in a plot to murder the crew. The conspirators were isolated and all prisoners broken up into groups distributed among the various ships.

On the afternoon of June 5th the squadron sighted

the mainland and, simultaneously, an enemy sail. *Dutchess*, being in the van, gave chase, overhauled and captured her. "She was a Vessel of about 90 Ton, bound from *Panama* to *Guiaquil*, call'd the *St. Thomas de Villa Nova.*"

This ship carried little of value, her cargo being chiefly iron and cloth, but she had some forty people aboard, including eleven slaves, the incumbent governor of Baldivia and a lady with her newly married daughter and son-in-law. The daughter was eighteen and very pretty, and the bridegroom, from that point on, suffered relentless doubt and torment. Certainly he was in an unenviable position, and perhaps he had some slight cause for worry; but probably he had heard too many lurid accounts of piracy.

He was not, of course, among pirates. "We assign'd them the Great Cabin aboard the Galleon and none were suffer'd their Company; yet the Husband (I was told) shew'd evident Marks of Jealousy, The *Spaniards* Epidemick Disease; but I hope he had not the least Reason for it amongst us; my third Lieutenant, *Glendall* alone having charge of the Galleon and Prisoners: For being above 50 Years of Age, he appear'd to be the most secure Guardian to Females that had the least Charm, tho' all our young Men have hitherto appeared modest beyond Example among Privateers; yet we thought it improper to expose them to Temptations."

The prisoners on this latest prize were first interrogated by Courtney. From them he learned some reassuring news: nothing was as yet definitely known, at least north of Guayaquil, of the presence, much less the whereabouts, of any English squadron in the South Sea, though there had been wild rumors and alarms that a strong fleet under the command of Lord Peterborough, Admiral and General, had sailed to strike Spain in a two-pronged attack: one force to hit the West Indies, the other the Pacific coasts.

The curse of the Encantadas seemed to be lifting. On June 7th, safely and as expected, they came to anchor in thirty fathoms of water off the east side of the island of Gorgona. They began taking in water and preparing a place ashore for the sick. By then, it was the evening of June 7th and too late to do more for that night. Early the following morning, the will-o'-the-wisps, the foxfires and false lights were back with them.

At eight o'clock that morning "we spied a Sail to the Southward of the Island, between it and the Main . . ." While the frigates continued to take in water from Gorgona, their boats went after this latest victim, captured her without trouble and returned with her to the anchorage in the late afternoon. She was a small bark and carried no cargo but had aboard some gold dust and a large gold chain. She aimed to buy salt and brandy at Guayaquil.

Her officers and crew confirmed the fact that there was as yet no news of any English squadron in these waters. As the questioning continued and further information was obtained, Dover and Courtney and many of the other officers conceived a brand-new, brilliant idea: to raid the Spanish gold mines at Barbacore. They resolved to proceed at once and held a meeting on board the *Dutchess* at six o'clock that evening to decide the matter. Rogers, ill and unable to attend, sent word that he would, according to agreement, abide by the majority vote. "After they had examin'd the Prisoners, they resolved to go to *Malaga,* an Island which had a Rode, where we design'd to leave our Ships, and with our Boats row up the River, for the rich Gold Mines of *Barbacore.*"

They had barely taken in enough fresh water to last a few more days. There were still many sick and dying aboard who had always desperately needed rest and refreshment ashore and now needed them even more, after all the luckless time wasted at the Galápagos. Dover's responsibility as a physician was weighed against his thirst for loot, and the golden resolution carried. At midnight the squadron weighed anchor and sailed for Malaga.

The next day Rogers was on his feet again, fortunately, and began asking questions of his own. Captain Morell, the former commander of the *Ascension* galleon, informed him that there was no fit anchorage at Malaga for ships such as theirs; other prisoners confirmed it. Rogers examined separately two men taken in the latest prize, who had recently been to Malaga. Their stories were the same. The entrance to the only harbor was narrow and treacherous, and the banks of the river heavily wooded. Once they started up river in boats or canoes, the enemy could easily block both their advance and any possible retreat, by felling trees. The attackers would then be pinned down, stationary targets to be smashed by fire from the concealment of the forest and riddled by the poisoned arrows of the Indians, who, for a change, were warmly allied with the Spaniards.

"I was surpriz'd," Rogers said, "that the Council had not inform'd themselves better before they resolved on going to this Place, and immediately sent Mr. *White* our Linguist with the two Prisoners, on board the *Dutchess*, to undeceive Capt. Courtney and his Officers. . . ."

Reason prevailed. The enterprise was abandoned. Courtney and Cooke came aboard the *Duke* and agreed that the squadron should alter course immediately to return to Gorgona. What Dover said or felt is not recorded. He had lately been distinguishing himself in so many various and mulish ways that relations between him and Rogers could not have been less than strained; in fact, it was not very long after this that the indomitable doctor had himself transferred, bag, baggage and chests, to the

Dutchess, where he could breathe more freely. He always got on better with Courtney, anyway; Courtney could be much more easily prevailed upon to agree with some sound, bold, or merely precipitate stroke, and often could be persuaded to see the wisdom of Dover's singular opinions.

The decision to turn back had been taken when they were little more than twelve hours out of Gorgona. They were a lot longer returning. On the night of June 9th they ran into squalls and thunderstorms. *Havre de Grace* lost her main topmast. She had been proving cranky all along, and this could have been an indication of things to come. However, they all confidently expected that as soon as she had been converted and refitted at Gorgona as an English privateer, everything would be different.

At daylight on June 10th Rogers went aboard the *Havre de Grace* and the *Dutchess* to see what assistance was needed. "This morning died *Jonathan Smyth,* a Smith by Trade and Armourer's Mate of our Ship . . . our men being very much fatigued, many of them sick, and several of our good Sailors dead, we are so weak, that should we meet an Enemy in this Condition, we could make but a mean Defence. Everything looks dull and discouraging, but it's vain to look back or repine in these Parts."

On the eleventh they tried to come to anchor but failed. On the twelfth they were more or less becalmed: frequent rain but almost no wind. At four on the morning of June 13th, they finally anchored again at Gorgona in forty fathoms of water. They were right back where they had been a week before.

Tents were set up ashore for the armorers and coopers. Work parties began cutting down trees and clearing away undergrowth to make a station for the sick.

It rained heavily, mostly thunderstorms at night. The

vegetation was tropical. Gorgona had plenty of snakes of various species and sizes, most of them venomous. A Negro from the *Dutchess* was bitten by a small, brown, speckled snake, and died within twelve hours in spite of the best efforts of the doctors to save him. Even with all possible precautions, it was dangerous for anyone to walk abroad on the island.

They started at once to careen in order that the two men-of-war might be seaworthy again and in fighting shape as soon as possible. Since they had every reason to believe that Gorgona, unlike the Galápagos, was a place to which the French and Spanish squadron would come in search of them, one frigate stood guard on patrol while the other was being scraped, cleaned and refitted. They were hampered by the heavy rains and by swells in the harbor. Nevertheless, in two weeks both had all their provisions back on board, guns mounted again and scaled for range—"so that in 14 Days we had Calk'd our Ships all round, careen'd, rigg'd and stowed them again, both fit for the Sea; which was great Dispatch, considering what we had to do was in an open Place with few Carpenters, and void of the usual Conveniences for careening. The *Spaniards* our Prisoners, being very dilatory Sailors, were amazed at our Expedition, and told us, they usually take 6 weeks or 2 months to careen one of the King's Ships at *Lima,* where they are well provided with all Necessaries, and account it good Dispatch."

There was a tent city ashore for the sick, as there had been at Juan Fernández, this one christened "Little Bristol." The plague seemed at last to have been beaten, and though a number of men had died, the mortality rate was far below what could reasonably have been expected. Dover's treatment may have been drastic and some of it would be strictly contraindicated today; but the men owed him a lot—both for what he did and did not do.

While the remaining sick men recovered, and after the frigates had been careened, work was concentrated on repairing and refitting the captured *Havre de Grace* to turn her into a fighting ship. She proved to be in sorry condition. Her rudder and cut-water were eaten away by the marine worm; her masts and yards were unserviceable, her canvas rotten, most of her cordage not fit to be used. They got masts and yards from the big trees—fitted her out with new sails, rerigged her almost completely. Soon she looked trim and yare and promised to be a formidable reinforcement to the squadron.

A boat was sent out daily to catch fish, and came back loaded. Rogers and Courtney also went fishing by themselves at least once—possibly to get away from Dover —landed the limit, which was what the boat would carry, and had a fine time. They also explored the island together, particularly during the search for timber suitable for masts. There were other excellent opportunities to discuss plans and procedures at length and without interruption; and it would be heartening to think that from this point on Rogers and Courtney, who already agreed with each other on most points, were solidly aligned together in most of the council's controversies. Unfortunately, one day's fishing or a few walks could not entirely erase the influence of Dampier's cautious hesitations, citing past experience, and Dover's booming self-assurance, citing his investment.

In addition to the snakes, little and large—"I saw one as big as my Leg, and above 3 Yards long; their Bite proves generally mortal"—Gorgona had an abundance of monkeys, guinea pigs, hares, lizards, insects. Hunters shot monkeys to make broths and fricassees for the sick: "none of our Officers would touch them, Provisions being not yet so scarce; but Capt. *Dampier* who had been accustomed to such food, says he never eat anything in *London* that seemed more delicious to him than a Monkey or Baboon in these Parts."

There was also a species of animal that dumbfounded Rogers. He supposed it to be some kind of monkey, but described it accurately enough, three toes and all. Dampier who had thoroughly observed the creature in Central and South America, did better: "The Sloth is a Four-footed, hairy, sad-colored Animal; somewhat less than the Ant-Bear, and not so rough; Its Head is round, its Eyes are small; it has a short Nose, and very sharp Teeth; short Legs but extremely long sharp Claws. . . ."

The squadron had now been at Gorgona for a month. Everything was just about ready and in order. It was time to be going. The reconversion of the *Havre de Grace* had been completed, and she was rechristened *Marquiss*. The *Duke* put two of her main guns aboard her, as did the *Dutchess*. These, with four cannon they had taken at Guayaquil, plus twelve she had in her hold when captured, amounted to an armament of twenty good guns. "The Carriages are all new, or very much repair'd and as good and strong as if mounted in England . . . We saluted each of the other Ships with 3 Huzzas from on board her, distributed Liquor among the Company, drank her Majesty's and our Owner's Health, and to our own good Success. The Ship look'd well, so that we all rejoic'd in our new Consort to cruize with us." Unfortunately, this invaluable *Marquiss* soon began to leak badly.

The bark commanded by Selkirk was cleared to transport most of the prisoners, now seventy-two in all, to the mainland—something which could not have been done earlier without the danger of alerting the countryside and having word get to the French and Spanish men-of-war that the squadron was at Gorgona and in no condition either to run or to fight.

With Selkirk's bark went the two pinnaces under orders to raid and plunder ashore wherever possible and return in eight days. Among the prisoners the Morell brothers, who had commanded the *Ascension* galleon, and Captain Navarre, of the latest ship captured, were appointed to negotiate for the ransom of the galleon, the bulk of its cargo and the cargo from the other prizes. Rogers wanted at least 120,000 pieces of eight. The emissaries suggested they might just possibly raise half as much, and then became vague about even that. "They told us that Trade with Strangers, especially the *English* and *Dutch* was so strictly prohibited in those Seas, that they must give more than the prime Cost of the Goods in Bribes, to get a License to deal with us; So that they could not assure us of Payment, unless we sold the Goods very cheap."

Rogers suspected that the Spaniards, knowing the squadron could not sail on further missions encumbered by the galleon, the two latest prizes and all the cargoes, counted on getting them eventually either as an outright gift or through their being abandoned at Gorgona. To correct this misapprehension, he declared that if the Morells and Navarre were not back by ten days with adequate payment, he would burn the prizes and everything else he could not carry with him. Then he sent them off to make the best deal they could.

The parting was amicable. The prisoners had, as usual, been well treated. The lady and her family, her daughter and the jealous husband, had no great cause for complaint. It is true they were relieved of their jewels and ornaments and gold chains; but the rest of their belongings were returned to them and they were given three mulatto slaves. "They confess'd to our People, who put them ashore, that we had been much civiller than they did expect, or believe their own Countrymen would have been in the like case." Later they "sent back the Husband with Gold to purchase some Goods and two Slaves of us."

The incumbent governor of Baldivia, captured sometime before, gave a young lieutenant on the *Dutchess* a jeweled ring in gratitude for the lieutenant's having turned his cabin over to him when he was sick aboard. The prisoners had also, and again in accordance with Rogers' regular procedure, been permitted the full practice of their religion. "We allow'd Liberty of Conscience on board our floating Commonwealth to our Prisoners, for there being a Priest in each Ship, they had the Great Cabbin for their Mass, whilst we used the Church of *England* Service over them on the Quarter-Deck, so that the Papists here were the Low Churchmen."

Two days after setting the prisoners ashore on the mainland, Selkirk's bark and the pinnaces returned. They had raided a small village and brought back several head of black cattle, twelve hogs, six goats and some limes and plantains. All that countryside, they reported, was poor—so poor that they gave the liberated prisoners and Negroes some cloth, nails and other goods to trade for food and assistance along the way. This humane gesture was also plainly practical. If the prisoners, particularly the emissaries, did not reach some civilized place safely and promptly, there would be no ransom at all coming back for the prizes and cargos.

A couple of days later a Negro freedman, named Michael Kendall, originally from Jamaica, made his way to them from the mainland in a canoe. Kendall had been part of a mixed force of a hundred and six men which had set out from Jamaica under three English captains to attack some Spanish mines that lay up river from the Gulf of Darien. This force had run into an ambush, and half the men were killed. The rest, many of them wounded, were promised their lives and honorable treat-

ment as prisoners of war if they surrendered. Being out-
numbered by something like ten to one, they accepted.
They were then put into canoes and carried up river.
Shortly thereafter, at the command of the chief Spanish
officer, nearly all of them were butchered. Three white
men and twelve Negro freedmen escaped, through the
intervention of a priest, and were sent as slaves to the
mines. Kendall labored some time in the mines, and then
was sold by his owner to the recently plundered village,
from which he got away after the English raided it.

He was welcomed aboard and eventually given a
small command; in this he conducted himself with such
zeal that his fellow freedmen conspired to murder him.
But that came later. Meanwhile, his story provoked a
certain amount of natural rage. Rogers wrote: "This is
enough to shew what merciless and cowardly Enemies
we have to deal with in these Parts of the World. I have
heard of many such Cruelties in the *Spanish* Parts of
America, to the eternal Scandal of those who encourage
or connive at them."

As negotiations for ransom continued (the Morells
and Navarre returned on July 17th with some money as
earnest of their good intentions, and hurriedly departed
to raise more) the cargoes of the *Ascension* galleon and
of the newly christened *Marquiss*, were completely overhauled and examined for the first time. It may seem
strange that this had not been done before, since both
ships were captured in April, three months earlier. But
until the squadron reached Gorgona, there was no time
and no place to unload, and at Gorgona the first order
of business had been careening the frigates, attending to
the sick, and refitting the *Marquiss*.

When she was being refitted, they had found in her
hold "near 500 Bales of Pope's Bulls, 16 Reams in a Bale
. . . These Bulls are imposed upon the People, and sold

here by the Clergy from 3 Ryals to 50 Pieces of Eight
a-piece, according to the Ability of the Purchaser. Once
in two Years they are rated, and all the People obliged to
buy them against Lent; they cannot be read, the print
looking worse than any of our old Ballads, yet the Vulgar
are made believe it's a mortal Sin to eat Flesh in Lent,
without being licensed by one of these Bulls, the Negro
Slaves not being exempted. This is one of the greatest
Branches of Income the King of *Spain* has in this Country, being a free Gift from the Pope to him, as the *Spaniards* and Natives told us."

The Protestant English could neither take advantage
of such dispensations nor sell them—which they would
unquestionably have been happy to do at any price at
all—and therefore, Rogers said: "we throw'd most of
them overboard to make Room for better Goods, except
what we used to burn the Pitch of our Ships Bottoms
when we careened 'em."

The better goods were what they expected to find in
the hold of the *Ascension* galleon, but for some of these
the English could find even less use. They discovered, for
example, "a great Quantity of Bones in small Boxes,
ticketed with the Names of Romish Saints, some of which
had been dead 7 or 800 years; with an infinite number of
Brass Medals, Crosses . . . religious Toys in Wax, Images
of Saints made of all sorts of Wood, Stone and other Materials, I believe in all near 30 tun . . . All this came from
Italy and most from Rome, design'd for the Jesuits of
Peru; but being of small Value to us, We contented our
selves to take only a Sample of most sorts to shew our
Friends in *England*, and left the rest."

Fortunately for an expedition underwritten by English merchants for their own personal profit and the honor
of the Realm, this was not all. The bulk of the galleon's
cargo consisted of dry goods and hardware, easily con-

vertible into cash. There were 320 bales of linens and woolens, many boxes of knives, scissors and hatchets, silver-handled swords, silver buckles, buttons and snuff-boxes, finger-rings, earrings and chains of gold.

The examination of this haul—much of which was legitimate plunder to be divided directly among the officers and crews—started a mutiny over shares. Sixty men on the *Duke* cheerfully signed articles to fight for their rights. Many more were involved on board both the *Dutchess* and the *Marquiss*.

Rogers broke this mutiny as he had broken the earlier one in the Atlantic, by arming all his officers, and putting the ringleaders in irons. But this time too many men were involved, and they had just causes for griev-ance. "There being so many concern'd in this Design, Captains Dover and Fry desired I would discharge those in Confinement upon their asking Pardon, and faithfully promising never to be guilty of the like, or any other Continuation again . . . The Reason we shewed 'em this Favour was, that there were too many guilty to punish them at once . . ."

The rules for plunder and shares in it were again re-vised. Rogers and Courtney with some bitterness sur-rendered a still larger portion of their own rightful shares; and nonsailor, noncombatant supernumeraries or super-cargoes like Mr. White, the linguist, and the vulture-shooting, Indian-shooting Carleton Vanbrugh had their shares reduced to next to nothing. With this the crews were content, particularly since Rogers faithfully prom-ised them full justice and a full review of all cases when they returned to England.

The mutiny moved him to some reflections: "Sailors usually exceed all Measures when left to themselves and account it a Privilege in Privateers to do themselves Jus-tice on these Occasions, tho' in everything else I must own, they have been more obedient than any Ship's Crews engag'd in the like Undertaking that I ever heard of. Yet we have not wanted sufficient Tryall of our Patience and Industry in other things; so that if any Sea-Officer thinks himself endowed with these two Virtues, let him command in a Privateer, and discharge his Office well in a distant Voyage, and I'll engage he shall not want Opportunities to improve, if not to exhaust all his stock."

There were other troubles. *Marquiss,* which had been so bravely launched with so many toasts and such cheering, sprang a leak and shipped eight inches of water in an hour. That leak was no sooner stopped than another opened. If she behaved like this while lying quietly at anchor in harbor, what would she do when the seas got to work on her? Captain Cooke, who had been given command of her, was worried; so were her crew, and so was Rogers.

Meanwhile, the Morells and Navarre had been returning regularly with more money. It must have been enough because the Peru galleon was turned over to the Morells, and one of the two latest prizes (the other, beached in an emergency, had sunk) was given to Captain Navarre. Navarre's son-in-law sailed that one away. Navarre himself was retained on board the *Duke* as a hostage. He had also the expectation of picking up some bargains in shipping when the English finally wound up their operations.

So the ransom must have been enough, but what it amounted to precisely or even vaguely or even in the most general, ambiguous estimate, Rogers does not say. He drew a careful and cautious screen around all such transactions.

These scrupulously kept accounts, reserved for the owners and Courtney and Dover and himself, were not

brought out into even the dim light of a swinging lant-
horn, either then or later. Who paid how much and
when, what the actual value of the various prizes were
(seventeen had been captured to date), and what sums
they finally brought—most of these were matters that he
left purposely clouded.

The squadron stood out to sea on the late afternoon
of August 7th. By six that evening, Gorgana lay some
eighteen miles behind. Cooke said that the value of what
they carried with them at that time amounted to 20,000
pounds in gold, plate and jewels and 60,000 in goods. And
the main chance, the really big gamble was yet to come.

The island they were leaving behind had been a
springboard for the original Spanish invasion of Peru.
Pizarro and twelve of his men had encamped at Gorgona
for seven months, waiting for a relief vessel from Panama
in order to proceed to the Bay of Tumbez on an explora-
tory voyage preliminary to launching the attack on the
Inca empire. Gorgona had now provided an invaluable
base for the English. It had afforded them two months in
which to repair and refit, to lay in supplies, settle their
affairs and complete preparation for what they hoped
would be their main strike against the power of Spain in
this sea.

The squadron headed first for Tecames, an isolated
spot on the Peruvian coast near Cape San Francisco. At
Gorgona the guns had been fired to sight and scale them
in after careening—firing heard by the scattered inhabitants on the mainland. Now the ships held regular battle
practice. As the bows dipped and rose through the hot
August days and nights, the cannon pounded and jumped
and recoiled against the breeching ropes. Everyone, from
captains to powder boys, knew that the Manila Galleon,
if they ever caught up with her, would be by far the most
formidable opponent they had yet faced, by the strength

of her sides, by the weight of her armament. It was very probable that she might finally have to be taken by boarding. That would require a lot of men and cost a lot of lives.

Rogers mustered the Negroes on board the *Duke,* some thirty-five in all, and made them an offer; if they joined up, they would be freed, given arms and trained in the use of them, be considered and treated as Englishmen and not as Spanish slaves. It was a humane gesture, in one way, because thirty-odd additional fightingmen could not be expected to count numerically for much and a considerable cash value in slaves would be lost by freeing them. It was also a practical measure because Rogers needed, or thought he needed, all the reinforcements he could get and it was just about unanimously agreed among impartial observers that the mulattoes and Negroes, when properly armed and aroused, were much tougher fighters than their Spanish masters in that area.

Under the leadership of Kendall, the Jamaican freedman, thirty-two Negroes signed up. Rogers then and thereafter kept his word to them, where others might not have when the emergency was past. The freed slaves were armed and dressed as Englishmen and treated as Englishmen from then on, with only a single but notable exception. Once when rations ran short, they were allowed something less, by a fifth, than the others.

In that instance, as in the matter of the frequent capture and resale of slaves, it must be remembered that Rogers was part of his time. But he was also in some ways a little ahead of it. Just as his discipline, while strict, was much more merciful than that of most captains of his time and a good deal more merciful than the legal justice administered everywhere ashore, so his treatment of those who fell into his hands, whatever their creed, color or status was almost uniformly decent. In a sense, it is the more to his credit, since he was neither a reformer nor a philosopher.

Now they were at sea again and preparing for the final strike, and it was time to review everything they knew and could learn that might help to bring it off.

Among the many books Rogers had with him were four fat folios of voyages—most of them translations from foreign sources—compiled by John and Awnsham Churchill and published in 1704. He had consulted these sources frequently and refers to them in his own book, particularly to the narrative of an enterprising Italian named J. F. Gemelli Careri.

Toward the end of the seventeenth century, when nobody went to sea as a passenger who could possibly help it, Careri, a doctor of civil law, prudently provided himself with plenty of money and set out from his native Italy to tour the globe.

According to his account, he traveled through Turkey, Persia, India and the East Indies, and visited the imperial court of China. Whether or not he went everywhere he claimed, his contemporaries who were in a position to judge accepted the fact, and almost all later authorities have agreed that in May, 1696, Careri was in Manila, preparing to embark on the galleon for the eastward passage to Acapulco. It was this and the subsequent part of his narrative that Rogers and his officers carefully studied and must have reviewed now, together with all other available information about the prize they were after.

Careri reached Manila from Macao early in May, and consequently had more than a month wait before the galleon was due to sail. He put the time to good use, indulging his curiosity and recording what he observed.

"The Voyage from the *Philippine* Islands to *Amer-*

ica," he wrote, "may be call'd the longest and most dreadful of any in the world." The historian Padre Casimiro Díaz termed it "the longest, most dangerous voyage in all the seas." Rogers and the rest knew, from a variety of sources other than Careri, a lot about the history of the line, the commerce and the route. Dampier himself, in his earlier "Voyages," had published a fairly accurate resumé.

The first galleon to make the eastward crossing, after several others had failed, was piloted by an Augustinian Friar, Andrés de Urdaneta, in 1565. Fra Urdaneta discovered the general route which all the Manila ships followed: north to the high latitudes to take advantage of the prevailing winds and the eastward flowing Kuro Siwa, or Japanese Current, east to the coast of North America and then south along the coast to Acapulco. The sister ship from Acapulco, to take advantage of the westward currents and the trade winds, went south to the low latitudes, west to the Ladrones, or Marshall Islands, and from there to Luzon and Manila. The westward crossing of the Acapulco ship averaged two to three months and was generally uneventful. The eastward crossing of the Manila ship averaged five to six months, and was never uneventful.

The two great annual events at Manila were the departure of the galleon for Mexico and the arrival of the one from Acapulco. "This trade," it was written, "is so great and profitable and easy to control that the Spaniards do not apply themselves to, or engage in, any other industry."

The government at Madrid, under pressure from merchants and manufacturers in Spain who saw their Central and South American trade dwindling toward nothing, restricted the number of galleons that might sail from Manila to one, or at most two, each year. There was also a restriction on the sailing date, imposed by the weather. If the Manila ship was to get safely out of the straits, she could not sail before May, when the southwest monsoon set in. And if she sailed later than the end of June, she might be caught in the tropics by the typhoons, called *"baguíos,"* whose general period was from July to October.

That more or less placed her probable time of arrival—if still only vaguely and generally—given a sailing date sometime in June and five to six months for the passage.

She approached the California coast at approximately the latitude of what is now San Francisco and when she sighted the first signs of land several hundred miles off shore, altered course to head southeast for her destination. The best possible points to intercept her would be off Cape San Lucas at the tip of Lower California, or off Cape Corrientes on the Mexican coast above Acapulco, and the time would be, or should be, somewhere between the beginning of November and the first weeks of December.

Rogers and the other captains had long been studying her strength and her vulnerability. Both were considerable; and many of her weaknesses were due to overreaching greed.

Because of all the restrictions, because the prosperity of Manila depended on this trade, because a man, any number of men, could become rich and retire on a single investment in some part of the cargo carried annually to Acapulco, the galleons were built as big as possible, to carry all the cargo possible, often at the sacrifice of seaworthiness, armament, food and water. The cargo was often improperly stowed; frequently the ship was poorly careened and refitted; some sailed with timbers already rotten, some without sufficient extra tackle for emergencies.

But not many sailed in such an altogether sorry condition. It was much more dangerously common for the galleon to be incompetently commanded and inadequately manned. The line had difficulty in retaining experienced pilots, captains and commanders, because these, too—those that survived—could just about retire on what they made from a voyage. In the early part of the eighteenth century the lowest subaltern could pocket 20,000 pesos and a captain or general did poorly if he cleared less than 150,000 or 200,000 pesos. When an officer could clear that much, he was more likely to retire or to ship out elsewhere than to continue the ordeal of the crossing.

It was as difficult to retain experienced sailors. Crews received only a fraction of their pay when they reached Acapulco, the bulk of it being withheld until they returned to Manila because of the certainty that if they were paid off in Acapulco they would jump ship. Partly for this reason, the crews were generally three- to four-fifths Malays and one- to two-fifths Spaniards.

Bribery and corruption often determined the appointment of officers. Since command of the galleon was the richest gift the Viceroy or the Governor at Manila had at his disposal, it was often sold, along with many other offices, to the highest bidder or given to some relative or favorite. A few years before Careri arrived in Manila, the King of Spain had written his Viceroy expressing his astonishment that command of a galleon had been given the royal accountant "being a person of so different a profession. . . ." And just as an accountant could be made a captain, so one governor appointed as the galleon's accountant a favorite of his who could not write.

The pilots, *pilotes-mayores*, the chief navigating

officers, were generally much better qualified and for all practical purposes exercised the actual command during a voyage. But there was as great a turnover among experienced pilots as there was among other competent officers and for the same reasons. Over the years a number of them of various nationalities were hired: English, Scots, French, Irish and Germans, in addition to Spanish. But some of these proved as incompetent to pilot as their nominal superiors were to command. One, having navigated only ninety miles from Manila, put the galleon athwart a reef, and the shipwrecked passengers immediately hanged him.

There was, of course, a further and obvious conclusion to be drawn from all this: many of the factors that seemed to work in favor of the English—the condition of some of the galleons, the failures in seamanship and command—also worked against them. Rogers' squadron might find itself on a long patrol at sea, while its supplies slowly ran out, waiting for a vessel that had long since sunk. Galleons clearing from Manila later than the end of June were often caught, by the time they were into the open ocean, by typhoons, and they were ill-fitted by construction to ride out a typhoon. Those that reached the high latitudes faced the terrible storms and seas of the North Pacific, the widest stretch of empty ocean on the globe.

One galleon, the *Santa Margarita,* after beating about for eight months finally went aground on the Ladrones, her sails and masts stripped, only a fifth of her original complement of crew and passengers left alive. The Manila ships grounded on Luzon and Saipan; they disappeared without trace in the North Pacific. They caught fire and blew up; they were beaten and hammered to pieces, split open on reefs, or only survived to limp back into Manila, dismasted and sometimes rudderless.

And yet, of course, the majority completed the voy-

8*

age. At Careri's time the line had been in successful operation for a hundred and thirty-five years and would continue for nearly a hundred and twenty years more. So the
general odds were that the galleon would come—though
Rogers and his officers could not count on them for one
particular vessel and though they could not pinpoint the
time and place of possible interception.

There were other odds, if they found her, to be figured. Against possible attack the Spanish merchants depended on the prohibitive factors of time and distance, on
an efficient intelligence system to give ample warning in
Manila of any ships preparing an attempt, on basic armament and, above all, on the galleons' construction. Most of
them were much more strongly built than any European
ship; they had the best hemp in the world for cordage and
the hardest and toughest wood for keel and timbers and
ribs and planking—Philippine teak and ironwood and mo-
lave, with a sheathing of lanang wood so strong and
resilient that small cannon balls embedded themselves in
it and large ones bounced off. Careri observed: ". . . the
Planks are made so thick, and So lin'd both within and
without, that they receive little Damage by Cannon-Balls.
That Vessel which fought some years since, with fourteen *Dutch* that came to Lake Cavite, had 90 balls taken
out of her sides, which stuck there as if they had been in a
Wall of soft Stone."

The galleon might not, probably would not, have all
or even most of her guns mounted and scaled in; the
English might count on surprise, provided she had been
not too thoroughly forewarned. And even if she had been
and was prepared, they could count on the fact that she
was bound to be weakened, if not in some distress, after
what she had come through.

Careri's narrative, combined with all the other available reports and accounts, provided Rogers and his officers

with a lot of varied information about this prize and what
their chances were, in spite of all the Spanish measures
for secrecy, mystification and concealment. But they also
knew that no matter how carefully they studied and prepared, the odds for and against them evened up or canceled out in the long run; what remained was an unknown
quantity, guesswork, substantially hope. They had planned
better, learned more, were better armed and organized
than any before them; but they could remember that
everyone before them, except one, had failed; had arrived
at battle stations either too late or too soon, like the Dutch
fleet and Davis with Dampier and Swan; or had cruised
futilely for a ship that never arrived, never would arrive,
or had almost miraculously come up with her like Dampier
on his last voyage, only to be beaten off and left sinking.

They might also, as a kind of afterthought, remember
what could stand for the enterprising Italian's last words
on the galleon. At one point, following a consideration of
how much money all hands—but particularly the officers
—could make on a singular voyage, Careri wrote: "For
my own part, these nor greater Hopes shall not prevail
with me to undertake that Voyage again, which is enough
to Destroy a Man, or make him unfit for anything as long
as he Lives."

These ships now comprised the squadron, bound
toward Tecames, cannon periodically jarring and booming against the hopeful day to come: *Duke, Dutchess,
Marquiss* and the fifty-ton bark *Joseph,* which they had
kept with them ever since her capture in April. They
went there to bargain, to release prisoners and to collect
ransom.

Marquiss was acting the way everybody was afraid
she would after her gloomy behavior at Gorgona. She
continued to leak, was a cranky sailer, her rigging was

bad. Cooke was advised to heave overboard two of her heaviest guns, two spare topmasts, some lumber she carried and twenty boxes of snuff to lighten ship. This he did, except for the snuff, which was much appreciated by his men. After that, she handled somewhat better, but not much.

Rogers wanted to get rid of her. He considered her an encumbrance that would only slow them up, prove of little or no use in any attempt on the Manila Galleon and be a continual drain on their food and supplies. He proposed sending her with a small crew to India and from there to Brazil, where her goods could be sold to the Portuguese at a neat profit. Courtney and Dover opposed this, and the majority of the Council voted with them. Apparently they were growing nervous again—this time about their chances of taken the galleon—and felt they needed all the support they could get. Rogers also wanted to dispose of the *Joseph*, now commanded by Alexander Selkirk. Again he was overruled. Dover and Courtney carried that vote, too.

What Selkirk felt at this particular point has not been noted. If there were those on board the ships who had been slaves and were now free, he who had been free was now, in a sense, a slave. He had been through the action off Lobos, had stormed ashore through the gunfire and smoke and stench of Guayaquil, survived the plague and the delusions of the Encantadas. He had been wet for weeks on end, cramped, depressed, sick, hungry and thirsty. He may have presumed that when he got back to England, if he lived to get back, the wisdom of his choice and the benefits of his return to civilization would become apparent. Meanwhile, he discharged his duties faithfully and efficiently, and Rogers relied on him.

As the squadron approached Tecames, a Spanish ship was sighted shortly after dawn on August 18th. *Dutchess* overhauled and captured her within an hour. A fair-sized vessel, christened the *Concepción*, bound from Panama toward Lima, she carried a number of passengers and some slaves but no cargo of any value. It developed that the coasts of Spain from Central America to Chile had now been alerted to the operations of the English squadron.

Rogers and his officers pumped the latest prisoners for further information, particularly news from Europe. They heard that their benefactor, Prince George of Denmark, Lord High Admiral of England, had died—"which we were not willing to believe, but drank his Health at Night, which can do him no Hurt if he is dead." As a matter of fact, His Royal Highness, suffering from dropsy and grown so huge he could not get up a flight of stairs without being hoisted, had succumbed to congestive failure in October of the preceding year—before the squadron rounded the Horn, before it had even left Grande.

There was further information. "We read several Letters from *Panama*, by which we understood, that when they heard of our taking *Guiaquil*, they kept their Gates shut Day and Night for above a Week, and that the Inhabitants kept Guard on their Walls, being afraid we should attack them next, and by what I can guess, we might have taken that Town as well as *Guiaquil* . . ." Could have taken it, even if its new walls were so high and so costly that the exasperated King of Spain had wanted to know if they could be seen from his windows in the Escorial. Could have taken it, that is, except for one slight reservation: ". . . had we but double our Number of Men."

On August 24th they dropped anchor off Tecames. The bark commanded by Selkirk had gone in first; then Mr. White, the linguist, and a Spanish prisoner, imprudently and without orders, went ashore to see what kind of deal they could negotiate with the local Indians. The deal they got nearly did for them what dropsy had done for Prince George; it consisted of showers of bullets and poisoned arrows and spears. The ambassadors only survived to tell the tale by dint of crawling on their bellies through the brush until daylight.

Order was restored by a young padre, presumably one of the passengers from the Panama ship. He went ashore to give assurances of the honorable character of the English, their upright conduct and their unshakable determination to trade peacefully. He was also asked to point out to the Indians and the local padres ". . . how easily we could land and burn the Church and Houses, and lay waste all the adjacent Parts; but that we were full of Charity and very kind to those in our Power."

Everyone was convinced; hostilities ended, and the Padre was followed by men bearing gifts and brandy. An Indian chief, offered a drink out of a quart bottle, drained most of the quart . . . "and went away extremely pleas'd. . . ."

They began to trade briskly. They heeled and cleaned the ships, laid in stores of water, bought pineapples, limes, bananas, coconuts, plantains, hogs and cattle. By then it was time to be heading for their appointment. They still had a margin. If the galleon sailed from Manila in June she would not be off Cape San Lucas before the beginning of November, and it might even be December. But this was, at best, an estimate. Moreover it would take the squadron weeks of sailing to reach the possible point of interception; and much yet remained to be done.

They set ashore most of the slaves and freed most of the Spanish prisoners. Among those freed was Captain Navarre, a man whom they had come to admire and trust. In return for the slaves and a quantity of goods, he gave them a promissory note for 3,500 pieces of eight payable from Portobello to Jamaica.

The council voted to give two Negroes to Captain Cooke and Mr. Frye as a reward for distinguished service in the capture of the *Havre de Grace*. Rogers considered it inappropriate and inadequate for the bravery Cooke and Frye had shown and the risks they had voluntarily run, and thought it would hardly prove an encouraging example for the future.

The council also gave a slave and some cloth to the Tecames padre. As for the young padre who had been so coöperative, they set him ashore and "gave him, as he desir'd, the prettiest young Female Negro we had in the Prize, with some Bays, Linnen, and other things . . . the young Padre parted with us extremely pleas'd, and leering under his Hood upon his black Female Angel, we doubt he will crack a Commandment with her, and wipe off the Sin with the Church's Indulgence."

There were, after all, others who had cracked commandments, including the strict orders of Woodes Rogers. On August 29th there is the ominous entry: "*Captain Cooke* buried one *John Edwards*, a Youth who died of a complication of Scurvey and the Pox, which he got from a loathsome Negro, whom we afterwards gave to the Prisoners, that she might do no further Mischief on board."

On the eve of sailing, Cooke presented the Indians with four large wooden statues of saints, carved and painted in Spain, for their local church. Rogers and Courtney gave three more. All these had been in the hold of the *Ascension* galleon, and were jubilantly received by the Indians and their padre. The last prize captured, the ship from Panama, was handed over to the former prisoners. At six in the morning of August 31st, the squadron sailed from Tecames.

They were headed back to the Galápagos—islands

which they need never to have left, if they had found
the enigmatic and elusive sources of fresh water. They
had bought all the hogs and cattle available at Tecames,
everything but the breeding stock, but the supply was not
enough to last more than a couple weeks. They had a long
way to go and maybe a long wait on the swell off Cape
San Lucas, and beyond that, if there was anything beyond
that, the course lay clear to Guam.

As they sailed from Tecames, Rogers noted that they
were leaving a place with certain historical associations.
It was off this Cape, Cape San Francisco, that Drake had
captured the Lima plate ship, the *Cacafuego,* in 1578; and
here, as a different kind of reminder, Sir Edward Hawkins
had been taken in 1594 by the Spaniards.

Cooke simply reported, the first day out: "Saw several
Grampusses and young Whales, engag'd with the Thrash-
ers and Sword-Fishes, also several Dolphins and Flying
Fishes, and Abundance of Water Snakes, one of which
was coming up the side of our Ship, and our Men beat
it off; the *Spaniards* say there is no cure for such as are
bit by them."

The squadron reached one of the Galápagos on September 10th and anchored in thirty fathoms of water about
two miles offshóre. They had already exhausted many of
the provisions laid in at Tecames, so limited was their
cargo space and so rapidly were such supplies used up.
Cooke had reported on September 9th: "This last day
made an end of our Plantains, every Man being allow'd
four a Day, instead of Bread, since we left *Tecames.*"

On their return to the Encantadas, Circe was kind
to them. They were no longer pressed to the limit; they no
longer desperately wanted anything of her, but only
came somewhat idly, so to speak, to stock up on the overwhelming abundance of tortoise and turtle and fish. It
may have been a little like a man who after a prolonged,

hopeless and tormented chase finally gives up and turns away; then the woman suddenly reaches out and touches him.

This time there were no tricks, or almost none. Rogers, going ashore one day, was attacked by a sea lion "as big as a large Bear," but fortunately was armed with a pike and finally beat the animal off, after wounding it several times.

They found a rudder and bowsprit which they thought might be part of Hatley's bark, until they discovered the wreckage was much older. Rogers, haunted by the thought of Hatley and his men lost and perhaps still alive among the Encantadas, had another search made and again fired guns. But, of course, if Hatley and his men had actually been trapped for so many months on any of those waterless rocks, they would by now have been long past hearing any gun.

The ships headed north, stocked with quantities of salted fish and all the live turtles they could carry, to provide fresh meat until they made their next landfall at the Tres Marías, a group of islands lying off the Mexican coast near the mouth of the Gulf of California.

And again there was the endless problem of food, of what they could stock and keep against time and consumption and an essential reserve. "Tho' our Men," Rogers noted, "have their Fill of Land and Sea Turtle, which keeps them from Scurvy, yet I find them weak, it being but a faintly Food, except they had sufficient Bread or Flower with it."

Cooke reported that the ration of bread and flour, rotten and packed with insects, was now down to a pound and a half per five men per day. He also noted that his ship, the *Marquiss,* sprang two more serious leaks en route to the Tres Marías. One of the leaks was sealed off with lead; the other, being somewhere under the stern, could not be properly located, and the pumps were kept going continuously.

Gunnery practice and sham battles presumably continued, such as the one that had been staged shortly after leaving Gorgona. During that maneuver, the *Duke* bore down on the *Dutchess*, which was flying Spanish colors. One of the *Duke's* crew, supposing the consort to be an actual enemy, loaded his musket with shot and was about to let fly when he was forcibly restrained. Rogers observed: "By this it appears, that blundering Fools may have courage. During this sham Engagement, everyone acted the same Part he ought to have done, if in earnest, firing with Ball excepted." The surgeons on the orlop deck had their canvas-topped tables ready and their bright instruments laid out. ". . . to imitate Business for them, I ordered red Lead mixt with water to be thrown upon two of our Fellows, and sent 'em down to the Surgeons, who, as well as the Prisoners in the Hold, were very much surprized, thinking they had really been wounded, and the Surgeons actually went about to dress them, but finding their Mistake, it was a very agreeable Diversion . . ."

Particularly agreeable for those who—after maybe an anxious moment or two before the matter could be explained—did not this time actually have to go under the knife. There would be plenty of them who would have to go under it soon, if all promises held.

14

A
BLOOD-RED
SEA

AT THE MIDDLE ISLAND of the Tres Marías they found firewood, plenty of turtles to restock their stores, and enough
water; but most of the water was bitter and some of it
acted as a cathartic. They also came on a trace of the
late Captain Swan's visit to these islands, a memento he
had left in the form of a human skull whitening in the
sun. The skull, they concluded, was that of one of two
Indians Swan had marooned there twenty-three years
earlier; "for Victuals being scarce with these *Buccaneers*,
they would not carry the poor *Indians* any farther, but,

after they had served their Turns, left them to make a miserable End on a desolate Island." And by now, of course, Swan's own skull had long since been picked clean by fish in an estuary of Mindanao.

It was at the Tres Marías that relations between Rogers and Dover had reached a point where Dover requested to be transferred to the *Dutchess*. The request was instantly granted. Dover, with his chests, necessaries and servant, had himself rowed over to the smaller ship to make life simple for Courtney.

In between stocking firewood, fish and turtles they spent a lot of time looking for the *Marquiss* and Selkirk's bark, both of which had wandered off, and for a work party of Negroes. Ten had been sent ashore to cut wood, and only three returned, the rest having taken off into the trees and dense scrub. It was learned that they had become so strongly disaffected with their leader, Michael Kendall, the Jamaica free Negro, that they had decided, if everything else failed, to kill him.

Notices were posted at strategic points promising the deserters their freedom if they returned, and anything else they could reasonably want except, presumably, Kendall's head. "My Reason for doing so," Rogers explains, "was to prevent those Fellows from giving notice of us on the Coast, if they reach'd the Main on Bark Logs, which they could make with the Hatchets they had to cut Wood for us."

When the *Marquiss* and the bark finally turned up, a committee meeting was held on board the *Dutchess* and a final, formal resolution at last drafted—that everything might be legal and in order—to attack the Manila Galleon: ". . . we have examin'd the Opinion of *Capt. Dampier*, appointed Pilot by the owners of the Ships *Duke* and *Dutchess* in *Bristol*, and have been well informed from all the Intelligences we have frequently had from Prisoners since our being in the *South Seas,* and do now finally determine to cruize off *Cape St. Lucas,* the Southermost Cape of *California,* in such Methods, and with such Signals to each other, as shall be agreed on in our next Committee.

"We resolve with the utmost Care and Diligence to wait here the coming of the *Manila* Ship belonging to the *Spaniards.* and bound for *Acapulco;* whose Wealth on board her we hope will prompt every Man to use his utmost Conduct and Bravery to conquer. . . ."

Then they sailed. But not without a certain regret, at least among the officers. "We the chief Officers," Rogers said, "fed deliciously here, being scarce ever without Hares, Turtle Doves, Pigeons, and Parrots of various Sizes and Colours, many had white or red Heads, with Tufts of Feathers on their Crowns. I wish 'twould hold, but 'tis in vain to tantalize our selves; for we must soon fare otherwise, and take to our old Food of almost decay'd Salt Pork and Beef, which we must prize, and heartily wish we had more on't."

They sailed from the Tres Marías on the morning of October 24th, and once more they could be reasonably sure they had slipped away from any pursuit. Whatever force was out against them would presumably still be searching the waters far to the south, off Gorgona or Tecames, or even among the blackened Galápagos, not knowing where the raiders were, not guessing where they were headed.

As they approached Cape San Lucas, Rogers wanted the ships to separate in order to double their chances of intercepting the galleon and to facilitate provisioning. He suggested that part of the force cruise off Cape Corrientes, where Dampier had met the Manila ship five years earlier, and that the others cruise off Cape San Lucas. But again, and this time fortunately, he was overruled. The majority voted to concentrate their forces near San Lucas.

They did agree "to spread as we ran to the North-ward, that the *Acapulco* ship might not pass us, if they should arrive sooner than we expected: We agreed to be to the Leeward, the *Marquiss* to Windward, and the *Dutchess* between us, and all to keep in sight of each other . . ."

The wind was intermittent and the heat extreme. Though they had only some forty leagues to go, they made no headway at all for two days against a strong southward current. They lay and baked on the swell, as if held or de-tained until something obscure at a far remove from any of their purposes or intentions, of no importance to them but still affecting them, had been accomplished: something, in the superstitions of cause and effect, like an insignificant knot which had to be untied before they could move on upon their business.

At any rate, whatever way the signs or auspices were to be read, on October 30th ". . . one of our Negro Women cry'd out, and was deliver'd of a Girl of a tawny Colour; *Mr. Wasse* our chief surgeon was forced to discharge the Office of a Midwife in a close Cabbin provided for that Purpose; but what we most wanted was good Liquor, to keep up or imitate the Womens laudable Custom of a re-freshing Cup, on such an Occasion. I accidentally found a Bottle of thick, strong *Peru* Wine, a good Part of which was given to the sick Woman, who desir'd more than we could spare her."

Concerning the accouchement, Rogers carefully noted: "She had not been full 6 months amongst us, so that the Child could belong to none of our Company. But to prevent the other she-Negro (call'd *Daphne*) from being debauch'd in our Ship, I gave her a strict Charge to be modest, with Threats of severe Punishment if she was found otherwise. One of the *Dutchess's* black Nymphs having transgressed this Way, was lately whip'd at the Capston. This I mention to satisfy the censorious, that we don't countenance Lewdness, and that we took those Women aboard, only because they spoke *English*, and begg'd to be admitted for Laundresses, Cooks and Semstresses."

A wind came up, the ships ran, the next day they sighted the Cape.

On November 2nd they spread out. *Duke* was the outermost ship, *Dutchess* in the middle, and *Marquiss* holding between six and nine leagues offshore. They could now sight anything that might pass them within sixty to eighty miles of the coast.

The men stood their watches; they lay packed in their hammocks in the swinging darkness. The food was beginning to crawl again, and the stock of turtle laid in at the Tres Marías was exhausted. The gunners checked and rechecked their guns. Nothing came. They could wait.

On November 7th Rogers noted: "Sir *Thomas Cavendish*, in Queen *Elizabeth's* Time, took the *Manila* Ship in this Place on the 4th of *November*."

The only think that had happened to them on the fourth of November was that one sailor had been put in irons for threatening the cooper; and another, "an ill abusive Fellow," got the same treatment for shouting that he wished he were aboard a pirate and would be happy if an enemy strong enough to capture them all were already alongside.

The ships beat back and forth, day after day, to the bells, to the turning of the glass and the sand running through it every half-hour. East of them were the bare cliffs and eroded promontories of Cape San Lucas, where huge granite molars and incisors stood up from the sea and the surf smashed on the waterworn rock. West of them was a tilting distance, a vastness beyond visualization, always empty.

For something, anything, the crews had been gambling again. Another agreement to cease and desist was drawn up and signed by all the officers and men of each ship. Then there was very little break in the strain and monotony as the loop of time and space and consumption tightened around them. Sometimes the sea turned red again in wide streaks and bands, mud-red and blood-red, and there is an entry early in November about the discolored water.

A week passed: another and another. They had come this far from Bristol, and Teneriffe and Grande, around the freezing Horn, and to Juan Fernández, north through the current to Lobos and Guayaquil and the slag-heap Galápagos—they had come through storms, cold, heat, sickness, gunfire, nightmares—for one chance in a thousand on their appointment. But it was late. It was getting very late.

And still they could hope. Still at any point in time and place—in the instant of a few grains sliding through the waist of the glass—the horizon could fill and deliver to them a pinpoint, a topmast, a speck, getting bigger. And since the time had not yet altogether run out on them, they could still laugh. The bark was sent ashore to look for water and provisions. The crew found some naked Indians, subsisting on just about nothing, who had never before encountered any European. "After they got safe on Shore the *Indians* led each of our Men betwixt two of 'em, up to the Bank, where there was an old naked Gentleman with a Deer-skin spread on the Ground, on which they kneeled before our People, who did the like, and wip'd the Water off their Faces, without a Cloth; those that led them from the Water-side, took the same Care of 'em for a quarter of a Mile, and led them very slowly thro' a narrow Path to their Hutts, where they found a dull Musician rubbing two jagged Sticks a-cross each other, and humming to it, to divert and welcome their new Guests."

There was an exchange of gifts, and two days later, on November 21st, Rogers sent the bark and boat ashore "with one of our Musicians, to shew that we could at least equal them in Musick."

The boat returned next day with "an Account, that they had found a very good Bay, with a fresh Water River, and that they saw near 500 *Indians,* who lived there in small Hutts, but had no Recruit for us, besides a little Fish. They met them as customary, and pilotted the Bark to that Place, which we suppose was the same that Sir *Thomas Cavendish* recruited at in *Queen Elizabeth's* Time, *Anno* 1588." So there was Cavendish again, and the small harbor, Puerto Segura, could, or might, serve them as it had served him after he had taken his prize. They could look at it as a kind of encouraging omen, against all the rest, or as a bitter reminder.

Duke resumed her patrol; all the ships were at sea again. And after that it was dark, a whistling waste. They had been cruising now off Cape San Lucas for nearly a month, a month of hope deferred, of hope, as the days went on, slowly strangling.

On the afternoon of November 27th, *Marquiss* suddenly fired a gun, and *Dutchess* answered. Something had been sighted. Rogers, in the outermost ship, immediately tacked and made all possible sail. *Dutchess* bore after. But the sea was as empty as ever. After a period of futile maneuvering, Rogers was dumbfounded to learn that *Marquiss* had mistaken the *Duke* for the Manila Galleon and *Dutchess,* under the same illusion, had been chasing her sister ship. Perhaps it was the strain of endlessly staring into a vacancy until everything became distorted in the heat and the light and the waves and reflections. Perhaps it was something like the city hunter who goes out after deer and shoots at the glint of a horn in a thicket and kills a cow—the man all along knowing, at some deeper level, that it is a cow but hoping, in the illogical processes of buck fever, by shooting at it to force the fact that it should be a stag.

They resumed the patrol, but now, of course, after hope having so suddenly ballooned and collapsed, it was even worse. There were few entries. One of them detailed something that might have seemed a little bizarre and fantastic, except among this company on these ships. It concerned a sailor who had broken open the *Duke's* lazerette door and stolen some bread and sugar. "I blam'd the Steward for his Remisness; he told me he lay next the Door, with the Key fastned to his Privy Parts, because he had it once stoln out of his pocket, I suppose by the same Thief, who was so dextrous to get it now without disturbing him; but not being ingenious enough to fasten it to the same Place, he was discover'd."

Stealing food, no matter how dextrously, was a serious offense at this point. Supplies were very short, and they would get no more till they reached Guam. And this was the big squeeze, the final squeeze; for if they delayed here much longer, they would not make it to the East Indies. They would not make it to any place at all.

The ships pitched and rolled on the swell, the bows rising and falling, spanking down with a shuddering splash, while the light burned unbearably and the watches stared into an endless distance of sky and ocean, a vacant, heaving horizon.

It had to be; she had to come. This was the time and the place for her, long overdue; if she had sailed in June, as they always did; if she hadn't hung herself up on some reef at the very beginning, months ago; if she hadn't burned or blown up, or been simply swallowed by the inconceivable distance in one black crack of wind snapping her masts, smashing her, capsizing her in the smother of enormous waves, with no more trace after than the wind when it has passed and the seas rolling; if, conceivably, making better than average time, she had not already passed that way some weeks before, so that they might be, in fact, in the position of waiting at this station for an arrival that had long since taken place. The emptiness rising and falling, slowly, endlessly breathing, gave back no answer.

By December 9th they had just about lost all hope. On December 14th they took stock of their provisions and knew that they had, at the outside limit, just eight more days to continue the patrol. They were beaten, or being beaten, by the odds. No wonder only one galleon had ever been taken in the whole 140-odd years' history of the line. The odds were too great—time plus distance plus the steadily dwindling supplies plus the imponderables were too much.

Here, exactly here, the heaving emptiness of time and space had beaten the Dutch fleet under Schapenham ninety years before, had squeezed and beaten so many others since. And the ghosts of all those other attempts— the ghosts of those who, you might say, started young and fresh and confident to declare: "My life won't be like that. My life will be different. They gave up too soon; or they weren't able, weren't strong enough. But this thing they fumbled, missed, couldn't get, *I* will get"— these ghosts rose and bobbed and nodded idiotically on the wave crests.

On December 19th Rogers figured the remaining food supplies, particularly the bread. This followed an earlier conference with Courtney and Cooke to determine how much was left in their ships. "On board the Ship *Duke*, cruising off Cape St. *Lucas* in *California* this 19th of December 1709 . . ."

The squadron had only enough bread, stretching everything, to last seventy more days. They decided they must allow a minimum of fifty days for the Pacific crossing to Guam, plus an additional period of nine days which would be required to refit the ships, lay in stocks of water and wood, etc., before they even attempted the crossing. This made a total of fifty-nine days which, for any margin of safety, must be reserved from their meager stocks right then. "By this Account, which is the utmost, 11 Days Bread will be left when we come to *Guam*."

And that was supposing they reached Guam in the most favorable time and made their landfall exactly. So they could not count on any eleven-day margin to continue the patrol; they could not count on waiting any longer at all. ". . . I doubt not will be full Satisfaction to our Imployers, that we have prolonged our Cruize to the utmost Extent, in hopes to meet the Rich *Manila* Ship: but since Fortune has not favour'd us, we must think of other Methods to promote our Safety and Interest." A resolution to set course for Guam was drawn up and signed by the council. ". . . we all looked very melancholy and dispirited, because so low in Provisions, that if we should not reach Guam in the limited time, or accidentally miss it, we shall not have enough till we arrive at any other Place."

Soles occidere et redire possunt:/Nobis cum semel occidit brevis lux,/Nox est perpetua una dormienda.

They stared, for the last time, at the vacant, meaningless line of sky and sea with which they had deluded themselves so long. No hope, said the emptiness, there is nothing. You can ride here and rot your lives out and the lives of your children and grandchildren and there will still be nothing. Only this rolling immensity indifferent to man.

There was no more to do here, or that could be done. It was finished. They gave up, and turned away. And then in the moment of turning away, the curve of sky and sea bulged and distended and the emptiness, extending off into unlimited space, produced a speck, a point— something almost protozoic or protoplasmic, and like that, it might be said, viable: because it grew and enlarged; until its masts became thin and short as a needle, carrying squares of canvas half the size of a thumbnail.

The lookout, high at the masthead of the *Duke*, yelled and yelled again. She was coming on with a good wind. She was coming on with her topsails filling, right for them. Here, here—the sky and sun and sea and the rolling horizon might have been saying—here, here, since you wanted it—in spite of everything, against all the impossible odds, here she is in your hands, in your laps, the ultimate, absolute prize, six months from Manila, in silks, pearls, spice, gauze, rubies.

But, of course, as might be expected after all that time, they couldn't entirely believe it. As the *Marquiss* three weeks before, had mistaken the *Duke* for the galleon, so now many said that what they took for the galleon was actually the *Marquiss*—particularly since no fore-topmast could be discerned. The *Marquiss* actually was undergoing final repairs for the long voyage west and was at anchor in the small natural harbor of Puerto Segura, near the Cape; but they thought that somehow, for some reason, she had slipped out and put to sea. This was merely a kind of uncontrollable trembling; a fit like buck fever. *Duke* hoisted her ensign and bore after the sail. It was morning of December 21st.

They closed the distance very slowly. There was little wind, and that began to drop. By afternoon the strange sail was only a little bit larger, maybe now the size of a stamp. Men laid money on whether it was the galleon or the *Marquiss*, the way some people will lay a bet against themselves on what they want most: partly, to insure that if they don't get it they'll at least pocket something but, actually, to make a sort of sacrifice to fortune, so that the goddess will smile, collar the small bet and let them have the big one.

There was activity aboard *Dutchess*. She put out a boat and it returned. Rogers sent Frye in the yawl to reconnoiter, fired a gun and hoisted a French ensign; the stranger distantly answered. By nightfall Frye was back. The *Marquiss* was where she ought to be. What they had in front of them was nothing at all but the Manila Galleon. It was as good as done. Except, of course, for the business of taking her.

They kept a boat out that night with lights, in order not to lose her. At one point during the night *Dutchess* passed near this boat and twice fired on it wildly. The vessels rose and fell in the darkness, the occasional lights gave back nothing. It was almost as if the whale had sounded.

And then it was daybreak of December 22nd, and daybreak disclosed her, not a league away, off the weather bow, towering, huge: *Dutchess* ahead of her to leeward, and all riding silently in the still, first light.

Everyone knew now. On each ship the boatswain shouted, "Up all hammocks." Each man ran to his hammock, rolled it up, corded it and carried it to the quarterdeck, poop or forecastle, as assigned. The hammocks were stowed, under the direction of the quartermaster, between the two parts of the protective netting that ran along the decks, as a shield against small shot. Hammocks and bedding were also packed against bulkheads and cabin walls to stop the splinters. Other bulkheads, chests, casks, mess tables, everything movable that might splinter, had already been pitched into the hold.

The boatswain and his mates secured the lower yards, slinging them with chains and doubling the important sheets, ropes and braces. Nets were spread under the masts to catch any wreckage falling from aloft.

There was no wind, and the distance of even one league was still too great. They had to come to point-blank range. *Duke* got out eight of the big oars and began to row. Carpenters and their crews assembled the tools and spare parts to repair the iron machinery of the chain pumps, against a hit. They got out their shot-plugs and mauls, plugs of oakum and sheets of lead to jam against holes opened up by hits at or below the waterline.

On each ship the surgeons in the holds had their platforms spread with canvas and the chests ready, the lanterns lit, the water standing in tubs; basins, tourniquets, ligatures, linens, powders, forceps, saws, tape and tow. *And at the corner of the Platform you are to place two Vessels, one with Water to wash Hands in between each Operation, and to wet your dismembring Blades in, and for other Services; and the other to throw amputated Limbs into, till you have an opportunity to heave them Overboard . . . also Basons to mix your Restrictives in. Pannikins to warm your Oyls in, and . . . have likewise your Cordial Bottle ready at hand to relieve men when they faint.*

A slight breeze sprang up. The oars were shipped. There was no liquor left; so Rogers had a kettle of chocolate made for the men.

Decks had been sanded, sails splashed with water to reduce the fire hazard. On the gun decks spongers and rammers were hooked to the beams above the guns. Spare matches, freshly soaked in saltpeter water, were coiled in small tubs. The heavy shot had been placed in shot racks beside each gunner, and from the magazines below the waterline stooping ship's boys had lugged up the cartridges in bucket brigades—charges of powder packed in canvas or parchment. The buckets were stowed amidships in barrels sealed with leather. Between the guns stood tubs of water: in some of them vinegar water for sponging the cannon; in others blankets soaking, to extinguish fires. The magazines were opened and hung with dripping blankets.

In each gun the cartridge had been rammed home: after the cartridge a wad of oakum; after that the ball, and then a second wad. The gunners opened the metal caps and filled the touchholes with priming powder. Rogers' ship was closing the range. *Dutchess,* still far back, couldn't come up. After the chocolate, the men of the *Duke* went to prayers; and while they were at prayers, the Manila Galleon opened fire on them.

The drums beat. At every hatchway the boatswain and his mates piped all hands to quarters. Gunports were opened, the lashings of the great guns cast loose, and the guns run out. All hatches were secured to prevent anyone deserting his post and hiding in the hold. In order that the force of the explosion might not blow the linstock from his hand, each gunner sprinkled a little train of powder from the touchhole to the base ring of his piece. The slow-matches lifted. The distance closed. From her stern-chase the galleon cannonaded them. Then the commands sang out, and the matches dropped, and the guns boomed.

Duke fired her fore-chase first, and then as she drew nearer, let go with a broadside. They were at point-blank musket range. One broadside and another and another. *Duke* fought alone. *Marquiss* was far off, and *Dutchess* almost becalmed.

The gunners stood on the opposite side of their pieces

from the cartridges, to prevent sparks from their matches igniting the ammunition. They applied the matches to the base rings smartly, whipped back their hands and jumped aside to avoid the recoil. Through the smoke and the pounding of cannon as the shot smashed home, small arms banged and rattled from the tops, waist, forecastle and quarter-deck. The galleon replied in kind, but could not work her big guns as fast.

And then Rogers was down on the deck and in agony, hit in the face. He could not speak, but wrote out his orders, lying where he fell. A shot cracked the mizzenmast. As the guns roared and came back, they were scraped to remove the burning fragments of cartridge-casing, sponged, reloaded and run out, blasting again. *Duke* moved ahead of the galleon and lay athwart her hawse, raking her. And then in a blast of flame, iron, splinters and stinking, fire-streaked smoke the action was over; the galleon struck.

Dutchess, finally coming up, excitedly fired five of her guns and let go a musket volley; but the galleon, having by then submitted, did not reply. The action had lasted three glasses, an hour and a half, and the price for the English was one man killed and two wounded. Rogers had been shot through the left cheek, the bullet knocking out a lot of teeth and smashing his jaw. He was in horrible pain; but he still commanded.

He ordered the pinnace over to bring him the galleon's captain and other officers. Nobody spoke about cheering, as the crew sat or leaned to rest, staring at what they had got; it was too soon; it was a little grim.

And a lot more grim, certainly, for everyone on board the prize and for her captains and officers as they were rowed back in the pinnace. *I am gall; I am heartburn. God's most deep decree/Bitter would have me taste . . .*

After the longest, and most terrible, continuous voyage in the world—after the gales and storms and the gigantic seas; after the cold to the bone and perpetual thirst; the lice, rats, weevils, and maggots swimming in the broth; after the beriberi, and scurvy and the pickled bodies awash in the bilge, when the whole ship swelled and stank with one gigantic infection; after the Te Deums and the hilarious celebration when they finally sighted, two or three hundred miles off the California coast, the *señas*—sea lions—and seaweed, the welcome first signs of land, and thought they were home safe and alive and all right—they had had to be met at this last Cape and be taken. Everything they had endured and survived, all those last-chance escapes, wound up under the guns of people they did not know, of whom they had barely been informed, who had sailed to meet them from Bristol, England, nearly a year before they had ever left Manila. So it was for nothing and worse than nothing, because they had lost not only all the possible profits and compensations which made men willing to undergo so much, but would now have to pay, out of whatever credit they had left, ransom money for "That Voyage . . ." as Careri wrote, "which is enough to Destroy a Man, or make him unfit for anything as long as he lives."

The Captain and officers were duly interviewed. "This Prize," Rogers noted, "was call'd by the long Name of *Nostra Seniora de la Incarnacion Disenganio*, Sir *John Pichberty*, Commander; she had 20 Guns, 20 Patereroes [a small, breech-loading swivel gun], and 193 men aboard, whereof 9 were kill'd, 10 wounded, and several blown up and burnt with Powder." *Sir John Pichberty* was an Anglicization of the name and title of the commander, who was French.

It was a glorious victory, its glory only a little diminished by the fact that though the galleon clearly outmanned the *Duke*, the *Duke*, in the cannon that counted, outgunned her. Still it was one for the record; the second in 140 years and maybe the richest. And still, considering reports, considering what was said to be the weight and size these things could be, the prize was not quite—not quite . . . The interrogation continued; and, as it continued, Rogers and his officers must have felt something like the man who has killed the biggest fish of its kind in the world, the record trophy, and then, while it is still being measured, turns and sees cutting the water far out one twice as big, something altogether fabulous and unbelievable.

The prize, they learned from the prisoners, had a sister ship of a good many more tons' burden and more than double the complement of men—"a brave lofty new Ship" making her first voyage. That one, the other, was named *Bigonia*; her tonnage was three times that of *Duke* and nearly four times that of *Dutchess*; she could carry sixty brass guns, had at least forty of them mounted and as many patereroes; and the crew to man and fight her, in addition to the passengers, numbered 450. "They added that 150 of the Men on board this great Ship were *Europeans*, several of whom had formerly been Pirates, and having now got all their Wealth aboard, were resolved to defend it to the last. The Gunner, who had a good Post in *Manila*, was an expert Man, and had provided the Ship extraordinarily well for Defence . . ."

It looked as if the only chance against this one was surprise—if there were a chance, because, while the two galleons had left Manila together, they had lost company three months earlier and Pichberty and his officers were certain that the *Bigonia*, which was not only much bigger but sailed much better, had already reached Acapulco.

The English frigates, escorting the captured galleon, put into the small, natural harbor of Puerto Segura to refit and prepare. They had combed that coast for nearly two months, and it seemed improbable that anything the size of the *Bigonia* could have slipped through. It was also learned that much of the goods on the two galleons were from India, and of these goods alone Cooke noted: "We were farther informed by the Prisoners that the Cargo in *India* amounted to two million dollars and that the other Ship was of much greater value." Since their food supplies would now be augmented by what they could expect to find in the captured ship, they decided to cruise for the second and biggest galleon eight more days.

The surgeons had been sent aboard the prize to treat and dress the wounded. Rogers himself was suffering badly. His face and throat were hugely swollen, he could barely swallow liquids, and he had been subjected to repeated probings for the bullet, which the surgeons could not find. On the night of the twenty-third, lying in the darkness, in that throbbing distortion of pain and fever which gets so much worse and more unmanageable in the hours for sleep, he felt something clog in his throat and swallowed it, thinking it either a piece of his jaw or the bullet. He may, or may not, have been somewhat relieved by a treatment then current among sea surgeons for head wounds: *Now Pain, Inflammation, and Fever in these Cases are almost inseparable; the one brings the other; and here bleeding must by no means be neglected, and that not only once but often, as is required, and especially if the Patient hath a Plethorick Body, and inject Clysters . . . But often through the vehement colour of the wounded Nerves, there happens convulsions, Palsies, etc. In this case you must anoint not only above the Wound but also along the Spine of the Back . . .*

On the following morning the Council met aboard the *Duke* and drew up a formal resolution to cruise for the second galleon. In view of her size and armament, Rogers wanted *Duke* and *Dutchess* to go after her together, with the crew of *Marquiss* divided between them. He pointed out that they would then be in sufficient strength, if they surprised her, to board and take her at once, before she could run out all her guns and screen her decks.

Again he was overruled. There was considerable jealousy over the fact that *Duke* had taken the first Manila Galleon alone and unaided. Now it was the turn of *Dutchess* and *Marquiss* to have the first honors, no matter what sense it made in the face of the odds. Some of the officers also considered Rogers' wound; the surgeons wanted him to stay where he could have rest and quiet. Accordingly, by majority vote, *Dutchess* and *Marquiss* put out to sea on Christmas eve. *God rest ye, Merry Gentlemen, let nothing you dismay.*

Captain-Doctor Dover did not sail with the *Dutchess,* to which he had lately transferred, but remained in the harbor aboard the *Duke.*

On Christmas Day in the morning, Rogers posted two men ashore on top of a bare hill to watch the ocean: there would be *Dutchess* and *Marquiss* far out on patrol. If the lookouts suddenly spotted on that glinting expanse three ships where there had been only two, they were to wave their colors three times.

The hours passed. On Christmas afternoon the lookouts abruptly signaled. Three sail out there now: the third ship, the biggest galleon of them all, had breached the horizon.

Rogers could not yet speak except with great pain and then barely above a whisper. Officers and surgeons still wanted him to remain in the harbor and safety, at least for the present. He ordered *Duke* out, to go to the aid of her consorts.

They put twenty-two well-armed men aboard the

captured *Incarnación*, to man and guard her, and transferred most of the prisoners to the bark. The bark was stripped of arms, rudder, sails and boat, and moored a mile away, with a few men assigned to her to keep order and issue rations.

Captain-Doctor Dover—the heroic physician who was some years later to write, "When I took by storm the twin cities of Guaiaquil . . ."—still preferred to remain in harbor, and at the last moment asked to be transferred to the anchored prize, where he exchanged places with one of the lieutenants on guard.

All this took time. *Duke* weighed anchor and got under sail at seven o'clock Christmas night. In the heaving darkness of this foreign sea there were flashes on the horizon. Rogers and his officers took them for the *Dutchess* and *Marquiss* signaling and making false fires. They did not learn until next day—because they were too far away for the sound of the cannon to carry—that it was *Dutchess* firing and being fired upon. The engagement had opened.

At daybreak on the twenty-sixth, *Duke* sighted three ships on the smooth, only slightly rolling sea; but they were too far away to distinguish which were Courtney's and Cooke's and which the chase. Again there was very little wind.

By nine o'clock *Dutchess* and the new galleon could be made out—*Dutchess* completely dwarfed even at that distance by what she was engaging—and still farther off, the little *Marquiss* crowding on all the sail she could in an effort to come up with them. Rogers' ship was some ten to twelve miles to leeward. He, too, had all available canvas out, but could make very little way. By noon he was not much more than a league nearer.

In the early afternoon, *Marquiss* finally came up with the great ship and went into action, while the men on the *Duke* strained and watched. There were small, black puffs of smoke and a rapid, barely perceptible jarring of the air; and then *Marquiss* fell back out of cannon shot and lay there for a long time, like a small hound mauled by a bear.

Rogers concluded that she was disabled; he ordered the pinnace manned and sent away to her—not only to determine her condition but also to keep track of the enemy after nightfall, if he didn't get enough wind to come up and close before then.

The pinnace had only just set out when *Marquiss* made sail again and went back into action to join *Dutchess*. This time the action lasted much longer—about four glasses, or two hours. The ships were outlined against the setting sun, the smoke puffs larger and more frequent, the reverberations more distinct, but still everything in miniature. They seemed like toy ships in an action of toys, everything except the rolling ocean plated with light that was supposed to belong to the King of Spain.

Just before darkness the toy that was the *Dutchess* drew ahead and to windward of the enemy to repair her rigging and stop the leaks where she had been smashed and holed. In the last light *Dutchess* and galleon and *Marquiss* fired one or two more broadsides; and then it was dark—the enormous being on which they floated, deeply and regularly breathing, with the firework phosphorescence in the waves and some fathoms down disc-shaped areas of faint light like the remote glow of the outer galaxies in space.

At midnight the *Duke's* pinnace returned with reports. The night before, when they had seen the flashes they mistook for signals, *Dutchess* had come up alongside the galleon. "At that time they could perceive the Enemy was in disorder, her Guns not being all mounted and consequently their Netting-Deck and Close Quarters unprovided; so that had it been my good Fortune in the *Duke* to accompany the *Dutchess,* as I desired, we all believe we might then have carried this great Ship; or if they in the *Dutchess* had thought of taking most of the Men out of the *Marquiss,* who did not sail well enough to come up to their Assistance at first, they alone might very probably have taken her by Boarding at once, before the *Spaniards* had experienc'd our Strength, being afterwards so well provided, as encouraged them to lie driving, and give us all Opportunity to board them when we pleas'd."

At any rate, Courtney had fought his ship for two hours, and then fallen back, foremast disabled and rigging shattered. Concerning the action on the following day, the twenty-sixth, beginning at two o'clock when the *Marquiss* engaged, Cooke reported: "She then fir'd two Shot at us, and we returned a Broad-side, and Volleys of small Arms, after giving three Chears. When we had fought two glasses, the *Dutchess* came up under her Stern, and Rak'd her fore and aft, and then fell a-stern again, we still continuing hot at her for five glasses; then war'd and stood to the *Westward,* to fetch up nearer to her, for firing so many Guns had lay'd us to Leeward. The *Dutchess* went up, and engag'd again very briskly for half an Hour or better, and then stretch'd ahead of her. We could perceive many shot plac'd in her betwixt Wind and Water, which oblig'd them to pump often. At Five we tack'd and stood towards the Enemy, half an Hour after engag'd again, and rak'd him fore and aft with our Star-Board Broad-side, then war'd under her Stern, and did the same with our Larboard Broad-side. . . ."

By this time it was getting dark again. The *Marquiss* fell astern to speak with *Dutchess* and to try to get more shot, having now only three rounds left for each gun. At eight that evening, Cooke went aboard the *Dutchess* and found she had taken considerable punishment, particularly in her masts and rigging, and had seven men killed and wounded. "Captain *Courtney* and I," Cooke reported, "agreed to be Yard Arm and Yard Arm with the Enemy in the morning, he to lie on the Bow and I on the Quarter; and if he boarded, I was to clap him aboard, and enter my Men over him."

When Rogers learned that *Marquiss* had expended nearly all her ammunition, he sent the boat to her with three barrels of powder and shot in proportion. During the hours of darkness, *Marquiss* and *Dutchess* kept up an intermittent fire "to annoy the Enemy, and to give the *Duke* Notice of where we were." They waited. The next day would do it, if it were ever to be done.

The *Marquiss* had been hurt, the *Dutchess* hurt much worse. She rode with her dead and wounded, while men worked to repair the foremast and the rigging and to clear away wreckage, the pumps constantly going, gulping and spewing out sea water.

But the galleon, too, had at least been shaken, and she was trying to break out. All through the previous day she had been desperately signaling the distant *Duke*, mistaking the *Duke* for her consort from Manila. Now, in the watchful patterns of the almost windless night, she edged away toward her supposed sister. It was as if in the depths below, in the endless distances overhead, a late audience were settling into place, all those fixed, indifferent eyes staring and a hurried whispering: "What's happening? What's going on? It is nothing. It is a big ship (to them) which has beaten her way here after some thousands of terrible miles, in the time it takes planet three to complete half an orbit; and she has fallen into this trap. Let's wait and watch how it turns out—who lives and who dies and what happens. Look, now, she is reaching—reaching . . ." And, in fact, for the galleon it must have been something like a man struggling in the darkness, who reaches his

9*

hand out to a friend for help and finds that what he has grabbed is a giant claw.

It was daybreak of December 27th. *Duke* was coming up. "Cast loose your guns . . . Level your guns . . . Load with Cartridge." The bags of powder were shoved down the barrels. Gunners rammed their priming irons down the touchholes to break the cartridges. "Shot your Guns." The cannon balls were rammed home. "Run out your guns . . . Prime." The gunners primed with powder from the horns on their belts, sprinkled powder from touchholes to base rings. The drums beat; all hatches were secured. The surgeons stood by their tables with the bright steel laid out under the swaying lights. The yards had been slung with chains, ropes and braces doubled. The decks, as before, were sanded so that men might not slip in the blood.

Duke, the friend for which the galleon had been groping, was nearest; but the wind veered, and *Dutchess* came up first. The galleon's gunports opened, and her guns boomed. *Dutchess* replied with a broadside and rolled and ran on ahead. *Marquiss*—eighteen guns in all and six of them small ones—came up on the enemy's quarter and raked her fore and aft, and then wore to get out of the line of fire of the *Duke,* which was now in position. On the *Duke* the orders rang out: "Point your guns," and then, as the roll of the ship brought the top sights on the target: "Fire." *Duke* was now on the galleon's lee, guns—one after one down the gun deck—rapidly crashing.

And ship by ship, or all together, the galleon lay and hammered them. As fast as a gun fired and recoiled, the gunport was closed so that the gunners might not be picked off by small-arms fire. The guns were scraped, sponged, reloaded, run out and fired as fast as they could be worked and the gunners, stripped to the waist, slipped on blood, in spite of the sand.

Duke and *Dutchess* had the galleon between them. *Dutchess* was firing rapidly, but her misses bombarded the *Duke*, which was therefore forced to lie alongside the enemy.

At that distance, the distance of a few yards, *Duke* pounded and was pounded—so close that muzzle-blasts scorched the planking. Wood splintered and smashed. The smoke stung and burned, and sweat ran down bare chests and bellies, and the air and heaving sea were filled with a continual, jarring concussion.

They fought for two hours. But even their largest shot appeared to do little damage to sides made of Manila timber. *Duke's* mainmast was disabled by a direct hit. *Dutchess* was sadly battered. Firing together, they engaged again, and at one point Rogers was so close under the galleon that he could barely use his guns. And still they could not board her. She had a netting-deck out—protective netting which extended fore and aft from the gunwales up into the rigging—and her crew were in close-quarters, hidden behind strong barriers of wood from which they fired through loopholes. A fireball from one of the galleon's tops landed on the *Duke's* quarter-deck, and blew up a chest of loaded arms and powder cartridges. Carleton Vanbrugh and a sailor were badly burned.

They got the flames out, but Rogers was wounded again. Just before the fireball hit, a shell-driven splinter had torn away part of his heel—"so that I could not stand, but lay on my Back in a great deal of Misery, part of my heel-bone being struck out, and all under my Ankle cut above half thro', which bled very much and weaken'd me, before it could be dressed and stopt."

Dutchess was out of the action. She stood in for the

shore and "lay braced to," trying to secure her foremast and repair sails and rigging which had been shot to pieces. She had now twenty-five men killed and wounded, and had again been holed at and below the waterline.

Meanwhile, *Marquiss* was back in the fight. She came across the galleon's bow, fired three broadsides, some odd guns and a volley of small-shot. *Duke* had also reëngaged. They had been at it now for hours, and the guns were very hot. They leaped and bucked crazily; they never recoiled twice the same way, and the hotter they got—in spite of the sponging, the bathing and washing after every eighth or tenth shot—the worse they recoiled. Sometimes a gun would snap its breeching rope, or leap and overturn, or slam clear up to the beams overhead, and all that weight of leaping, bucking, red-hot metal the gunners had to fight and avoid in a swirling darkness where they could just barely see, in batteries choked and blanketed by the smoke of black powder.

Duke was close up. The *Marquiss*, athwart the galleon's stern, delivered another broadside, another volley. Smoke clouds covered the ships and rolled across the sea. The great ship bombarded them slowly and accurately, concentrating on their masts and rigging. Cooke later noted that the *Marquiss* was by now a mere shell and that if the galleon had concentrated on his hull, she'd have sunk him. As it was, his mainmast was hit, his sails and rigging shattered, and he had to fall astern to repair these and to plug the leaks made by twelve-pounders. At that point, *Duke* received a second direct hit on her mainmast, and the mainmast settled. They were afraid it might go by the board and maybe carry another mast with it. *Duke* sheared off and bore to westward, securing the mainmast for the moment with "Fishes"—two long pieces of curved hardwood, like halves of a cylinder, fitted around the cracked mast and lashed together to hold it.

Cooke was getting ready to try again, when he saw the *Duke* and *Dutchess* signal to speak to one another, and he brought to.

They considered their condition. Beginning with the action Christmas night, they had been at it, off and on, for two nights and a day and for some six solid hours that morning. The great ship was just about as strong as ever. The *Duke's* mainmast and the *Dutchess'* foremast were in such shape that the least thing would bring them by the board. In this place new masts would be difficult, if not impossible, to find. Worse, if they engaged again and the masts went, taking other masts and yards with them, the two frigates would be disabled under the guns of the galleon, which could then proceed at leisure to blow them out of the water.

Any attempt to take her by boarding seemed equally hopeless. There were by this time only 120 men fit and available for the effort, and even these men had been weakened by having been on short rations for a long time. They would now have to fight their way through the net-ting-deck, false-deck, bales and close-quarters manned by an enemy who was thoroughly prepared and who out-numbered them more than three to one.

The odds were too great. Even to try was to risk losing everything: "If we had boarded her, and been forc'd off, or left any of our Men behind, the Enemy by that means might have known our strength, and then gone into the Harbour and took Possession of the Prize in spight of all we could do to prevent it."

Finally, their ammunition was almost gone. The little *Marquiss* alone had fired more than 300 great shot, fifty crossbars, two great chests of steel bars, nine barrels of powder. All together, they had put not less than 500 six-pound shot into the *Bigonia's* hull, battered her sails and rigging, shot two men out of her tops: that much damage and no more. "These large Ships are built at Manila with excellent Timber, that will not splinter; they have very thick Sides, much stronger than we build in Europe."

Only enough ammunition remained, by actual count, to engage her for a few more glasses, with nothing to be accomplished by it. They had a long way to go, and what was left in the bottom of the powder barrels and in the shot-racks was their only safeguard home. Once they blew that away, they would be simple targets for every hungry hunter eyeing them and their prize—from this cape to Guam, from Guam to the Philippines and the Spice Islands and Batavia.

The problem now was how to let go. They decided to accompany the *Bigonia* until nightfall, and then lose her in the darkness. As they came up again, she was ready, and opened her gunports; but they kept out of range, and there was no further action. The night settled down, no longer so watchful, covering everything.

At dawn, on December 28th, they had the deserted horizon to themselves. The white, airborne seabirds banked on the updraught and wheeled and dived and squawked; here and there bits of wreckage and refuse still bobbed, and now and then the water swirled, and something was pulled under. The ocean was empty. The biggest of them all had gone.

Part Three

THE
REQUIEM
SHARKS

15

LONG RUN
WEST

THE BIGGEST of them all had vanished. But what they had
captured in the smaller galleon, the *Nuestra Señora de
la Encarnación y Desengaño,* was still fabulous. The overwhelming question now was whether or not they would
ever be able to bring her safely home. For one thing, they
knew that from this point on, because of the nature and
value of their prize, the pursuers would become in earnest the pursued.

They had to consider the possibility of being caught
here by the squadron of Spanish and French ships now
presumably cruising for them somewhere southeast by
south. They knew that if they succeeded in crossing the
Pacific they would have to avoid the Philippines and

enemy squadrons that might be operating out of Manila. They knew that if they finally reached Batavia, they would have to cope with the cupidity of the crafty Dutch.

And beyond there, beyond Batavia, on the long voyage down through the Indian Ocean and around the Cape of Good Hope, there would be the chance of being attacked by their own loyal countrymen, the English East India Company. If anyone entertained any doubts as to the attitude and intentions of this monopoly, these doubts were immediately settled when Rogers questioned officers of the captured galleon. He learned that one of the main reasons for Manila having sent out two galleons, with the principal riches aboard the one most heavily armed, was that the British in India had long ago prudently warned the Spaniards. "The Enemy was the better provided for us, because they heard at *Manila* from our *English* settlements in *India*, that there were two small ships fitted from *Bristol*, that design'd to attempt them in the *South Seas*."

Cooke said: "The French Captain inform'd us, that they had Advice from *Maderas* two Months before they left *Manila* that two Bristol Privateers were coming in quest of them into those seas, and that Capt. Dampier was Pilot; which was the Reason they had so many *Europeans* aboard the great Ship, most of whom having their Wealth aboard, they would fight to the utmost . . . The two Ships were to have join'd at Cape St. *Luke*, expecting to meet us off Cape *Corrientes* or *Navidad*." So the English East India Company, or John Company, had made sure that Spanish Intelligence, efficient as it was, got all possible help, even to practically pinpointing the place of attack. *Arriba con el comercio de Inglaterra.*

Meanwhile, quite in keeping with such dealings and with what lay ahead, the Bristol captains had a savage quarrel among themselves, as soon as there was time to take stock and they fully realized the extent of their success.

Almost as soon as the treasure ship was captured, Dover had transferred himself to her, ostensibly to keep an eye on things. He had remained safely aboard her all through the engagement with the second galleon. Rogers now demanded that someone competent to sail her be put in command for the difficult voyage west, and suggested Frye. Cooke later said that he was himself first offered the command but refused because he already had a ship. Courtney and Cooke, since Rogers was more or less immobilized by his wounds, went to talk things over with Dover, and were gone some hours. When they returned, they brought a paper appointing Dover "to be Sole Commander, without the least Restraint . . . to order everything as he should think fit." This resolution had been signed by the officers of the *Marquiss* and the *Dutchess*, who constituted a majority of the Council. The signers incĺ ided not only Dover, obviously, but Courtney, Dampier and Cooke.

Rogers, in fact, suddenly found that nearly all his principal officers were aligned against him. Courtney, of course, was a shareholder, like Dover and unlike Rogers, and could presumably have been motivated by some obscure interests on behalf of their fellow owners. And Dover and Courtney and Dampier had been more or less making common cause ever since the ruinous delays and postponements at Guayaquil, for which they were largely responsible. Now Cooke had joined them, in a proposal that should have made no sense to any competent seaman. And this alignment against Rogers was to continue, off and on, for the rest of the voyage.

Rogers' own officers on the *Duke* remained loyal. He and they objected violently to Dover's appointment. They refused to sign the resolution. That brought a strong protest from the dominant Dover faction, declaring that Rogers would be held personally accountable and pointing out that this was the first time anyone had refused to abide by the majority vote. Rogers and his officers, in reply, merely agreed that for the time being they would not board the vessel and remove Dover bodily. "We therefore (being inclin'd to Peace and Quietness aboard and not to use any Violence to remove the said Captain *Dover* out of the aforesaid forc'd Command, although he is utterly uncapable of the Office) do hereby publickly Protest against the aforesaid Commander, and every one of those that have already, or shall hereafter combine to place him in."

The galleon was the culmination, the reward of all their efforts and suffering. They faced "a long Run through dangerous unknown Passages, into the *East Indies*, and most of the Recompence for our great Risques and Hardships lay in her Riches." Ahead of them loomed not only the threat of losing her to the enemy, or even to their own allies and countrymen, but the much greater threat of the sea itself, of all those oceans they would have to cross. And they were about to put in command of her a man who could not sail a ship or navigate, who was dogmatic and intractable, had an ungovernable temper and generally considered his own unsupported opinion to be self-evident truth.

The dispute continued for two days. Rogers reflected: " 'Twas our great Unhappiness, after taking a rich Prize to have a Paper-War smongst our selves." Being weak from his wounds and in great pain, he could not attend the council's interminable meetings but sent his protests in writing. The next was even more blunt. "My Opinion is, That 'tis not for the Safey of the rich *Spanish* Prize, that Capt. *Dover* command her, because his Temper is so violent, that capable Men cannot well act under

him, and himself is uncapable. Our Owners directed me
to use the securest Method to bring the Ship home, if we
should have the good Fortune to take her; and 'tis not so,
if an Ignorant Person have the Command. . . ."

Finally, they settled it. Rogers had no objection to
Dover's remaining aboard the prize to keep an eye on the
treasure, if that was what troubled the doctor, and to
have any title he liked, as long as the actual operation of
the ship was left to others.

The majority of the officers accordingly, and at last,
agreed that Dover should be called the Ship's Captain
but that Frye and Stratton, in equal posts, should be in
command of all the sailing and navigating and of all operations during an engagement. They agreed, as Rogers
wrote, that Frye and Stratton, though nominally under
Captain Dover, "were to be no ways molested, hinder'd
nor contradicted in their Business by him, whose Duty
'twas to see that nothing should be done contrary to the
Interest of the Owners, and Ships Companies, in the
Nature of an Agent, almost in the same Manner I proposed at first, only he had the Title of Chief Captain in
that ship, which was so small a Difference where Titles
are so common, that we all consented to it . . ." Alexander
Selkirk, the old reliable, was appointed ship's master.

Meanwhile, they had freed all the galleon's officers,
except the pilot, all the passengers and most of the crew,
turning over to them the bark formerly commanded by
Selkirk. The bark's cargo was included and ample water
and supplies provided so that the prisoners might proceed
to Acapulco. The two remaining hostages for the balance
of ransom owing from Guayaquil were also released.
Bark, cargo and hostages were part of a deal they made
with the captain of the galleon, Sir John Pichberty: ". . .
the Captain of the *Manila* Ship (who was a *French*
Chevalier) having given us 5 Bills of Exchange for the

same, payable in *London* for 6000 Dollars, being 2000 more than the Ransom Money, for which we allow'd him the Benefit of the Bark and Cargo, the Captain and Hostages giving us Certificates, that it was a Bargain concluded at their own Requests, and very much to their advantage. Sir *John Pichberty* being, we hope, a Man of Honour, will not suffer his Bills to be protested, since we have so generously trusted him . . ." The prisoners, particularly the captain, his chief officers and their priest, were given back all their clothing and personal effects, such as their instruments for navigation and their books and anything else—except jewels or hard cash—they personally valued.

The remaining time at Cape San Lucas, with the ships riding at anchor in Puerto Segura, was spent refitting and laying in stocks of water and firewood. They were happy to discover in the treasure ship enough bread to fill out their own dwindling supplies and last them on the 7,000-mile run across the Pacific.

On the night of January 11th, the four ships weighed anchor—*Duke, Dutchess, Marquiss* and galleon, now rechristened the *Batchelor Frigate*. It had been agreed that *Duke* would put thirty men on board the prize, *Dutchess* twenty-five, and *Marquiss* thirteen, ". . . which with 36 *Manila Indians*, call'd Las-Carrs, and other Prisoners we have left, her Complement will be about 110 Men."

Each ship put many guns down into the hold for the long run to Guam; but after Guam, as everyone knew, the guns would have to be taken up again and mounted and sighted-in, against all comers.

The ordeal of the 7,000-mile crossing began. They agreed "that in case of Separation, the Place of Rendezvous was to be *Guam,* one of the *Ladrones* Islands, where we design'd to touch at, God willing, to get Provisions."

Their supply of certain essentials was short, above all, food. It had been, of course, this shortage of rations they could count on that had made them give up and decide to break off their long patrol and turn west, when the first Manila Galleon was providentially sighted. From the time they left the Tres Marías, during the entire time they were at, or cruising off, Cape San Lucas, they had been able to replenish their diminishing stocks only by some fish and a few yams obtained from Indians and by what stores they found in the captured galleon.

Water, and some firewood, had been taken aboard at Puerto Segura; but between the amount they could stow and the rate of daily consumption for so long a crossing there was a narrow margin. Rogers noted: "We were forc'd to go away with little or no Refreshment, having but 3 or 4 Fowls, and a very slender Stock of Liquor, which we got out of the *Batchelor*. Several of our Men were in a weak Condition, besides my self, Mr. *Vanbrugh* and the rest that were wounded. We were forc'd to allow but 1 pound and half of Flower, and 1 small piece of Meat to 5 in a Mess, with 3 pints of Water a Man for 24 Hours, for Drink and Dressing their Victuals."

Again the wounded and the sick lay in the darkness above the stinking water sloshing in the bilge. On February 1st, the Englishman Boyce, who had escaped to them when they took Guayaquil, died and was tipped into the Pacific. This was the man captured by the Spaniards in the distant Bay of Campeachy and held a prisoner or slave in Peru for seven years; and his lease on freedom had been brief.

On February 5th, ". . . a Negro we named Deptford died, who being very much addicted to stealing of Provisions, his Room was more acceptable than his Company at this time." He and others may well have been so addicted. "We agree to give 6 Negroes the same Allowance as five of our own Men, which will but just keep those that are in health alive."

All the ships were now leaking badly, and the crews had to man the pumps continually. A few men began stealing food again—a deadly serious matter at this point, so serious that Rogers punished the thieves with a grim severity he had never before shown toward such an offense. ". . . the Steward missing some Pieces of Pork, we immediately search'd, and found the Thieves, one of 'em had been guilty before, and forgiven, on promise of Amendment, but was punish'd now, lest Forbearance should encourage the rest to follow this bad Practice; Provisions being so short, and our Run so long, may prove of ill consequence. I order'd 'em to the Main Jeers, and every Man of the Watch to give 'em a Blow with a Cat of Nine-tails, and their Messmates being privy to the Theft, were put in Irons."

Attempts to supplement their rations with fish failed dismally. A month after leaving San Lucas they had caught only one albacore. This part of the Pacific has, in fact, been described in recent times as a great ocean desert—weak currents, warm water, no stirring of nutrients up from the bottom, few if any fish in the surface waters and even deep-net filterings bringing up few organisms from the depths. Dampier knew what to expect, having recorded from an earlier crossing: "It was very strange, that in all this Voyage we did not see one Fish, not so much as a Flying-Fish, nor any sort of Fowl, but at one time, when we were by my account 4975 miles west from Cape Corrientes, then we saw a great number of Boobies, which we supposed came from some Rocks not far from us."

On February 13th the Spanish pilot of the Manila Galleon died: "we kept him, thinking he might be of use to us, if he recovered of his wounds: but he was shot in the Throat with a Musket-ball which lodg'd so deep, the Doctors could not come at it."

They celebrated St. Valentine's day according to custom. Rogers drew up a list of fair ladies in Bristol who were in any way concerned or connected with the privateers, and sent for his officers to come to his cabin, "where everyone drew, and drank the Lady's Health in a cup of Punch, and to a happy Sight of 'em all . . . On the 17th I was troubled with a swelling in my Throat, which incommoded me very much, till this Morning I got out a Piece of my Jaw Bone that lodg'd there since I was wounded."

This ocean was still so little known that Rogers and Cooke later published in their journals tables of each day's run, with the latitude, longitude and variation between Cape San Lucas and Guam: "We resolved to keep an exact Account of the Distance and Variation not being certainly known to us from any former Voyages."

They averaged somewhat over 100 miles a day, which was very fair, considering the nature and condition of the ships, but still barely enough. "On the 18th, we threw a Negro overboard, who died of a Consumption and Want together. Our Men began to be very much out of order, and what adds to their Weakness is our continual Pumping, nor can we pretend to make any further Addition to their Allowance.

"On the 25th, *Tho. Williams*, a *Welch* Taylor, died; he was shot in the Leg at engaging the second *Manila* Ship, and being of a weak Constitution, fell into a Dysentery, which kill'd him . . . On *March* the 3rd we buried a Negro call'd *Augustine*, who died of the Scurvy and Dropsy."

Eight days later they sighted Guam. They had made, fortunately, a good landfall. After a two-months' voyage there were just enough provisions left, even on a slow starvation allowance, to last them little more than a week.

They had no trouble obtaining supplies at Guam. The governor, it turned out, was overjoyed to see them, and so was every other inhabitant in any position to do business. The Spaniards and natives of the Ladrones in general, and of Guam in particular—like those of many other Spanish possessions—had been fuming for a long time over the restrictions on trade imposed by their government's monopoly.

At one point, after a galleon from Manila had put in at Guam two years in succession to check on things and deliver instructions from the King of Spain, the governor decided to move his residence to another island in order to get away from this incessant interference with his private affairs.

The ships began laying in water, firewood, cattle, and fowl, rice, limes, oranges and coconuts. "Our Misunderstandings at *California* have been very much augmented since by our Want of Provisions, one Ship's Company being jealous the other had most and best; but now being arriv'd at a Place of Plenty, we were all indifferently well reconciled, and an Entertainment was provided aboard the *Batchelor* for the Spanish Gentlemen . . . I being not able to move my self, was hoisted in a Chair out of the Ship, and also out of the Boat into the *Batchelor*."

There was another Entertainment later on board the *Marquiss*, and in return the governor had the captains and chief officers to dine at his residence, receiving them with an imposing guard of honor and serving them a banquet of some sixty different dishes. They presented him with twenty yards of scarlet serge, some pieces of cambric, and two Negro boys dressed in scarlet liveries, "which he seem'd wonderfully pleas'd with . . ." In addition, "we gave him and the rest of the Gentlemen what they esteem'd double the Value of what we received of them . . . and parted very friendly."

At daybreak on March 21st the *Duke* hoisted her colors and fired a gun as a signal for her consorts to unmoor. On her deck was stowed a strange craft presented to Rogers by the governor: a native proa, or *"Prow,"* as Rogers called it, a sailing outrigger, "The *Spaniards* told me 'twould run twenty leagues *per* Hour which I think too large; but by what I saw, I verily believe, they may run 20 Miles or more in the Time, for when they viewed our Ships, they passed us like a Bird flying." Rogers intended to exhibit it in London, if he ever got back there.

A last piece of unfinished business remained. Rogers still held one Spanish prisoner and had been holding him a long time. This was an elderly Spaniard "call'd *Ant. Gomes Figuero,*" who had been aboard the first prize they captured in the South Sea, the bark later rechristened the *Beginning,* taken off the coast of Peru nearly a year before. Rogers and Courtney had intended to carry him with them back to London, where he could testify that all the ships they had seized were lawful prizes; but the long months and the ordeal had been too much for him. He was old and ailing and ". . . being now in all appearance not likely to live, we agreed to dismiss him, he giving us a Certificate that he saw us attack and take several Prizes, all Subjects to *Philip* V, King of *Spain,* &c. I gave him some Clothes and other odd things to help him in his Sickness, and then put him ashore to the Deputy Governour, and the rest of the *Spanish* Officers . . ."

Then the ships sailed, decks loaded with provisions. But again there was the problem of what they could stow against the rate of consumption, and they knew that if they were delayed long in the labyrinthine passages among the islands ahead of them, everyone would again be on a starvation diet.

Three weeks out of Guam they were somewhere off the Spice Islands, and they were in trouble. All their charts of the area were unreliable. The course they had plotted lay to the west of the island of Morotai and down through the Molucca Passage to Ternate. But they could get no land bearings and they could not determine their own positions with any accuracy by celestial navigation. Moreover, the *Duke* was again leaking badly and her crew "wearied almost to Death with continual Pumping . . ."

On April 13th and again on the 14th, they sighted islands they could not identify. They also saw three waterspouts, "one of which had like to have broke on the *Marquiss*, but the *Dutchess* by firing two Shot broke it before it reach'd her."

Then they encountered strong westerly gales and storms which, continuing for six days, drove them still farther off course. Walls of thunderheads rolled over the ships; lightning flashed and flared in the high shoulders and crevices of the clouds and from the clouds to the sea, and the sea shook with continual, rolling blasts from horizon to horizon. Rain beat at them in solid sheets; the wind split their sails. Cooke reported: ". . . such terrible *Westerly* Winds, and *Storms* and Thunder and Lightning that I could compare it to nothing but Doomsday . . . The Weather prov'd such, as broke most of our Main Shrouds, several of our Stays, most of our running Ropes, and the Mizen Gears; so that the Yard came by the Board, broke in several pieces, and knock'd down Mr. *Pope*, my lieutenant, who lay speechless for some Time, but soon after came to himself. Most of our Sails were split, and I bent others. I was supply'd with new Shrouds by Capt. *Rogers*, and with others from Capt. *Courtney*: besides all which, my Ship was very leaky. The *Duke* and *Dutchess* far'd not much better, and the Prize split most of her Sails, but the

Ship is so strong, that no Weather could well damage her. I could not imagine we should have met with such boisterous Weather in that Latitude, so near the Sun. It was as bad as what we met with at Cape Horn, and only warmer."

When the weather finally cleared, not even Dampier could calculate approximately where they were, though he had been twice to these waters and explored them on earlier voyages. They thought they might have missed the Molucca Passage and be now to the east of the big island of Halmahera, known to them as Gillolo, instead of to the west of it, the side of the island off which Ternate lies. They were, in fact, somewhere between Halmahera and New Guinea.

By now the food ration had been cut so short that Cooke reported: "The Men give a groat or Six Pence a Piece for Rats, and eat them very savourly."

Dampier was gloomy about the prospects. He informed Rogers that if they did not reach Ternate or find the island of Tulur, "we can reach no Port or Place to recruit at, and that it will be impossible to get Provisions for us on the Coast of *New Guinea* should we be forced to go thither . . ." That coast was mountainous. The timid natives living along the shore would disappear with everything they had at the first sign of strangers, whereas the shy inhabitants of the high interior were dedicated cannibals.

Rogers and his captains decided to try for Ternate again, and now ran into calms and strong currents. On May 3rd they sighted some islands which they identified from their charts as a small group near the northern tip of Celebes. They concluded that they were now in the Molucca Passage after all, between Celebes to the west and Halmahera to the east. Accordingly, the ships bore south-southeast. Since they were already east of the Passage, they were turning away from it and were headed toward ferocious New Guinea.

Nine days later they discovered, by the nature and extent of the coastline they sighted, that they were off New Guinea, and realized that they had no choice but to continue south and try to reach the settlement on Amboina. The old suspicions and jealousies about food and water erupted again; on each ship the crew thought it was being held to a shorter ration than the others. "Upon Enquiry I found the Ship's Companies far'd all alike."

Each ship was ordered to check her supplies and report. They found they had enough food to last them, at the longest, three more weeks at sea. The squadron poked and groped its way through unknown passages among unidentifiable islands. On May 20th Rogers recorded: "The *Dutchess* generally kept a-head in the Night, with her Pinnace a-head of her, because the Currents are so very uncertain, and being in an unknown Track, we cannot be too careful in the Night. We are still in sight of the High Lands of *New Guinea*, and several Islands to the Northward, which we find laid down in no Draught, so we noted them as we past by."

Then the southeast monsoon set in. Winds beat and drove them, and they gave up any hope of fetching Amboina. By May 24th they were so far from being able to determine their position that they did not know whether they were off Ceram or had already gotten well past Buru, to the southwest of it. The following day: "We came to a Resolution . . . to make the best of our Way to the Straights of *Bouton,* where if we arrived safe, we might get Provisions enough to carry us to *Batavia.*"

Two months had passed since their departure from Guam, and by now almost no provisions were left. The *Dutchess* had no water except what could be caught when it rained. Rogers sent her a butt of water, as he had earlier sent twelve hogsheads and a barrel to the *Marquiss*.

They sailed or groped their way through a bewilderment that grew steadily worse—baffled by strange currents, driven by contrary winds, their charts either partly or wholly wrong and error compounding error until they were faced with the certainty that the only chance they had left was to reach Buton.

In the early hours of May 25th, in darkness and stormy weather, they were a little to the east of it and among a small group of islands on which they would have been wrecked if the weather had not suddenly cleared. They wore the ships and stood off northeast until daylight, when *Duke* and *Dutchess* hoisted out their pinnaces and sent them ashore. The pinnaces returned with some coconuts and word that the Malay inhabitants were friendly and willing to trade.

Rogers' squadron was able to take aboard some food and water, enough to proceed in considerably less distress to Buton. It reached Buton, after more storms, calms, contrary currents and errors of navigation, four days later.

But there were further troubles. First, after negotiating a 100-mile-long strait, they couldn't locate the port. Some Malays came out to the *Duke* but for want of a linguist no one could understand their directions. There was a linguist aboard the *Batchelor* and Rogers sent for him, "but Capt. *Dover* refus'd to let him come to me, altho' he had no use for him."

Finally, a pinnace was dispatched with a crew under the command of Dampier to find the town and arrange terms for trade with the local sultan. With Dampier went the linguist and Carleton Vanbrugh.

Everything proceeded with deceptive smoothness. "We made a Present to the King of a Bishop's Cap, being of little or no Value to us, but what he highly esteemed and gratefully acepted of." He even more highly esteemed and gratefully accepted of the hard bargains he and his subjects were able to drive; the Bristol privateers were forced to the stiffest prices they had so far paid for supplies. Rogers noted that it was said the sultan could raise a force of fifty thousand men and added: ". . . they boast of not valuing the *Dutch,* but I am satisfied their Poverty is their greatest Security."

They were not, however, so poverty-stricken that any among them would consent to act as a pilot for the run to Java, though the English offered to pay very well. A native pilot was obviously needed—considering the state of the charts and the squadron's recent experience in trying to navigate from the time it sighted, or did not sight, Morotai.

On top of the failure to obtain a pilot at Buton, Rogers and the other captains were faced with a fresh conspiracy to mutiny, led by an officer aboard the *Duke* and some officers and men aboard the *Dutchess.* This could have been extremely serious, if not fatal. Piracy was always inviting to some and now a distinct possibility to many, in view of where they were and the prize, apparently worth millions, they had with them. Why sail all the way home to turn everything over to the owners? Why not go on the account? Or take service with the great Mogul as some of Swan's good men had done? Or some equally harebrained scheme hatched on decks in the darkness, over the snuff and pipes and arrack.

Fortunately, the plot was discovered before it had made real headway and this attempt smashed, as had been earlier ones, by putting everyone concerned in irons "on board different Ships, to break the Knot, which might otherwise have ruin'd the Voyage."

By June 4th the squadron had all the supplies it needed for the run to Batavia and was ready to sail. Then there was another hitch. The sultan had locked up Carleton Vanbrugh and some of the boat crews and was holding them for ransom.

The day Rogers learned this a Portuguese linguist and resident of Buton, who had previously been aboard the *Duke,* returned with some private goods he wanted to sell. They decided to keep him as a hostage to exchange for Vanbrugh "but he got out of the Ship before we were aware (he being jealous by his cold Reception, that we were uneasy) and rowed away as fast as possible. I sent the Yawl after him, which overtaking his Canoe, the Men all jumpt over board, but the *Dutchess'* pinnace took 'em up, and our Boat brought the *Portugueze* Linguist aboard us, where seeing he was likely to be confin'd, he sent the boat with the Men up to the Town, to desire our People might be dismiss'd as soon as possible."

Vanbrugh and the others were released. Everyone parted on the most friendly and agreeable terms imaginable; it was nothing, mere business. The squadron weighed.

Two days out of Buton, they caught the pilot they needed. A proa was sighted, chased and, in spite of her superior speed, finally captured by the pinnaces. Her master, a Malay from Macassar, was thoroughly familiar with the passage to Batavia and had, in fact, frequently served as a pilot for the Dutch. "We promis'd him," said Cooke, "a suit of Cloaths, and as much Money as he could in Reason ask, to go with us to *Batavia.*"

These inducements persuaded him. He agreed to be their pilot, with the sole provision that it be kept secret "for fear of the Dutch." Thereafter, the run to Java was uneventful. When, by their reckoning, they were a couple of days from Batavia, they armed to full strength, taking up from the hold those guns that had been put down to trim ship after they sailed from Cape San Lucas, mounting and scaling them in—just to be prepared. The Dutch were their allies, but the Dutch East India Company was an enormous, going concern, and profit was its own excuse. Against overwhelmingly superior forces the English squadron would, of course, have no chance; but it could defend itself and make any attempt at simple expropriation fairly expensive.

On the afternoon of June 20, 1710, the ships entered the road of Batavia. "By our Reckoning here, we alter'd our Account of Time, having as customary, lost almost one Day in running West so far round the Globe."

As *Duke* came to anchor, she fired thirteen guns in salute and *Dutchess* as many, and the Dutch replied, cannon for cannon. Officials and burghers and merchants must have rushed to their windows and the streets, and there could be no doubt what vessel the English ships had with them. By her lines, by her size, by the type of construction, this could be nothing but the historic Manila Galleon, the prize for which Holland had unsuccessfully tried almost a century earlier and for which it had once sent a fleet of eleven big men-of-war around the world. And here she was now in the road of Batavia, riding beside two fourth- or fifth-rate English ships of the line, mere Bristol privateers —appearing out of nowhere, coming suddenly without prior news or notice or warning over the rim of the horizon. Officials and burghers and townspeople, the solid Dutch, must have stared with astonishment and wild surmise and definite malice.

16

BROTHERHOOD
OF
MERCHANTS

IT HAD BEEN nearly two years since these men had seen any
kind of city at all; they had not even seen a town, except
for battered, pestilential Guayaquil. Batavia must have
represented something fabulous, like legendary Baghdad
or Byzantium with its moonlit domes.

A sailor could stroll through these streets and bazaars
like a king or a caliph—neat, well-paved streets full of
singers and music and cages of birds, streets where there
were pageants and side shows and cockfights and Chinese
theaters; all sorts of dishes, all sorts of women, all sorts of
drink.

As the Spanish conquerors of Tenochtitlán kept trying to drain its lake in order, presumably, to turn Mexico City into something as familiarly arid and harsh as much of their homeland, so the Dutch, in reverse fashion, had lined Batavia with canals.

The population was a mixture of Europeans, Chinese, Malays, and a remnant of those Hindus who had long ago conquered Java and ruled it for centuries through a succession of kingdoms until the Mohammedans took over.

The city had been built foursquare. The streets along the canals were straight, some of them more than thirty feet broad and all paved with brick, and the banks of the canals were faced with stone. "The Country Seats and Buildings round the City, are well contriv'd with handsom Gardens for Fruit and Flowers, and adorn'd with Springs, Fountains, Statues, etc. The vast Quantity of Coco nut Trees, every where afford delightful and profitable Groves."

For most of the officers and crews of the squadron the first and prime interest was not, obviously, fine buildings and neat canals and enchanting prospects of gardens. Rogers, who underwent considerable surgery for his bullet wounds on the second day in port and had been weak and ill thereafter, could not visit the ships except occasionally, and when he did, found the behavior of his own men amazing, "During these 10 Days, I was not able to go much on board, and whenever I went, found, that till then I was a Stranger to the Humours of our Ship's Company. Some of them were hugging each other, others blessing themselves that they were come to such a glorious Place for Punch, where they could have Arrack for 8 Pence *per* Gallon, and Sugar for 1 Peny a Pound; others quarreling who should make the next Bowl, for now the Labour was worth more than the Liquor, whereas a few Weeks past, a Bowl of Punch to them was worth half the Voyage."

The second day at Batavia the captains waited on the Governor-General to acquaint him with their urgent need to careen. He read and approved their commissions as privateers, said he would refer the matter to his council, and promised a decision in short order as to what could be done toward providing them with the help they needed.

Ten days later they were still waiting, and would be waiting much longer. Meanwhile, Rogers had suffered his surgery: "the Doctor cut a large Musket Shot out of my Mouth, which had been there near 6 Months, ever since I was first wounded; we reckon'd it a piece of my Jaw-bone, the upper and lower Jaw being much broken, and almost closed together, so that the Doctor had much ado to come at the Shot, to get it out. I had also several Pieces of my Foot and Heel-bone taken out, but God be thanked, am now in a fair way to have the Use of my Foot, and to recover my Health. The Hole the Shot made in my Face is now scarce discernable." Rogers was optimistic; it was going to be a long time before he recovered his health or before the hole in his face would be scarcely discernible. Considering all he had been through since he received his wounds, the strains and hardships of the voyage, the operations to which, in a sick and weakened condition, he had been subjected and the methods then in use, the wonder is that he survived.

On the last day of June the council met aboard the *Batchelor* to settle various matters of business, the first being the preservation of the cargoes and particularly that of the prize by having all water-damaged goods unpacked and repacked and the rest re-covered with new waxed tarpaulins. It was agreed that the legitimate plunder aboard the captured galleon should be examined and assessed by Dampier and Glendall and divided among the crews. The council voted to give a reward of 100 Rix dollars to the Malay master who had piloted them to Batavia. Carleton Vanbrugh, back in favor, was reappointed owner's agent for the *Duke*. Then, duly deliberating the pastimes and diversions to be had at Batavia, they voted that a sum of 10,000 pieces of eight be made available for the officers to draw on against future shares.

They had arrived in the best month of the best season of the year. "Here are Hospitals, Spin-houses and Rasp-houses, the same as in *Amsterdam*, with all other publick Buildings, equal to most Cities in *Europe*. The *Chinese* have also a large Hospital in this City for their Aged and Sick Persons, and manage their Charity so well, that you never see a *Chinese* look despicable in the street."

Altogether, the capital of the Dutch East India Company's empire was a fine and impressive place, and the Dutch intended to keep it that way and to themselves, though Englishmen such as these, with money to spend, were tolerated as long as the flow of money went one way and one way only: into Dutch pockets. There were great magazines of naval stores defended by platforms of guns. The river of Jacatra running through the city formed fifteen canals, and over these there were bridges at almost every street, and booms which were lowered at sunset so that no boats might enter or leave the waterways. The Company had seldom less than twenty men-of-war in the harbor, ships of "from 20 to 50 and 60 guns each," as Rogers observed thoughtfully, "with Men enough for them on all Occasions . . . Their Soldiers are very well train'd, and there's a Company always on Duty at every Gate of the City and Citadel."

Batavia was, in fact, as impregnable as Manila was reputed to be and a lot more formidable. Rogers considered that the Dutch could at that time muster a force sufficient to drive the English not only out of all those regions but even out of India, "should we ever have an unfortunate War with them." These were matters to be weighed and reported, for later consideration by the government in London.

Meanwhile, in respect to the happier aspects, Rogers concluded: "this City is one of the pleasantest in the World." There were dice and fan-tan and buffalo races, and the Chinese, inveterate gamblers here as elsewhere, were often reduced to betting their hair, fingernails, wives and children. There were all the diversions of a mixed population, and, as the crews had instantly discovered, plenty of cheap liquor. The Dutch women presumably would not look at a common seaman, but they might look at an officer, and apparently they had the liberty to do so. "The *Dutch* Women have greater privileges in *India* than in *Holland,* or any where else; for on the slightest Occasions they are often divorc'd from their Husbands, and share the Estate betwixt them."

In any case, there were probably more accommodating and provocative choices among the Javanese and Malay women: "The Women are not so tawny as the Men, and many of them handsom, but in general amorous, and unfaithful to their Husbands or others, being very apt to give Poison, which they do very cunningly."

All this was fine—aside from the poison, of course—but the ships continued to leak badly and were in foul condition; and the English squadron, nearly three weeks after it dropped anchor, had still not received any permission from the governor to careen. On July 8th Rogers and his officers finally received this permission but were ordered to proceed to the Island of Horn instead of to Unrest, the place where the Dutch careened their own ships and where there were all the needed facilities. Dampier's former companion and enemy, William Funnell, had earlier written about Unrest: "The *Dutch* careen their Ships here; and it is very well fortified, being (to use a sea phrase) all round a Bed of Guns."

They were not allowed to hire any Dutch carpenters and were instead assigned, at a price, eight or ten Malay calkers. No adequate vessels were assigned to them, at any price, to help unload their cargoes and to heave down. When they tried to protest to the Governor-General, they found they were barred from even seeing him. The Sabandar, or Chief Customs Officer, through whom it was necessary to proceed, refused to arrange a meeting.

On July 20th Rogers and some others finally obtained an interview with the governor by bribing his guards. They presented a petition stating their troubles and grievances in diplomatic language and concluding: "Delays are very prejudicial to our Ships, that have been long without the Benefit of a Friend's Port . . . We hope for a Continuance of the common Benefits and Refreshments, and on our Parts shall persevere to behave our selves with all due Regard and Respect to the Governor and Customs of this City."

That brought results. The governor ordered them a careening vessel, and on July 23rd they proceeded to Horn Island. Meanwhile, a preliminary examination of the *Marquiss* had revealed that her bottom was honeycombed by marine worms. She was only single-sheathed and could not possibly make the voyage back to England, unless they undertook a rebuilding job which would not have been worth the cost and for which, in any case, they were not allowed the facilities and carpenters required. They decided therefore, to sell her at a public auction in Batavia. However, when they applied for permission to hold the auction, the Sabandar informed them that the governor and council had resolved to publish a decree that any Dutch freeman who bought her would have to rip her up or burn her.

There was more here than simple obstructionism and more than the simple, fixed determination that all money

passed should be into, and none out of, Dutch hands. The
citizens of Batavia were divided into two groups: servants
of the Company and free citizens. The servants of the
Company were under the Company's rule in every detail
and aspect of their lives, and the free citizens had just
about no freedom at all, being hedged about and confined, allowed to engage only in certain occupations and
even more rigorously restricted in any trading they
might carry on. The Company kept a cold, steady eye on
its profits, its prerogatives and its monopoly. It maintained the high price of spices, among other commodities,
by limiting their production and availability. It did not
intend that any free citizen should acquire a vessel, however honeycombed, in which he might secretly go off to
trade among the islands and so nick, by even a guilder,
the Company's lawful return.

This zeal and determination had long ago been noted
by Dampier, among many others: "For the Dutch being
seated among the Spice-Islands, have monopolized all the
Trade into their own Hands, and will not suffer any of
the Natives to dispose of it, but to themselves alone. Nay,
they are so careful to preserve it in their own Hands, that
they will not suffer the Spice to grow in the uninhabited
Islands, but send Soldiers to cut the Trees down . . ." After
citing instances of this and other examples of Dutch behavior in the Indies, Dampier concluded: "I believe
there are no where greater Thieves."

Together with its business acumen, the Company
sometimes displayed plain savagery. It indulged in massa-
cres and atrocities; and while the principal victims were
native populations, Europeans also suffered. At Amboina
the members of an English post, though not proved guilty
of anything at all, were seized at gunpoint and summarily
condemned on a charge of "conspiracy." Ten Englishmen,

10*

nine Japanese and one Portuguese were tortured extensively to produce "confessions" and then executed.

It had been said that in the Indies the Dutch "would do no right and take no wrong," and Sir Thomas Lynch observed, in 1683, that no wonder there was a proverb in Holland "Jesus Christ is good, but trade is better."

At Batavia, the clerks of the Company rose at 5:30 in the morning, began working at six and continued, with only intervals for breakfast and dinner, until six in the evening. If there was much to be done, they were sent back to their desks at night. The Governor-General himself held his first audience at 6:00 A.M., went on working until 6:00 P.M., and did not enjoy a single day's vacation in the entire year.

They worked in the heat, which is high, Batavia being nearly on the equator, and in the humidity, which is much worse. During the good months, the city is cooled by sea breezes, but the inhabitants considered these noxious and believed that fresh air caused colds; therefore, all doors and windows were tightly closed every morning.

Not many servants of the Company or free citizens lived to return to Holland. They died of tropical fevers and diseases and of contagions bred in the canals, which were used as sewers. Gin being considered a good antidote, the average Batavian, as soon as he awoke, drank a glass of it neat on an empty stomach and continued with frequent glasses throughout the day. Jan Pieterzoon Coen, the conqueror who established the Company's East Indian empire and who founded Batavia, wrote in 1619: "Our nation must drink or die."

Tobacco was also thought to be a preventative, and everybody smoked continually and prodigiously—often cigars, which were very cheap, but mostly long clay pipes. It was a wonder that the Company's servants,

agents, officers—wracked by fever, stupefied by gin, suffering, presumably, from chronic nicotine poisoning—
should have been able to persevere as grimly as they did
and that the Company should have been able to continue
its good works with such thoroughness and efficiency.
Nothing that might contribute to that efficiency was over-
looked.

When it was observed that the mortality rate among
the Chinese was next to nothing compared with that of
Europeans, savants attributed this to the Chinese habit of
drinking tea. The Directors in Amsterdam, therefore,
circulated leaflets recommending tea as a health beverage
and advocating a minimal intake of forty cups per person
per day.

Rogers' squadron suffered almost equally from the
endemic diseases. Horn Island not only lacked adequate
facilities for careening and repairs but also proved to be
singularly unhealthy. Men began dropping with "Fevers
and Fluxes." Cooke himself became seriously ill. And as
the weeks ran on into September, the weather grew
worse. "We buried here *John Bridge* our Master, as also
the Gunner of the *Dutchess,* with another of her Crew,
and one belonging to the *Batchelor.* The Season being so
far spent, and the Wind blowing fresh on *Horn* Island, I
could not go again thither to careen my Ship, tho' she
needed it much; therefore we try'd to get an Order to
careen at *Unrest,* where the *Dutch* careen their own, as
we might have done ours, in a few Days, and with little
Trouble." Protests and petitions got them nowhere.

One day a member of the *Dutchess* crew went swimming and was killed by a shark. Cooke recorded it: *"John
Read* a young Man belonging to the *Dutchess,* venturing
to swim, had both legs snapped off by a Shark, which at
a second Bite, before we could get him aboard, took off

the bottom of his Belly, so he was quite dead before we could take him up."

Even if Cooke and the others did not make it, a comparison certainly existed between the fate of this young man and their own situation. The term "Requiem shark" today is applied to a species that more or less confines itself to other fish; but during that period and earlier, particularly among the Spanish and the French, killer sharks—the true man-eater, the white shark, and the occasional man-eaters—were all appropriately called Requiem sharks.

The English knew, at any rate, that they were surrounded by people and interests ready to rip at what they had and, if possible, seize it whole: the Dutch here, the English East India Company in the months to come. Rogers obviously did not think the Dutch Company would proceed so far at this point as to appropriate the galleon itself, though they sometimes expropriated the vessels of their own countrymen. However, it was well to be prepared; and just as he had all his guns mounted when approaching Batavia, so now he ordered the magazines repeatedly checked, to make sure the powder was dry. In the process of doing this they discovered a fresh leak in the *Duke:* "Rummaging to day in the Powder room, we found a Leak 3 or 4 Foot under Water." It was now September 15th and nearly time for them to sail.

They had done their best to avoid giving any provocation, not only to the Dutch but to their own watchful compatriots in the English East India Company. As early as the meeting of June 30th, the council adopted a resolution: "for our general Safety that all trading be prohibited by any of us with the Inhabitants of this City of *Batavia,* or this island of *Java,* or any part of *India.* And to the End that no Person may plead Ignorance, a Protest shall be drawn up and published at the Mast of each Ship, prohibiting the aforesaid Commerce . . ."

They continued to pay exorbitant prices for everything. ". . . our Boats are not suffer'd to bring the least thing off Shore, without being first severely searched. This, tho' we pay more, will likewise hinder all manner of Traffick with any one here. Our chief Officers have also prevented it aboard, and narrowly watch our Crews; so that I doubt they'll want several Necessaries that this Place affords. This we do to avoid giving the *India* Company in *England* any Pretence to clamour against us at home, on account of our trading here without their Permission."

By the middle of September, with changeable, blowy weather, it became impossible to continue careening at Horn Island, which was exposed to the winds. Rogers and Courtney made a last attempt to see the Governor-General. They had a petition drawn up in Dutch asking permission to use the shipyards at Unrest to complete their repairs and protesting the fact that they were neither allowed to employ the Dutch carpenters and facilities needed to make the *Marquiss* seaworthy, nor permitted to put her up for sale.

The Sabandar, as usual, refused to obtain an audience for them with the Governor-General. Rogers and Courtney proceeded to the Castle anyway, accompanied by two interpreters, one of whom was Carleton Vanbrugh. And there they waited. This time the guards could not be bribed and "told us, They had Orders, that no *Englishman* should be admitted without the *Sabandar*, and that they durst carry no Paper or Message from us to the Governour-General."

The hours passed. Rogers and Courtney at least had a chance to admire the place. "In this Pallace is the Council-Chamber, the Secretary's Office and Chamber of Accounts. The Great Hall is hung with bright Armour, Ensigns, Flags, etc. taken by the Dutch here . . . Here is also a Church within the Castle, and an Armory with

Apartments for all the Artificers belonging to the Castle, which has 4 Gates, and all the Avenues well defended, the whole being surrounded with Ditches and the Works well mounted with Brass Cannon, as are the Bastions of the Town with Block-houses within the Walls, so that they can fire upon Mutineers within, as well as upon an Enemy without . . . The Governour-General lives in as great Splendor as a King; he has a Train and Guards, having a Troop of Horse, and a Company of Foot, with Halberds, in Liveries of yellow Satin, richly adorn'd with Silver Laces and Fringes, to attend his Coach when he goes abroad. The Guards are as well equipp'd as most Princes in *Europe:* His Lady has also her Guards and Train. He is chosen but for 3 years, out of the 24 Counsellors call'd Rads of *India,* 12 of whom must always reside in the City."

More hours passed. Rogers and Courtney had been waiting since early morning, and it was now well into the afternoon. Finally they gave up and went to the house of a high official, one of the Rads, who had been sympathetic to the English. This official received them handsomely and agreed they had been very unjustly dealt with, but declined to intervene, for fear of making a personal enemy of the Sabandar, a close-relation of the governor. His best advice was for them to go through the proper channels—i.e., the Sabandar, and ask him to arrange the audience they wanted.

They went back to their still leaky ships. It was time to sail, if they were to take advantage of the now favorable prevailing winds and currents in the Indian Ocean for the passage to the Cape of Good Hope. As soon as the word got out, a number of hands promptly jumped ship, "tho' we look'd upon our Hardships to be over, several ran from us here that came out of *England* with us, being stragling Fellows that can't leave their old Trade of De-

serting, tho' now they have a good Sum due to each of
them, so that their Shares are by Contract due to those
that continu'd."

In spite of the fact that the straggling fellows were
giving up their share in the loot, whatever it might amount
to, they might have had sufficient reasons. They had now
been on these ships for more than two years, and the
Indian Ocean, the South Atlantic and North Atlantic still
lay ahead—with the certainty, at least for those aboard
the *Duke,* of constant work at the pumps. That ship,
thanks to the coöperation of the Dutch, had been so inadequately careened and calked that she sprung still
another leak while still in the harbor of Batavia, two days
before the squadron sailed.

To replace the men who deserted and a number of
those who had to date died or been killed, the *Duke*
shipped seventeen Dutch sailors, and the *Dutchess* and
Batchelor about the same number each. At the last moment they were able to dispose of the *Marquiss* after all,
though hardly for what she was worth. A Captain John
Opey, commander of an English frigate recently arrived
from London, bought her for 575 Dutch dollars, "being
an extraordinary Bargain . . ."

The squadron weighed from Batavia, taking advantage of the land breeze, and proceeded to Princess' Island
in the Sunda Strait near Java Head, where it spent four
days laying in firewood and water for the passage to the
Cape of Good Hope. On October 24th it put to sea. "At
4 in the Afternoon *Java* Head bore N.E. by E. distant 10
or 12 Leagues, which being the last Sight we had of it,
from that we took our Departure."

Cape Falso was sighted a little over two months later.
On December 27th the ships let go their anchors in Table
Bay at the Cape of Good Hope, and saluted the Dutch

fort with nine guns. Rogers wrote that nothing particularly remarkable had occurred on the long passage except that a week after leaving Java Head his ship was leaking so badly that she had three feet of water in her hold, her pumps were choked and "we were in such Danger, that we made Signals, and fir'd Guns for our Consorts to come to our Relief, but had just suck'd her as the *Dutchess* came up."

There had been, of course, the usual mishaps and accidents. And there had been the same crawling food and pestilential conditions and sickness, principally scurvy again. Rogers himself continued weak and very ill and was confined to his cabin, except for rare intervals, from the time they left Batavia. The day they anchored at the Cape, the chief surgeon, James Wase, died. Sixteen other very sick men—among them Carleton Vanbrugh—were at the same time sent ashore for immediate treatment, and it was obvious that at least several of these would not survive.

Cape Town was no Batavia. "The *Dutch* have here a well built small Town, containing about two hundred and fifty Houses, with a Church, and several fine Gardens and small Vineyards near it." But if Cape Town did not provide as many pastimes and diversions as Batavia, the attitude of the Dutch here was downright friendly. During a stay which stretched into several months, about the only trouble the English had was among themselves.

The first order of business initiated by the ships' council was to make available a certain quantity of silver plate and unwrought gold and a considerable amount of gold and silver coins to pay for the supplies and services they needed. The second order of business was to sell part of their cargoes at the best possible price, to avoid exchanging too much gold and silver. They could trade at Cape Town, as they could not at Batavia, because here

the English East India Company would have no grounds
for a case that they had violated its monopoly in respect
to British subjects in the Indies. It was therefore settled
that numerous bales of goods be disposed of—particularly those that had been repeatedly soaked by sea
water and were beginning to rot.

The third order of business was another violent dis-
agreement. The general proposal had been to wait at
Cape Town until the Dutch East India Company fleet
arrived from Batavia and enough homeward-bound ships
had assembled for the frigates and their prize to proceed
in a convoy. They would need its protection again enemy
men-of-war when they reached the North Atlantic.

Rogers made a counterproposal which he submitted
to the council in the form of a letter, since he was too
ill to attend a meeting. He pointed out that it would be
still some time before the Batavia fleet arrived and weeks
more before it would be ready to put to sea again. Meanwhile, they would be forced to lie idle at Table Bay, in-
curring continued expense, the condition of their ships
not improving and the perishable part of the cargoes
rapidly deteriorating. He recommended that the squadron
sail at once for Portuguese Brazil, where the goods could
be sold at a considerably higher price than they might
bring in Holland or England and where there would be
no question of who had legal right and title to what. He
almost certainly was thinking that if the ships reached
England with empty holds and hard cash, the East India
Company would find it much more difficult to prove any
claim that its legal monopoly had been violated, and
could not, in fact, impound cash as it could cargo. This
was a point that merited very serious consideration. However, the proposal was almost unanimously turned down.
He then recommended that one of the frigates, with all
the cargo she could carry, proceed alone. That, too, was

voted down. Finally, he proposed that they at least transfer some of the galleon's riches to the *Duke* and *Dutchess*: "That if any Accident should happen to the *Batchelor*, we might have Part of her Value in another Bottom. I desir'd if any amongst them were not of this Opinion, they would give their Reasons to the contrary in Writing; but we could agree to nothing."

Dover would not even agree—so bitter had the feud become between him and Rogers—that the badly leaking *Duke* be properly careened. How could anyone like Dover ever forget what Rogers had long ago put in writing and submitted for everyone to see? "My Opinion is, That 'tis not for the Safety of the rich *Spanish* Prize, that Capt. *Dover* command her, because his Temper is so violent, that capable Men cannot well act under him, and himself is uncapable."

Cooke, Frye and Stetton were appointed as impartial observers to go aboard the *Duke* and make an inspection with the carpenters to determine what should be done. "After some Rummage, they agreed 'twould be very dangerous to attempt any thing with-in-board, and no other way but Careening would do . . ." Dover still voted against it and got a majority of the council to agree with him. They may have been considering the expense. In any case, Rogers was left to adopt such temporary measures and expedients as he could: ". . . we are forced to lie in as bad a condition as ever, only now and then mitigate the Leak with a Bonnet, which is of no long continuance in the Harbour, much less when we come to Sea."

The fact that Rogers was still very ill and confined most of the time to his quarters ashore probably accounts for the way Dover was able to ram resolutions through the council practically unopposed.

They continued to sell bales of goods—principally those from the hold of the *Duke*, where sea water had done the most damage—and Rogers disposed of twelve Negro slaves. Late in February the Batavia fleet arrived, eleven big ships bound toward Holland, and immediately began refitting. Rogers observed of Cape Town: "Amongst other Advantages, the *Dutch* have here a noble Hospital, furnished with Physicians and Surgeons as regularly as any in *Europe*; and this Hospital is capable of entertaining 6 or 700 sick Men at one time; so that as soon as the *Dutch* ships arrive here, their distemper'd Men are put ashore, and they are supplied with fresh Men in their stead. They have all sorts of Naval Stores here, with proper Officers to attend on all Occasions, which is a mighty Addition to their Strength, and enables them to preserve their *India* trade."

More arrivals and departures, among them four more Dutch ships, much damaged by storms, from Ceylon. In January the frigate *Oley*, commanded by the captain John Opey to whom they had sold the *Marquiss*, arrived from Batavia and departed ahead of them for England. Rogers sent letters by her to the owners in Bristol, to keep them informed—which later proved fortunate.

By April the fleet was ready at last, and at daybreak on the fifth the flagship of the Dutch admiral hoisted a blue ensign and fired a gun as a signal to unmoor. Rogers and the other captains had already received a strict briefing from the admiral. "About Noon I came aboard very thin, and in no better Health than I was when I went ashore at our Arrival here. Presently after I went aboard the Flag, there being a Signal made for all the *English* Commanders. We had before received our Orders, which were very particular, and as obligatory to be punctually observed."

Rogers listed the men they had left at Cape Town: four more deserters and four men who, following James Wase, Chief Surgeon, died and were buried. Carleton

Vanbrugh—who had got himself into a futile mess at Teneriffe, been disgraced for killing an Indian at Grande, was ridiculed and again disgraced at Lobos, conducted himself well and was badly burned during the battle with the second galleon, was kidnaped at Buton, and next appointed interpreter and distinguished emissary at Batavia —ended as simply a note: ". . . buried ashore here . . . Owners Agent, 3 *Feb.*" Or, at least, that is all the obituary Rogers gives him.

But Vanbrugh was not so abruptly or offhandedly interred. His obsequies were conducted with due pomp, as Cooke reported: "During our Stay here, we buried on the 12th of *February*, Mr. *Carleton Vanbrug* [sic] the Owner's chief Agent, which was done as he desir'd of me, being one of his Executors, in a decent Manner in the Churchyard, most of the *English* Gentlemen there attending the Corps to the Church, the Ships firing Guns every half Minute, as is customary on such Occasions."

So Vanbrugh, brave enough but often rash, often inept, sometimes the clown, was in fact carried to his burial like another Hamlet, to the solemn, measured pounding of cannon.

And then it was April 6th and they were homeward bound, with their prize still safe, still intact. "In the Afternoon we all weigh'd from *Penguin* Island, 16 *Dutch* and 9 *English* Ships, having a fresh breeze at S.S.E.

To take advantage of winds and currents and to avoid the dangerous coasts of Europe, the convoy steered a long course to the westward of the Azores. Dampier had observed: "But experience often shews us, that the farthest way about is the nearest way home, and so it was here. For by striving to keep near the *African* Shore, you meet with the Winds more uncertain, and subject to calms; whereas in keeping the mid-way between *Africa* and

America, or rather nearer the *American* Continent, till you are North of the Line, you have a brisk constant gale."

From the Azores, their course lay toward Ireland, then north up the west Irish coast and clear around the Shetland Islands, to avoid the sea lanes where enemy warships were operating. The convoy moved very slowly. Thirty-eight days after leaving the Cape, it crossed the Line—giving it an average speed of no more than three knots, a little more than three miles per hour. Rogers noted: "On the 14th at Noon we found we had just cross'd the Equator, being the 8th time we had done so in our Course round the World."

The galleon was the slowest ship in the convoy. "The *Dutch* Commadore was very civil to us, and because our Prize sailed heavy, he allow'd her to keep a-head in the Night, which he did not to any other Ship." By day, *Duke* and *Dutchess* frequently took turns towing her. Rogers was still very ill and his ship leaking as badly as ever. With the pumps going continually, each hand must have found some way of expressing the general fervent feeling about Dover and those who voted with him against a proper careening at Cape Town.

On the seventh of June, the convoy reached a latitude approximately midway between the Cape Verde and Canary Islands. The Dutch ships at a signal from the admiral hauled down their flags and hoisted pennants at their main-topmast heads, in order to appear more like men-of-war. Rogers has a note of admiration: "Now we draw near home, they scrape and clean their Ships, bending new Sails, so that they look as if newly come out of *Holland.*"

If Dutch seamanship was admired, Rogers also recorded, without complaint, that Dutch discipline was strict. The days of free and easy visiting between ships—

when Rogers might have a boat lowered, no matter what seas were running, to go and dine with Courtney and Cooke, or when Courtney and Cooke might come aboard the *Duke*—were over. During the entire run from the Cape, the admiral "kept an exact Discipline in the Fleet, not suffering any of the Commanders to go out of the Ships to visit each other at Sea without his Signal or Leave."

Eighty-one days after leaving Cape Town, the convoy was in 51° North and somewhere off the southwest coast of Ireland. Here it ran into thick, foggy weather ". . . so that the Flag fired two Guns every half hour; each Ship answer'd with one. This continu'd several Days, which consumed a great deal of Powder, but by the Noise of the Guns it was easy to keep Company, tho' sometimes so thick for several Hours that we could not see three Ships Lengths."

Since rounding Cape Horn, two and one half years earlier, Rogers' squadron had been continuously in climates ranging from warm to hot; now, though it was summer, there was often a chill at night and the spray of the cold blue-green North Atlantic bit and stung. By July 14th the convoy was north of Ireland, north of the Orkneys, almost to the Shetland Islands. That day they spoke with a Danish ship bound for Ireland. She informed them that the wars still continued and that a fleet of ten Dutch men-of-war was waiting as planned to rendezvous with them at the Shetlands and escort them safely down through the North Sea.

Rogers' most recent letters to the Bristol owners had been sent from Cape Town. For double precaution he now gave copies to the Danish vessel to be forwarded. The next day the convoy reached the Shetlands and its rendezvous with the Dutch men-of-war. It laid in some supplies at the islands: ". . . the Boats came to and fro all Night, and supply'd us with what we wanted." Rogers dispatched by way of a fishing boat further letters to the owners, giving them the latest information in respect to the ships' present position, meeting with the Dutch men-of-war and probable date of arrival at Texel.

Then he was treated to a fresh bit of business by his captains. Dover and Courtney and Cooke got their heads together, and, as Cooke reported, sent Rogers and his officers a peremptory message demanding that he turn over to the *Dutchess* and galleon all the "Gold, Plate, Pearls and Jewels," aboard the *Duke* and adding that if he did not comply, they would "protest against the Officers for refusing to deliver the same . . ."

Rogers, of course, refused. This was a piece of gall and impertinence which certainly outraged him, and nobody cared to press him too far, though it might have looked for a moment as if the Bristol privateers, in the middle of a Dutch fleet, would start blowing each other out of the water.

The convoy and its new escort weighed from the Shetlands on July 17th. In evidence of the power and prestige of the Dutch East India Company, Rogers noted: "The *Dutch India* Admiral, tho' but a Company's Ship, wears his Flag, and gives Signals and Orders to the *Dutch* Men of War, which is not suffer'd among the *English* . . ."

On the evening of July 23rd, convoy and fleet dropped anchor at Texel, one of the West Frisian Islands on the Wedden Zee and the principal port at the time for inbound and outbound Dutch shipping. "The Flag and all the *English* ships saluted the Commadore, and afterwards we saluted the Flag himself to welcome him in sight of *Holland*; and as soon as they got over the Bar, the *Dutchmen* fir'd all their Guns for joy of their safe Arrival in their own Country . . ."

The afternoon of the following day Rogers went up

to Amsterdam, where letters were waiting him from the
Bristol owners. He does not specify what the letters contained, except for instructions "to direct us how to act
and proceed from hence . . ."

The owners had written from Bristol on June 6, 1711,
nearly two months earlier: "sirs: we have received several
of yours from Sundry Places, particularly that of the 7th
of February last, from the Cape of Good Hope, by the
Oley Frigat, which is arriv'd in Ireland . . .

"By the Council's general letter, your Resolution
seems for Holland, unless you hear of a Peace, or meet
with an English convoy. The War continues, and Convoy
is doubtful. Upon Receipt of yours, we have consulted
and write to Sundry Friends in London, what proper
Methods must be taken, should you arrive in England. We
have also writ to several Friends in Holland, to be fully
inform'd how to proceed, should you arrive there. We
cannot yet expect Letters from Holland, but have receiv'd
sundry Advices from London; all of which confirm the
East-India Company are incens'd against us, and have
appointed a Select Committee to inspect their Charter
. . . and are resolv'd to take all the Advantages they possibly can against us. We doubt not but that you have
acted with all due Precaution Abroad, but there may be
Danger of offending at Home. Therefore we have writ
divers of these copies to several Ports, viz. Amsterdam,
Rotterdam, and five or six ports in Ireland, that it is our
opinion and Order, that at your Arrival in any Secure
Port in Holland or Ireland, you despatch any Advice, as
soon as possible, by Express or otherwise, and remain in
Port, 'till further Orders; and particularly to take Care
that nothing be landed out of your Ship or Ships, that
it may not be in the Power of any Informer to lay the
least Accusation against you; for we lye liable both to
the English and the Dutch East-India Company upon

any Mismanagement, and they are resolv'd to give us all possible Disturbance. And since it has pleas'd God to bless you and us with probable Success, after your long and dangerous Voyage, and since all your Company, from the Captain to the lowest Mariner, will have a good Interest therein, we doubt not but that you and they will be all unanimous to preserve their own and our Interest, and not commit any rash Act to expose and hazard the whole . . . We do recommend it to you, that you read this Letter and Order to your respective Crews, that everyone may be appriz'd, that if either Officer, Sailor, or any who shall come Aboard of you, do carry any Goods ashore, for Sale or otherwise, the whole is forfeited and lost; and no doubt, but there will be some employ'd by the East India Company to insnare some of you, who will use all imaginable Art for that Purpose. God send you safe to your discharging Port, that we may have a joyful Meeting, is the Desire and Prayers of Your Loving Friends . . ."

There had been several big English East India ships from Mocha and Bengal in the convoy from Cape Town, and relations between them and Rogers' squadron had, under the strict, vigilant eye of the Dutch admiral, remained friendly. The English East Indiamen were now about to sail for England with a Dutch convoy. On the evening of August 4th Rogers had information that some of the Bristol owners were at Den Hilder, just across from Den Hoorn on Texel. The following day the owners came aboard, and there were prolonged and intense conferences. "After a short Stay they went for the *Dutchess* and *Batchelor*, designing thence for *Amsterdam;* we welcom'd 'em with 15 Guns at their coming and going; the *English East-India* Ships and others bound for *England* weigh'd with the *Dutch* Convoy to Day, having a fine Gale at N.E.

On the 6th we weigh'd from the *Texel,* and went up to our Consorts, it being by a particular Order from the Owners for our better Security . . ."

It was well for their security. The owners brought news. The English East India Company had set in motion due legal processes to grab everything, down to the last bale of goods and the last piece of eight, that the *Duke* and the *Dutchess* had won in their three-years' voyage.

The formal resolution, according to the "Minutes of the Court of Directors of the East India Company," was "that the Court will seize the two Privateers of Bristol, called the *Duke* and the *Dutchess,* and their prize called the *Batchelor,* together with their cargoes." But the formal statement was more or less anticlimactic. Long before that, the Company had been busy, as far back as Cape Town and even as far back as Batavia. The moment the Bristol ships reached Texel, it immediately dispatched twelve of its agents to Holland to report any sale there of the cargoes in whole or in part.

The Bristol owners had not been idle themselves. As soon as they learned of the Company's intentions, and long before its formal resolution was adopted, they petitioned the Lord Treasurer of England and the Attorney General to intervene on their behalf. The timing was on their side, at this point. Some months earlier the Whig Ministry, partial to the East India Company and partly controlled by it through its subsidizing of ministers and candidates for Parliament, had fallen. Through the humble conniving of the Queen's new friend, Mrs. Masham, Harley had literally mounted the back stairs of the palace, to become in March, 1711, Lord Treasurer of England, then the highest office under the Crown.

Harley had no particular love for the East India Company, and was, therefore, on the side of the Bristol owners. His Attorney General dispatched a letter point-

ing out, among other things, that the Bristol ships had
operated with legality throughout, that they held commissions from the Lord High Admiral, that they had done
no trading or trafficking in the Indies except to obtain
essential supplies, and that they had only taken the route
home via the Indies because the ships were in no condition to attempt a second rounding of the Horn. Finally,
in an attempt to apply a little pressure, he informed the
Company that if it persisted in its attitude, the owners
would be forced to sell everything for cash in foreign
markets.

He might as well have dispatched his letter into a
barrel. The Company's directors simply replied by asking
him to convey word to the owners that their explanation
was not satisfactory. It referred the matter to its Committee of Lawsuits.

In Holland the owners got busy. They came down
from Amsterdam to Texel on August 10th. An abstract of
the voyage had been drawn up, and now officers and men
went before a Notary Public who took their affidavits
"that what was therein contain'd was true to the best of
our Knowledge, and that we had been at no other Places
than therein mention'd."

Two days later the ships' council met and resolved
to make available a certain amount of gold in order to
purchase necessary supplies in Amsterdam and to issue
officers and crews an advance pay allowance. The very
next day this resolve was changed, perhaps under some
prodding from the owners. "On the 13th we went away
for *Amsterdam,* but did not carry any Gold out of our
Ships, upon Consideration it might be prejudicial to the
Insurance made on our Ships, if we took any Value out,
and an Accident should afterwards happen . . ."

The muddying of the water had begun, and from

this point on neither Rogers' account nor Cooke's help much to clarify the financial transactions. This was the big game now, the really serious one, and they had no part in it. The mere officers and men who had survived everything to take these ships around the world, who had captured and brought home all the treasure everyone was grabbing for, were simple amateurs; now the competent men of affairs took over.

One captain, however, was conspicuously qualified to join them: Dr. Dover. He was ashore again and an owner among owners, the second biggest one of all. He no longer needed to maneuver or raise a quorum on any ships' council; he no longer could be insulted and shunted aside by Rogers and others as a captain in title only, unfit to command at sea. And, indeed, in the subsequent negotiations at Amsterdam, whatever they were, obscure as they were, he appears to have distinguished himself. Lord Drummond, an agent of Harley, now Earl of Oxford and Mortimer and Lord Treasurer, was sent to Holland during this period and reported that "one Captain Dover allias Doctor Dover seems to be the man of Sense and Conduct in all that affair."

Lord Drummond was not the only one who, in addition to the Bristol owners and the representatives of the East India Company, hurried over to Holland. In August there also arrived from England a lawyer named Stephen Creagh, whose only interest, oddly enough, was in promoting and prolonging whatever litigation he could. Creagh persuaded 209 members of the crews to sign a paper appointing him their legal representative and awarding him for his commission a modest 5 percent of whatever they got. Rogers was against the men signing. He and the crews and everyone else concerned lived to regret that they did.

There was a concerted attempt to play down the

value of the captured galleon. When he came to publish his book, Rogers inserted—in a chapter describing Mexico which immediately follows his account of the galleon's capture—the statement: "I must here observe, that the Ships which come from *Manila* use to be richer than our Prize; for she waited a long time for the *Chinese* Junks to bring Silk, which not arriving, she came away with a Cargo mix'd with abundance of coarse Goods." Unfortunately this does not exactly tally with an itemization of the galleon's cargo which Cooke published in his own book.

They had other news at Texel beside that of threats, writs, litigation and financial juggling—news that took them back more than two years and half a world away.

At Texel, Rogers met Captain Stradling, the privateer who had commanded the *Cinque Ports*, consort of Dampier's *St. George*, and had cruised the South Sea for a period with Dampier in 1704. It was he, of course, who marooned Alexander Selkirk on Juan Fernández. Stradling told Rogers that the *Cinque Ports* did not sink with most of her crew, as had long been supposed, but was run aground on an island, he and his men being captured by the Spaniards. The long years Selkirk spent on Juan Fernández, Stradling spent in prison at Lima. He escaped once and performed the formidable feat of sailing more than two thousand miles northward in a canoe, and almost reached Panama, "intending to cross the Isthmus and get to *Jamaica* by some of our trading Sloops . . ." He was recaptured and shipped back to Lima, where he was closely confined in a dungeon and threatened with a life sentence in the mines.

Stradling, who had only recently been returned to Europe on an exchange of prisoners, gave other news of long ago and far away. He was able to tell Rogers, for example, about the phantom ship the squadron had sighted off the Falkland Islands, which they had supposed to be a big French vessel homeward bound: an apparition they had chased and lost in the mist and found again and that had then unaccountably outrun them; an apparition in those desolate waters that brought a superstitious shiver. And perhaps, in view of her own troubles, she had been a kind of omen. But she was solid enough, for all that: a big French ship, as they had at first supposed, only not homeward bound. She had tried to round the Horn, been beaten back, and, when Rogers' squadron sighted her, was headed with her sick and dying for Rio de la Plata in Argentina to recruit. Later, she made the rounding and reached Lima; and it was on this same ship that Stradling—long after the *Duke* and *Dutchess* finished their business in the Great South Sea—had finally returned to Europe. Rogers' only comment on this solution of a mystery more than two years old and always worrisome was, "Had we been able to come up with her, she must certainly have been our Prize."

Stradling had further riddles to resolve. The avenging enemy squadron which Rogers and his captains had always expected just over the horizon, from which they had run and dodged and hidden but never sighted, had indeed been on their track. Three weeks after the long-expected English frigates hit Guayaquil, the news reached Lima and pinpointed their position. Three Spanish and two big French men-of-war immediately armed out and sailed north. If this squadron had proceeded to Gorgona, it would have caught Rogers' ships on the heel; and perhaps it did eventually proceed there, but, of course, there were a lot of places and a lot of ocean to search, and by the time the enemy warships reached Gorgona, if they ever did, Rogers and his men had long gone.

Or most of them. Simon Hatley and the others on the bark that disappeared around a headland in the dismal

Galápagos one fine day had not, after all, vanished into the enchanted air. He and his men, lost and without water for fourteen days, finally reached the mainland where they encountered "a barbarous sort of People, who are a mixed breed of *Negroes* and *Indians*. They voluntarily surrendered themselves, being in a starving Condition, yet these brutish People, instead of giving them Food, tied their Hands, then whipp'd and hang'd them up, so that they must unavoidably have lost their lives; had not a Padre, who liv'd in the Neighbourhood, came time enough by good Providence, to cut 'em down and save them. There are several Letters from Mr. Hatley since, which signify that he is a Prisoner at *Lima.*"

As a contrast to the treatment Hatley and his men received from the natives, Stradling was able to report that before leaving Peru he had met several of the Spaniards who had been Rogers' prisoners and that "they all own'd we had treated them very civilly, which has in part taken off the bad Impression they had conceiv'd of the *English* in those Parts; for not being used to War, they account all alike that come to cruize, because of the unheard Cruelties and Debaucheries which were committed about 25 years ago by the Buccaneers in those parts, which their Priests did improve to give them an ill Idea of all those they think fit to call Hereticks, not considering that most of those disorders were committed by *French* Buccaneers of their own Religion."

Stradling was not the only one at Texel with information about the past. Rogers met a sailor who had been on the *Bigonia,* the bigger galleon, when they engaged her off Cape San Lucas. This sailor said she had suffered heavily in the engagement and arrived at Acapulco much disabled. That she was well-armed and well-manned by competent fighting men Rogers and everyone else knew from experience. What he learned now was that her defense had been made even more desperate because of the fact that the master gunner had stationed himself in the powder room after taking an oath on the Sacrament to blow up the ship if she were successfully boarded. So netting-decks and close-quarters or not, whether the English squadron had attacked early and in full force, as Rogers had wanted, or not, there never was a real chance of taking her. Boarders and boarded alike would have gone high into the blue air and then on down into the depths. The English officers and crews could think now that the failure and mismanagement at the time had actually been their luck.

Meanwhile, at Texel, the principal business of buying and selling, jockeying and juggling, the shuffling of accounts and concealment of assets went on, or did not go on, according to later divergent testimony and possibly bought evidence.

On August 23rd the owners again came down from Amsterdam, this time to cross-examine the prisoners and get everybody's story straight about the taking of the Manila Galleon and the other prizes: "having Notice of our going over for *England*, and that a Convoy was appointed to come for us."

It had been decided to let the frigates and the galleon proceed to England, in spite of the fact that three of the owners had recently requested a personal interview with the directors of the East India Company to arbitrate the matter, and had been refused. The directors' best word had been that "if you will lay any Proposals before the Court in writing, they will give a speedy answer in writing, and are very inclinable to do anything that is reasonable in order to bring the Riches aboard these Ships to England. And no advantage shall be taken on either side. But in case no agreement be made all papers to be destroyed."

On August 31st a Mr. Hollidge, one of the busiest and most efficient of the owners, was back aboard. "We got all the Men off Shoar, who had been very troublesome to the Owners at *Amsterdam*"—no doubt through the activities of lawyer Creagh—"and everything in Readiness for Sailing . . . Mr. *Hollidge* came aboard (the rest of the Owners being gone over for *England*) and took Account of what Plate, Gold, Pearl, etc. was in the Ship. The same being done aboard the *Dutchess,* he likewise took a List of our Men to get Protections for them, from being impress'd after our Arrival in the River of *Thames.*" This was considerate. Unlike the crews of merchants' ships, who after one or two years at sea might be seized by the Royal Navy when within sight of their home port, the crews of privateers were not lawful game for impressment.

Finally, late in September, the frigates and the galleon sailed from Holland with four men-of-war sent from England to convoy them. The men were exceedingly pleased, having been at Texel "in the utmost Uneasiness of our long Stay, being just at Home, so that we had much ado to keep the Companies aboard till now."

On October 1, 1711, the ships anchored in the Thames' estuary. Several of the owners immediately arrived, reëxamined each ship and took some prisoners ashore to record fresh statements and affidavits. An agent of the English East India Company, a man named Spencer, who had been posted to watch for the privateers and their prize, rushed word to London.

Duke, Dutchess and galleon proceeded up the Thames and came to anchor at Erith on October 14th. The captains closed their logs and Cooke and Rogers their journals. The East India Company gave its agent, Spencer, three fellow employees to assist him in seizing the ships. Since this expeditionary force was not even allowed aboard, it was reduced to throwing onto the deck of each ship the following note: "We seize this ship and all goods aboard for the use and on behalf of the United Company of Merchants of England to the East Indies."

17

THE TUMULT
AND
THE SHOUTING

ROGERS CLOSED HIS BOOK with an entry: "*Octob*. 14. This
Day at 11 of the Clock, we and our Consort and Prize got
up to *Eriff* [sic], where we came to an Anchor, which
ends our long and fatiguing Voyage."

The Bristol privateers had been gone nearly three
years. Of the original complement of 330-odd officers and
men, a little more than a hundred had died or been killed;
and, even so, no long voyage with such a proportionately
small cost in lives would be made until much later in the
century.

They had accomplished everything they set out to do, had taken twenty enemy vessels, held a city to ransom, circumnavigated the globe. They brought home with them what had never been seen in the Thames before, never before seen in any European waters, the Manila Galleon. Only once before, as everybody knew, had a Manila ship ever been taken, by Cavendish in the days of Elizabeth, and Cavendish did not bring that one back with him. But there she was now, fabulous, incredible, riding at anchor in the Thames, two or three miles southeast of London.

They had a right to expect the fame and the solid rewards. And they did receive a measure of public acclaim; even after the general applause faded out and they were no longer a sort of nine-day wonder, their fame among those who could understand and appreciate what they had done continued. But as for any signal honors and solid awards, they landed in the law courts; and they were there a good long time.

The claims of the English East India Company turned out to be only a part, or only the beginning, of their troubles. The Company was fat and formidable. From the time of its incorporation under a Royal Charter granted by Queen Elizabeth, the profits had been rarely less than a hundred percent. From Charles II it had received five additional charters, giving it the right to acquire territory, to exercise civil and criminal jurisdiction, coin money, command troops, build fortresses, wage war and make peace.

But powerful as it was, it could be circumvented. For one thing, it had no legal grounds at all for its claims against the Bristol privateers and their owners; but that, of course, hardly mattered. What was more important, the owners had strong friends in the new government and, much more important still, they had recourse to the great instrument of bribery—an instrument which was almost universally effective at that time and which the directors of the company were congenitally unable to resist. To cap it, the directors had already tentatively applied to Doctors' Commons for an opinion on their chances in court, and had been informed that legal action would be unwise.

Dover and five of his colleagues set to work in London. They entertained extensively at taverns and coffee houses and other places of amusement—so extensively that the largest shareholder, Thomas Goldney, was moved to cry out for agony and loss. He issued a protest, listing expenditures by Dover and his colleagues totaling 10,000 pounds—equivalent to perhaps $200,000 today—among the items being "bribes to Custom House officers."

The East India Company took a bribe of 6,000 pounds, little enough for it, but apparently enough. Goldney complained that this sum "was weakly parted with," and he was further incensed that Dover's group paid an agent of the Company a bribe of 161 pounds to persuade the directors to accept a bribe.

At any rate, the scheme worked: the East India Company withdrew. Then, the Company of Silk Throwers and Throwsters, seeing how much money was being tossed around, entered a claim based on an act passed during the reign of William III which imposed a duty of 15 percent on all silk from the East Indies. The owners got the claim dismissed by proving that the silk goods on board their ships and the prize had all been made in Spain. How they were able to do this remains a mystery—particularly in view of the fact that Cooke published a list of the galleon's cargo which included, among a lot of other valuable things, "Chintz, divers sorts—24289 . . . Silk Stockings—4310 pairs; Silk raw of China—28502 pounds; Ditto thrown—11990 pounds; Ditto Sewing—

1370 Pounds; Ditto Bengal—61 Pounds; Ditto Sleve—
6581 Pounds," etc., etc. It also should have offended almost anyone's reason to think that even the Spaniards,
who could have shipped goods directly across the Atlantic, would have shipped them all the way around the
world to Manila for transhipment to Mexico—quite aside
from the fact that the Manila Galleons were always and
primarily "silk ships" and it was on the goods from China,
Japan, India and the Indies that the whole commerce
depended. Presumably, however, most of the evidence
had by now vanished, along the way at Cape Town and
Texel and, most recently, from the London warehouses.

The East India Company had settled with the owners. The claim of the Company of Silk Throwers and
Throwsters had been thrown out. Now it was lawyer
Creagh's turn. Acting ostensibly on behalf of "The poor
South-Sea Sailors" but actually on behalf of himself, he
began filing suits and claims. Another year passed. Finally, the Lord Chancellor ruled that the prize goods
should be sold and that one-third of the proceeds should
go to the seamen and two-thirds to the owners. He also
ruled that Creagh was entitled to receive a commission
only from those crew members who had actually signed
a paper appointing him to represent them.

The majority of the goods, or the majority that remained, was sold at public auction and the proceeds
amounted to £147,975 12s. 4d. A neat, tidy and exact
figure that might be comparable to almost three million
dollars today. However, there is and was no accounting
of what goods were previously disposed of, what figures
juggled, what assets concealed, what profits siphoned off.
Later estimates of the actual profits of the voyage have
ranged from 200,000 pounds to 800,000 pounds. It may
be remembered that even as far back as Gorgona the ap-
proximate value of what the ships then had aboard, was,

as Cooke wrote: "In Gold, Plate and Jewels amounted to about £20,000 and in Goods at £60,000." And that, of course, was before they even captured the real prize, the galleon. The seamen were under the illusion that the profit ran into the millions of pounds, an estimate they presented in a subsequent petition.

At any rate, the owners were not satisfied. They objected to the fact that all the bribes and expenses of entertainment and the cost of all the lawsuits and countersuits were to be deducted from their share, and they therefore appealed against the Lord Chancellor's decision.

First they claimed that the crews were not entitled to storm money for the taking of Guayaquil, because Guayaquil had been "abandoned by the enemy." It might have been of interest to the men on both sides who were killed or wounded in that operation to learn that the place had not been defended. The claim was finally disallowed on the basis of Dover's evidence and Courtney's, who were not only among the owners but entitled to storm money themselves. The owners then asked that the bribe to the East India Company be proportionately deducted from the crew's share. This appeal, too, was denied.

It was now 1714, three years after the ships had completed their voyage, and the crews had still not been paid. Thirty-three of the seamen petitioned the House of Lords, accusing Creagh of deliberately prolonging the litigation solely in his own interest and accusing their commanders of having sold much of the prize cargoes abroad. The House of Lords declined to intervene because the case was still in the High Court of Chancery.

Fourteen more months passed. A second petition, longer and more explicit, was drawn up. Described as The Humble Petition of the Poor South-Sea Sailors, it was read before the House of Lords on August 31, 1715. After stating that the owners had "entered into Articles under their Hands and Seals, dated the 10th of *May*, 1708, to grant the Officers and Seamen, who should Enter with them for the Voyage, one Third Part of the Value of the Prizes and Treasure that should be taken (to be divided into proportionable Shares amongst them) and then to have no Pay; or else to have half Purchase and half Pay, as they should think fit to Enter . . ." the petition then enumerated the principal prizes, and made the wildly extravagant claim that the true value of the goods and treasure taken from the enemy amounted to "Three Millions Sterling, or Thereabouts, the greatest Part whereof consisted in Gold, Silver and Precious Stones."

That wasn't all. The sailors were convinced "a farther immense Treasure might have been taken, had they not been withheld by the Cowardice or Corruption of their Chief Officers from Storming the large and rich City of *Guyaquill*, when they first came before it, which they were desirous to have done, but were restrain'd from it for about two or three Days."

During this period, the petition noted, the citizens were busy burying their assets in the jungle or sinking them in the river; the sailors claimed that after the capture of the town, the inhabitants "declared to the Men, That at their first coming before the Town, There were therein Five Millions of Pieces of Eight of King *Philip's* Money, besides a vast Treasure belonging to the Merchants and other rich Inhabitants."

Next came the embezzlements abroad, beginning at Batavia, where the chief officers "took divers Chests of Plate (of many Hundred Weight a Piece) out of the *Duke* and *Dutchess*, and putting them on Board several Ships there, belonging to the *English East-India Company*, sent them whither they thought fit.

"At *Batavia* they stay'd about three Months, and the like at the *Cape of Good Hope*, at each Place breaking

Bulk, and selling and disposing of their Prize-Goods (at the latter in open Ware-houses) without having Condemn'd their Prizes in any Court of Admiralty."

And at Texel, of course, the embezzlements were even worse, what with the owners coming over like a flock of crows to descend on the harvest. The seamen, obviously, had an exaggerated idea of the profits of the voyage. But behind the language of the petition with its extravagant claims and accusations there is a plaintive note of desperation as the noncommissioned officers and seamen saw everything on which they had counted so much, for which they had gambled and fought and gone through such hell, slipping away from them. "Notwithstanding," said the petition, "such their Embezzlements Abroad may be esteem'd to amount to the Value of near Two Millions, Sterling, yet was the *Aquapulca* Ship, with her Cargo, worth about a Million, Sterling, at her arrival at the Port of *London,* besides what Treasure they had on Board the *Duke* and *Dutchess*—and after all, they have brought to Accompt (for the Whole) no more than the Sum of 148,700 £ or thereabouts, That not being a Fifteenth Part of the Value of the said Prizes and Treasure so taken; as, is not doubted, it would appear, were the Matter thoroughly Examin'd into."

The seamen pointed out the years all the suits and cross-suits had dragged out in the High Court of Chancery, "until the present Lord Chancellor (lately) put an end thereto." So it was apparently settled. "But there being nothing in either of the Bills requiring a Discovery of the true Value of the Prizes taken, or of what Embezzlements had been made of the same; the Matter thereof being chiefly concerning the Right of Agency, and who should have the Fingering of the Money; no Benefit has accru'd to the poor Officers and Seamen . . ."

But it was a lost cause; it was all water over the dam

by now. After hearing out the poor South-Sea Sailors, the Lords "Ordered y° s⁴ petition be Rejected."

So the legitimate, rock-bottom accounting of a sum of £ 147,975 12s. 4d., which no one could effectively dispute and in which no one apparently believed, was finally divided—two thumping thirds to the owners, one third to the officers and men, and of that slice the individual poor South-Sea sailors got much the least. It was understandable.

So much for the cash. There remained the credit for what they had done, the general acclaim, the possible dream of luxuriating at ease in coffee houses or taverns and regaling a rapt audience with the story of that voyage. But not many, after a few months, were listening.

The first volume of Captain Edward Cooke's account, *A Voyage to the South Sea and Round the World,* was published in London in 1712, and enjoyed some success. It apparently preceded the publication, also in 1712, of Woodes Rogers' *A Cruising Voyage Round the World.* (Rogers notes in his first edition that "Since I advertis'd my publishing this Book, the Booksellers have thought it their Interest to hurry out a continuation of Cooke's Voyage; in which they have attempted at the Views of several Harbours and Sights of Land in the South-Sea" etc.)

Rogers' book, being better written, wittier and much more informative, if somewhat less clear concerning the actual chronological sequence of events, had a much greater success. It became, in fact, the most popular book of voyages in England at the time. Elford's Coffee House, for example, immediately displayed a copy or copies for free reading in order to attract trade. The book ran into three editions, and was published abroad in French and Dutch translations.

Addison and Steele and Defoe paid attention, and

so did numbers of literate ladies and gentlemen and many men of prominence and position. But as far as the general public was concerned, the chief and most lasting impression of this voyage was that it confirmed, or appeared to confirm, good news about the possibilities of trade in the South Sea. That opened up a new way to get rich quickly by wise speculation and helped precipitate a rush to invest in a bubble that nearly wrecked the economy of England.

An opening sentence in Cooke's second volume, dedicated to Lord Harley, begins: "The great and wealthy Countries lying along the South Sea, being the object on which the Eyes and Thoughts of all Men are at present fixed . . ." Rogers, dedicating his book to the surviving Bristol owners, said: "I make no doubt it will be to your lasting Honour, that such a Voyage was undertaken from Bristol at your Expence; since it has given the publick a sufficient Evidence of what may be done in those Parts, and since the Wisdom of the Nation has now agreed to establish a Trade to run the South-Sea which, with the Blessing of God, may bring vast Riches to Great Britain."

Callander, who was to some degree an authority, wrote fifty years later: "I might, perhaps go too far should I assert that this voyage gave rise to the South Sea Company, but this much I can safely say, that the success of this voyage was what the patrons of that company chiefly insisted upon in their defence, when the plan of it was attacked as insufficient and chimerical."

The time, of course, was ripe. The middle and upper classes were not only prosperous, they were gripped by a frenzy for speculation that approached the compulsive and insane. There were companies for making salt water fresh, "for making Butter from Beech Trees," "for extracting Silver from Lead." There was a company capitalized at one million pounds "for a Wheel for perpetual Motion."

"Puckle's Machine Company" was set up to revolutionize the art of war by making both round and square cannon-shot and bullets, the round shot to be used against Christians, the square against the Turks. There was a company for "furnishing Funerals to any Part of Great Britain" and one "for assuring of Maidenheads." An entrepreneur of formidable gifts announced a company "for carrying on an Undertaking of great Advantage; but nobody to know what it is." He opened an office in the morning, by afternoon had sold one thousand shares of stock at two pounds a share, by nightfall was gone with the cash to the Continent.

All these companies combined—and there were some eighty-six of them whose operations the Lords Justices terminated shortly before the collapse of the really big bubble—were as nothing compared to the South Sea Company.

Founded in 1711 under the auspices of Harley, the South Sea Company was regarded as a Tory institution, the primary object of the government in the matter being the restoration of public credit. To this end the merchant-promoters assumed part of the national debt, in the amount of 10,000,000 pounds for which the government agreed to pay them six percent interest plus a further substantial sum annually for charges of management. The company was granted a monopoly of trade to South America and the South Sea, and prospered—particularly after the War of the Spanish Succession ended in 1713 with the Peace of Utrecht, when Spain granted various concessions and, by the Assiento treaty, gave the company a monopoly on the slave trade to South America. There were rumors that Spain would cede to England four ports on the coasts of Chile and Peru. Rogers and Cooke, Courtney and Dampier and Dover had confirmed the desire of the Spanish colonists to trade. Everyone with a pound to invest could see himself getting rich on the exchange of English goods and manufactures for the gold and silver of Mexico and Peru.

The prospect was so fascinating and irresistible that practically nobody paid any attention to the soundness of subsequent developments. After some complicated maneuvering, during which it outbid the Bank of England, the South Sea Company took over the entire national debt in return for due interest and other considerations and got a law passed by the Commons and the House of Lords to that effect in 1720. The lid was off, the bubble airborne and expanding as it rose.

A large part of the debt consisted of annuities—money lent to the government in return for a fixed income for life. The directors felt that most of the holders of annuities could be persuaded to exchange them for shares in the company, which they planned to issue at a high premium and so liquidate a good part of the debt at the cost of a relatively small amount of stock. The directors were right.

At the beginning of 1720, stock sold for 128½, by May it had climbed to 550. In June it reached 890, in July 1050. It was now selling at nearly 1000 percent of par. Steele had written: "As this Company grows rich, this Nation must grow poor. . . . The Stock of the South Sea rose 50 per cent in one hour's Time, which, by the Year, is 8760 Pounds per cent, and that . . . comes to £ 17,520,000,000,000. I am considering at this Rate, in what time the Company may purchase the terraqueous Globe, Gibraltar and Minorca included." In July, at the peak, the directors dumped five million shares. The bubble popped.

Innumerable people were ruined; dukes, barons and baronets; lawyers, doctors, clergymen, merchants, tradesmen, spinsters and widows. Those who had held annuities with the assurance of a comfortable fixed income for the remainder of their natural lives saw both principal and interest vanish into thin, blue air. Many were reduced to penury and even starvation. And among those who lost everything was one of the captains—believing, perhaps, too much in his own glowing accounts and his unalterable luck—who sailed with the *Duke* and *Dutchess*: Thomas Dover.

But, of course, if the long litigation and the indirect effects on the South Sea Bubble had been the only results of this voyage, it would have been forgotten entirely within the space of a very few years.

Rogers and his captains and most of the others who started out on the voyage were certainly driven by a desire for fame and fortune. They were also motivated, many of them and particularly Rogers, by the desire to serve their country in hitting her enemies where it would really hurt and, above all, in proving that it could be done by others to follow: that the Great South Sea need no longer be the private property of the King of Spain but that Englishmen, if properly prepared and commanded, could cruise and trade and explore there more or less at will.

They had proved that. They had established not only strategy and tactics but brought back a great deal of completely new, detailed information as well. Cooke wrote in his second volume, in respect to the financial success of the voyage: "Nor is this the only Advantage of our Attempt, having improv'd the Knowledge of those Seas and Coasts; not only by our own Experience but by bringing Home the *Spanish* Manuscript Coasting-Pilots, taken on Board their Ships, being the only Accounts to be rely'd on, by such as shall hereafter sail into these Parts, all our Adventurers having barely touch'd at some few Places, and never so much as seen the most; whereas these are Descriptions approv'd by the constant Practice of about 200 years that Nation has been trading to all the Ports along that Coast."

In spite of showing what could be done and the way to do it, all that came of their efforts was a miserable and mismanaged expedition that sailed from Bristol in 1719. It consisted of two frigates, *Success* and *Speedwell*, commanded by Captains Clipperton and Shelvocke, and they were out to raid the western coasts of Spanish America and capture another Manila Galleon.

The captains feuded; the crews were often mutinous and distrusted their owners, citing the example of the way the "poor South-Sea Sailors" before them had been treated. Shelvocke deserted Clipperton while they were still in the South Atlantic. The two ships rounded the Horn separately some weeks apart. Shelvocke, following at a good safe distance, eventually lost the *Speedwell*— after having been holed in a couple of engagements, she drove on the rocks of Juan Fernández and foundered.

Out of the wreckage he and his men constructed a cranky bark, captured a large Spanish merchantman and transferred to that vessel. Off the coast of Mexico he encountered Clipperton again, and an attempt was made to patch things up between the captains and organize some plan to try for the Manila Galleon. They couldn't agree to anything. Clipperton, in his turn, deserted Shelvocke and sailed for China. He eventually lost the *Success*, returned home aboard a Dutch East Indiaman, and died a few weeks after reaching England.

Shelvocke had earlier committed an act of plain piracy off the coast of Brazil; now he committed another by taking a large Spanish ship though peace had long since been signed between England and Spain. He and his men sailed the new prize to China, where Shelvocke sold her, falsified accounts, pocketed most of the profits, and returned to England with, it was said, some £7,000, little or none of which his owners and his former crew ever saw. He was arraigned and tried on two counts of piracy, acquitted for lack of evidence, according to one account, or, according to another, escaped from King's Bench Prison; in any event, he left England for a number of years.

There was one more curious note. In a book he wrote to justify his conduct on the voyage, he mentioned, in passing, that he had visited California and found gold there; but nobody paid much attention.

Though most of the officers and men of the *Duke* and *Dutchess* did not live to know it, their voyage did eventually produce many of the results they had hoped for, and it had other, far-reaching effects they could not possibly have anticipated.

Certainly the King of Spain's ocean was never the same again after them. What they had done was remembered and studied in various important quarters; it was clearly remembered when England for the fourth time in that century was engaged against France and Spain, in the War of the Austrian Succession, and the Royal Navy decided that what the Bristol privateers could accomplish, it could do better.

Lord Anson, then a commodore, sailed for the South Sea in 1741 under admiralty orders. He commanded a large unwieldy squadron poorly prepared and equipped, through no fault of his, and he carried with him a copy of Rogers' book.

Anson, after severe losses in men and ships, tried for the Manila Galleon, missed her, and then in his one remaining ship, the *Centurion,* sailed west across the Pacific and intercepted off the Philippines the Manila-bound vessel from Acapulco. She was a richer prize than Rogers had taken because she was laden with almost nothing but

Mexican gold and silver. When the *Centurion* reached England again and anchored off Sheerness, it required thirty-two oxcarts guarded by Royal Marines to convey the treasure to the Tower of London. There is one brighter contrast with the Bristol privateers; the Crown forwent its claims and rights, and the money—amounting to 500,000 pounds (maybe ten million dollars or more today)—was divided entirely among the few officers and men who survived the voyage.

But Anson's expedition, in view of the cost in lives and ships, was not as successful as Rogers'. Anson set out with six of His Majesty's ships, with a combined armament of 234 guns and a complement of 1683 men. He had, in addition, two supply ships, each one nearly as large as the *Duke*. He returned with one ship and less than 200 men. Anson could not be blamed. He was the victim of admiralty graft, of strangling red tape, of crooked contractors, political thieves and hopeless procedures. His ships were badly fitted and worse manned.

Yet Anson had learned from Rogers. He learned much more, of course, from his own voyage and his long years of service, and when he became Lord Admiral, he initiated those measures which transformed the Royal Navy from what it was at that point to what it became during the Napoleonic Wars. And, long after Anson's voyage, men still remembered the Bristol privateers.

But that was only part of it. After the raiders came the explorers and discoverers. Rogers had written: "I have often admir'd that no considerable Discoveries have yet been made in South Latitude from *America* to the *East Indies*: I never heard the South Ocean has been run over by above three or four Navigators, who varied little in their Runs from their Course, and by consequence could not discover much. I give this Hint to encourage our *South Sea Company*, or others, to go upon some Dis-

covery that way . . . there being a vast Surface of the Sea
from the Equinox to the South Pole, of at least 2000
Leagues in Latitude that has hitherto been little regarded . . ."

After Anson, then, came James Cook and his great
discoveries in the Pacific, and after him others. And still
the upsurgings, the effects continued; they spread out
and out in time to influence men of talent and men of
genius in many distinct and various professions. The voyage and the men who made it, particularly Dampier, were
studied by Howe and Nelson and Humboldt and Darwin.
The works and the lives of the Bristol privateers provided material for Swift and Steele and Coleridge; and in
Selkirk, Defoe found the inspiration for his most famous
book, *Robinson Crusoe.*

~~~~~~~~~~~~~~~~~~~~

18

FIN-OUT

SAILORS SAID of a dying whale when it surfaced, rolling and lashing the water with its fins, that it was "fin-out." The voyage of the *Duke* and the *Dutchess* had long since ended; there remained the fin-out or fate of the men who made it.

Captain Edward Cooke disappears. He must have received a certain share of the proceeds eventually, in addition to whatever advances he was given along the way; but after the publication of his book, everything is obscure—where he went, what he did, what happened to him—until 1732, when the September issue of the *Gentleman's Magazine* carried, under an obituary of his former

commander, Rogers, a brief reference to "Capt. *Cooke*,
lately drowned."

Captain Courtney's share of the profits of the voyage
was undoubtedly large. He was second to Rogers in command of the entire expedition. He must have profited, if
any of the commanders profited, by the transactions at
Batavia and Cape Town and Texel. He had his share with
Rogers—deducting the portion they had agreed to give
the crews—of the cabin plunder. He had his share in the
one-third part of the profits allotted to the officers and
men, plus his share of the storm money, plus—what was
even larger—his share of the two-thirds part awarded to
the owners. He apparently retired to an estate at Bristol.
Thereafter, one bubble drifts up—or maybe more like a
mist, an exhalation among his grottoes and gardens—to
indicate he is still there. In the *London Gazette* of July 5,
1715, a Mr. Pyne, postmaster of Bristol, undertook to pay
two guineas reward plus expenses for the return to Captain
Stephen Courtney of a Negro, aged about twenty, "having
three or four Marks on each Temple and the same on
each Cheek." And that is all of Courtney.

Simon Hatley left, if only indirectly, a more lasting
imprint. After his curious disappearance among the Enchanted Islands, he and his men reached the mainland,
were captured subsequently and spent some years in
prison at Lima. Hatley, after considerable efforts made on
his behalf by the Bristol owners, was apparently released
following the Peace of Utrecht. At any rate, he was back
in England in 1719, in time to sail with Clipperton and
Shelvocke as Shelvocke's second in command on the
Speedwell.

Later, in the South Sea, Hatley and shipmate Betagh
were detailed to a Spanish prize and deserted Shelvocke
or, as Betagh claimed, were deserted by him. Shortly
thereafter, the Spaniards captured them and, it is re-

corded, were extremely displeased to find Hatley again on their hands. His subsequent fate is obscure, and may well have been highly unpleasant.

But before that, Hatley had done something trifling and irrelevant whose effects, in the long run, would prove a good deal more lasting. Shelvocke reported that when the *Speedwell* was rounding the Horn: "We all observed that we had not had the sight of one Fish of any kind, since we were come to this southward of the Straits of Le Maire, nor one Sea-Bird, except a disconsolate black Albatross, who accompanied us for several Days, hovering about us as if he had lost himself; till Hatley, observing in one of his melancholy Fits, that this Bird was always hovering near us, imagined from his Colour, that it might be some ill Omen. That which, I suppose, induced him the more to encourage his Superstition, was the continued series of tempestous Winds, which had oppressed us ever since we had got into this Sea. But be that as it would be, he, after some fruitless Attempts, at length shot the Albatross, not doubting, perhaps, that we should have a fair Wind after it."

Nearly eighty years later, William Wordsworth, happening to read Shelvocke's account, suggested to his friend, Samuel Taylor Coleridge, that there might be an idea somewhere in all this. There was an idea indeed.

Hatley's contribution was indirect, of course; it consisted of a single act which provided Coleridge with the crime for his Ancient Mariner to commit.

The imprint of Alexander Selkirk, the Hermit of Juan Fernández, was more direct and unmistakable. He sat, without knowing it, for his portrait in what has been called the first English novel—over the years the most widely read work of fiction in the language, except one. But, in fact, this is not truly Selkirk's portrait at all: it exaggerates the features and fixtures, it diminishes and even misses the man. Nevertheless, there he is, in some shape or fashion, and it is as Robinson Crusoe he is remembered today.

Rogers, of course, had given a clear, concise account of Selkirk's experiences on Juan Fernández, and Rogers' book was widely read. Daniel Defoe had a copy in his library and relied on it later. Then, following the publication of *A Cruising Voyage Round the World*, a catchpenny pamphlet appeared with a title beginning "Providence Displayed, or a very surprising Account of one Mr. Alexander Selkirk." This tract was a verbatim reprint of the account Rogers had given, with the addition of an introductory paragraph. Selkirk was already on the way to becoming famous.

And before that, Selkirk had dined with Rogers, and Rogers' friend, Richard Steele, who two years later devoted to him the twenty-sixth issue of *The Englishman*, published on December 3, 1713. The issue begins: "Under the Title of this Paper, I do not think it foreign to my Design, to speak of a Man born in Her Majesty's Dominions, and relate an Adventure in his Life so uncommon, that it's doubtful whether the like has happen'd to any of the human Race. The Person I speak of is *Alexander Selkirk*. . . . It was a matter of great Curiosity to hear him, as he is a Man of good Sense, give an Account of the different Revolutions in his own Mind in that long Solitude. When we consider how painful Absence from Company for the space of but one Evening, is to the generality of Mankind, we may have a sense how painful this necessary and constant Solitude was to a Man bred a Sailor, and ever accustomed to enjoy and suffer, eat, drink and sleep, and perform all Offices of Life, in Fellowship and Company."

There follows a description of his first months after being marooned, a little about his period of black depression and emergence from it, and the subsequent serenity of his life on the island. The issue concludes: ". . . there was a strong but cheerful Seriousness in his Look, and a certain Disregard to the ordinary things about him, as if he had been sunk in Thought . . . The man frequently bewailed his Return to the World, which could not, he said, with all its Enjoyments, restore him to the Tranquillity of his Solitude. Though I had frequently conversed with him, after a few Months Absence he met me in the Street, and though he spoke to me, I could not recollect that I had seen him; familiar Converse in this Town had taken off the Loneliness of his Aspect, and quite altered the Air of his Face.

"This plain Man's Story is a memorable Example, that he is happiest who confines his Wants to natural Necessities; and that he who goes further in his Desires, increases his Wants in Proportion to his Acquisition; or to use his own Expression, *I am now worth 800 Pounds, but shall never be so happy, as when I was not worth a Farthing.*"

In any event, this one short article by Richard Steele in *The Englishman* came considerably closer to the heart of the matter and what was to prove, in a sense, Selkirk's tragedy than Defoe did in his whole book.

Selkirk himself, having unwittingly served as a model, did not simply vanish, at least not at this point. Just as after leaving Juan Fernández he had gradually grown accustomed to shoes again, to ship's diet and ship's stores, to pills and purges, to the smell of gunpowder and blood and to that overcrowding which now and then only intensified a feeling of essential isolation, so now ashore the last sense of that kind of fundamental freedom, that inner attention, seems to have collapsed. He was subject to periods of profound depression and was sometimes found weeping. At other times he seemed to have reverted, at least briefly, to the kind of conduct that in his youth, just before he ran away to sea, got him hauled up before the kirk-session for indecent behavior in church. In the records of the Court of Queen's Bench, Bristol, there is a process against "Alexander Salkirke" of St. Stephen's parish, Bristol, "Nauta," for having assaulted one Richard Nettle, shipwright, on the twenty-third of September, 1713.

Wherever he was, wherever he went, he never ceased to look back on Juan Fernández with longing and despair. "Oh, my beloved Island! I wish I had never left thee! I never was before the man I was on thee! . . . I have not been such since I left!" His attempt to recapture it by retiring to a cave in the valley of Keil's Den near his native Largo in Scotland did not work either. He shortly burst out of his cave and ran off to London with a girl named Sophia Bruce. Selkirk may or may not have married Sophia. In any event, he certainly did marry, sometime before 1720, a Frances Candis or Candia, who claimed what estate he had to leave. After the last marriage he went to sea again, either by preference or necessity, and shipped October 20, 1720, as Master's Mate on H.M.S. *Weymouth*. A little over a year later, off the west coast of Africa, he was entered in the *Weymouth's* paybook as "dead 12. Dec. 1721."

Cowper wrote a poem of sorts, and Branwell Brontë, brother of Emily and Charlotte and Anne, composed some undistinguished verse on Juan Fernández. Defoe, of course, did better; and, thanks to Defoe's book, Selkirk now has a big, gratifying bronze plaque on the island where he once piped and danced with his goats and his cats.

Dampier, too, sat for his portrait, in an odd sort of way, in *Gulliver's Travels*, as has been noted. But he did a lot better than merely to provide a kind of model. He left his own works to be read, studied and enjoyed. Quite apart from any use that was made of him, he was enough in himself.

Three years after his return from the voyage, he celebrated his sixty-third birthday, in September, 1714. He was an old man now, worn out by nearly half a century of adventuring and exploration. In an age when one long voyage might incapacitate a man for life, he had made many: three times around the world, four times to the South Sea, once to the icy waters of Newfoundland; to the Indies, to coasts of Australia never before seen by any European. Who alive had a record to match it?

In his sixty-fourth year he made his will, beginning: "I, Captain William Dampier, of London, Mariner, being diseased and weak in body, but of sound and perfect mind and memory, (praise be God therefore) considering the frailty and uncertainty of this transitory life, and that as nothing is more certain than Death, so nothing is more uncertain than the time of Man's dissolution, do therefore make and ordain this my last Will and testament in manner following . . ."

He was then living in the parish of St. Stephens, Coleman Street, and being cared for by his cousin, Grace Mercer. He made her his executrix and bequeathed her nine-tenths of his estate, the remaining tenth to go to his "loving brother, George Dampier . . ."

Like the rest of the officers and men, he waited for the settlement of the long litigation to receive what he was owed. He put in a claim for "eleven shares equal in value with those due the ship's company," plus "1/16th part of the nett profits," plus interest on the profits, dating from the time the owners had divided their shares among themselves. The sum he asked was substantial but does not appear to have been excessive.

He never received it. He was long gone to Fiddler's

Green before the case was settled. His executrix, Grace Mercer, did not receive it either; the Master of Chancery finally disallowed the claim. She was awarded, after sums advanced to Dampier had been deducted, twenty pounds.

Dampier was not penniless during his last years, as he had been after most of his other voyages. A schedule of payments made to him shows a share of the plunder money, advances at Batavia and in Holland, a substantial advance from one of the owners, John Corsley, and another advance from the Master of Chancery. In addition, he borrowed from friends against his expectations. These advances and loans amounted to more than 2000 pounds. Dr. Johnson said, later in the century, that a man could subsist on six pounds a year and even enjoy a degree of comfort on thirty pounds. So Dampier, during the time he had left, must have lived fairly well and at ease, if not in the affluence he had expected.

It was not what he wanted. He wanted a fortune, and searched for it from the time he was a log-wood cutter, from the time he shipped with the buccaneers. But it was not that, really, though he sometimes complained in his writings of lost chances for a fortune—some lost through almost incredible bad luck, some lost through the lack of vision or stupidity of his associates.

He had wanted fame, and he had gained that through his writings; but he was lapsing now into obscurity, and his fame would not be requickened until posterity acknowledged its debt to him as a navigator and hydrographer and explorer and naturalist.

If Dampier in his last years declined into a quiet obscurity, Thomas Dover's fate was almost exactly the opposite. In the course of his long life, and he lived to be eighty, the bombastic doctor became increasingly a center of controversy. Very few people who had any dealings with him remained neutral; many he managed merely to alienate, and he succeeded in turning even more into feverish enemies.

At first after his return, while waiting for the settlements of the long litigation, he lived fairly quietly in London—though he was apparently given to frequenting coffee houses and boasting of his exploits. Some years later, when he published his *Ancient Physician's Legacy to his Country*, he stated with his usual modesty: "When I took by storm the twin cities of Guaiaquil, under the line in the South Seas . . ."

He was not pressed for cash. As one of the owners he had already received some share of the profits of the voyage, prior to the final settlement. Furthermore, he had money of his own and a comfortable estate at Barton-on-Heath in Warwickshire. He practiced medicine merely as a hobby. In fact, he was not legally permitted to practice for fees in London or within an area of six miles around it because, although a graduate of Cambridge and Oxford, he had not troubled himself to become a licentiate of the College of Physicians. That did not bother him, as yet.

Viscountess Dupplin, writing to her aunt, the Countess of Oxford, said: "There is a famous man in town called now a doctor, who undertakes to cure the smallpox a new way; I believe you may have heard of him by the name of Captain Dover. He came here with the Agripulca ship in the Queen's time . . ." He was indeed becoming famous, and he lived as he pleased.

When, in 1719, all the suits and countersuits had finally been settled in the Court of Chancery, Dover received his part of the profits of the voyage. This included what was due him as the second largest shareholder, plus fees for acting as physician to the voyage, plus "storm money" for taking part in the capture of Guayaquil, plus plunder money, plus a sum for commanding the captured

Manila Galleon. In all, it came to an official 6,689 pounds, more than double the sum he had originally invested and a fortune itself at that time. And there is always the reservation, as with the rest of the owners and the principal officers, that it did not include whatever specie, goods and treasure had been secretly diverted and discreetly apportioned earlier.

Dover proceeded to sink all this, and more, in stock of the South Sea Company. For the time being, the stock continued to rise very satisfactorily. Dover, who was then residing in Cecil Street, near the Strand, made a leisurely trip abroad, crossing Europe to Asia Minor.

When he returned home, it must have seemed as if all the hounds of hell had been abruptly let loose. Stock in the South Sea Company all at once skidded, dropped from 1000 to 500, to 200. Dover tried to protect his investment by pouring in more money, all he could raise. He mortgaged his estate at Barton-on-Heath, house, acres, farm and farm buildings, everything. He had complete confidence in his own judgment that the South Sea Company was sound, would survive and eventually prosper even more spectacularly.

By November, 1720, three short months after the peak, shares in the South Sea Company were selling at 135. It became apparent even to Dover that it would be a long, cold winter, or several long, cold winters, before the fundamental soundness of his financial opinions could be demonstrated. Meanwhile, there was the simple, perplexing problem of money to live on, and he was forced to return to the practice of medicine. But in order to practice in London he had to be licensed by the Royal College of Physicians; he therefore applied for admission to the college in January, 1721. After several months during which various essential documents, including his diplomas, were lost or misplaced, he learned that he would be admitted as a licentiate, provided he passed the necessary examinations. For a man who had studied medicine six years at Oxford, thereafter received his diploma from Cambridge, been a house student of Sydenham, and had behind him, best or worst of all, some thirty-five years of clinical experience, this, too, must have been trying. He had, however, no choice, and doggedly set to work, passed all the necessary examinations and late in September, 1721, was proposed by Sir Hans Sloane and duly elected a licentiate of the College.

He was now in the business of medicine in London and its greater area but not, being Dover, for long. Five months after his election to the licentiate, he became embroiled with the institution in general, and one of its Fellows, a Dr. Wagstaffe, in particular, who charged him with unprofessional conduct for treating one of Wagstaffe's patients without proper consultation and blamed him for the patient's death.

Dover got off fairly lightly, being merely admonished by Sir Hans Sloane and the College Censors. However, this incident and the admonition became coffee-house gossip and hurt his practice. In addition, he was at war with the apothecaries, as usual, and the apothecaries refused to refer any patients to him. Eventually, he gave up and went back to Barton-on-Heath, but his stay there turned out to be brief and dismal.

First, his wife died. Then, as a result of the liabilities he had incurred during the desperate attempt to protect his investment in the South Sea Company, he was forced to sell his mortgaged house, lands and farm buildings to pay his creditors. He was left, when everything had been settled, with about 140 pounds. After all that time and all that voyaging, after all his efforts before and earlier, he was now widowed, homeless and nearly bankrupt.

He took refuge with his wife's relatives, the Tracys,

who had a fine estate and manor house, Stanway Hall, in Gloucestershire. He remained there two years, but not idly. Dover, obviously, was tough; he had lost almost everything, he was now nearing seventy, and he was not just about to give up. During the time he stayed at Stanway Hall, he kept professionally busy treating an epidemic that spread through the district for most of that period. He wrote later: ". . . I was called to several homes where eight or nine persons were down at a time; yet did not so much as lose one patient where I was concerned." If, of course, he did not lapse into weakness, he never lapsed into modesty either.

He left the Tracys and tried to rebuild a practice in Bristol without much success, though he appealed to Sir Hans Sloane and others to send him patients. Meanwhile, he had written a book. It was brief and to the point. Essentially a self-advertisement or exercise in public relations, it proved to be a tremendous success, in spite or because of its staggering title: *The Ancient Physician's Legacy to his Country, being what he has collected in Forty-Nine years' Practice: or an Account of the Several* DISEASES *incident to Mankind, described in so Plain a Manner, that any Person may know the Nature of his own Disease. Together with Several Remedies for each Distemper, faithfully set down.*

When this book was completed, Thomas Dover set out, at the age of seventy, to try London again. *The Ancient Physician's Legacy*, published in 1732, went into two editions that year, and the year following into five, two of these probably being pirated inasmuch as the author's name is misspelled. Eventually there were eight editions; the book was translated into French and widely read on the Continent.

Its popularity may have been largely due to the fact that it included within its hundred and fifty pages so astonishingly much. There were violent condemnations of many existing treatments and remedies, of the apothecaries and of his fellow physicians. There were some sound prescriptions, some novel forms of treatment, some efficacious remedies. There were testimonial letters from grateful patients and a number of tributes from Dover to Dover for his accomplishments. There were anecdotes and curiosities and dubious statements such as: "The Mahometan Women in the Greater Part of Asia destroy one testicle; no doubt they find their account in it because males make their addresses more frequently when there is less expense of spirits at each evacuation." He damned his colleagues for multiplying remedies in order, by enriching the apothecaries, to gain their favor in the matter of referrals. He damned the whole faculty of Physicians "who like Moles work underground, lest their practices should be discovered to the Populace."

Dover was back in the limelight and, as usual, embroiled. He was a pioneer in advocating inoculation for smallpox. He tried to popularize cold baths for certain skin conditions. He recognized, better than most of his contemporaries, the palliative and therapeutic value of remedies derived from opium. He prescribed quinine only for malaria and not, as did most of his contemporaries, as a sort of cure-all.

But Dover, like Sydenham, was addicted to bleeding his patients, often excessively and particularly in most cases of infectious fevers. And he developed a fanatical conviction about the therapeutic value of mercury, which he prescribed in such massive doses for so many different diseases that he was known in his time, and has gone down to posterity, under the cognomen "Dr. Quicksilver." He prescribed it as the miracle agent for such assorted afflictions as scrofula, asthma, syphilis, elephantiasis, scorbutic ulcers, acute appendicitis, sterility and worms.

While any number of patients were apparently able and willing to swallow considerable amounts of heavy mercury, almost none of his colleagues was prepared to do as much for Dover's claims. Lamentable incidents were cited, such as the case of a lady who had taken a large dose of quicksilver. It passed through her abruptly. She inadvertently and uncontrollably discharged the load while she was dancing the minuet, or, possibly, a gavotte. As the shimmering pellets rolled across the polished floor, a number of gallant gentlemen stooped in a hopeless effort to retrieve the baubles, under the misapprehension, much to the lady's embarrassment, that she had broken her necklace.

Once more famous and having stirred up for the last time as much hell as he possibly could, Dover retired at the age of eighty and went back to Stanway Hall, to whose owner, John Tracy, he had dedicated his book.

Like most physicians of the time, he subscribed to certain alchemical notions (he considered a concoction of dried toads to be an unparalleled specific for asthma), but he also compounded the remedy by which he is still remembered today. Originally intended as an analgesic for gout, his powder contained an amount of opium unusual even for that period. However, he buffered its dangerous effects by combining it with ipecac. His knowledge of opium he got from Sydenham, and of ipecac from Helvetius; but nobody before had thought of combining them. Dover's powder is now used as a diaphoretic; and in World War II it was standard issue with the Italian army, if that is any recommendation.

Dover died at Stanway Hall in 1742, and was buried in the Tracy family vault. No plaque or headstone now exists.

Woodes Rogers did not survive the voyage as long as Dover—very few did—and if he never again accomplished anything as spectacular as the command he held in his thirties, he did enough.

His book, under the title of *A Cruising Voyage Round the World,* had been published in 1712 with maps by the famous cartographer Herman Moll. It was translated into French and Dutch under the titles: *Voyage autour du Monde, Commencé en 1708 et fini en 1711,* and *Nieuwe reize naa da Zuid Zee, van daar naa Oost-Indien, en verder rondom de waereld.* He was famous now both for his book and, to the curious, as the commander who "took the Acapulco Ship." Men like Addison and Steele and Sir Hans Sloane became his close and lifelong friends; they influenced his subsequent career, and when he was not with them, he corresponded with them extensively.

In 1713, to improve his fortunes while the long litigation still dragged through the courts, he went to sea again, as captain of a 460-ton, forty-gun merchantman, the *Delicia,* bound for Madagascar to pick up slaves and sell them in the East Indies. The voyage was largely financed by his old opponent, the East India Company, and its primary object, naturally, was to make money. The secondary object was to confirm the possibilities of getting rid of the pirates on Madagascar and establishing a stable colony there. This idea for another venture combining patriotism and profits seems to have come to him when the *Duke* and *Dutchess* were still in Cape Town in 1711.

He put in at the Cape, renewed old acquaintances and began a correspondence with the Dutch Governor-General at Batavia, in whose antechambers he had once waited so long for a hearing. The *Delicia* then proceeded to Madagascar, where Rogers completed his survey and picked up a full complement of slaves, who were subsequently sold for a fine price at Sumatra, to the immense satisfaction of everyone except the slaves themselves. A number of his former subordinates and crewmen on the *Duke* and *Dutchess* insisted that Rogers also put in later at Batavia, to retrieve various goods, cash, jewels and valuables which he had embezzled during their voyage and prudently cached among the Dutch. Anything was possible.

Rogers was back in England by 1715 and certainly, on any count, no poorer. In addition, his eventual share of the profits from the voyage of the *Duke* and *Dutchess* has been estimated at 14,000 pounds. This seems high for an "official" figure, considering that Dover, with all his subordinate shares plus the larger percentage due him as the second principal investor, is recorded as receiving less than 7,000 pounds. But, of course, none of the official figures include possible hidden assets and secret dealings along the way; and whatever Rogers finally realized from his cruising voyage, it was certainly a small fortune. He was at last able to retire in considerable comfort to his fine residence on Queen's Square, then the most fashionable quarter in Bristol.

Retirement did not suit him; he was still young and ambitious. First, he advanced his proposal for a settlement of Madagascar. That came to nothing. Then, in the summer of 1717, he submitted to the Lords Commissioners of Trade a careful and comprehensive plan for colonizing the Bahamas and stamping out piracy; many of the costs to be underwritten by himself and partners in return for certain proprietary rights and reimbursements.

The Bahamas were strategically placed. Their settlements had repeatedly been attacked and stripped by the Spanish and French. The absence of any order or proper government was bad enough—what was worse, the islands, particularly New Providence and its town of Nassau, had become the headquarters of piracy in the

Caribbean. Vane, Blackbeard, Rackam, Horningold and any number of others made it a base for operations, and as a result British West Indian trade had just about come to a standstill.

Furthermore, the Caribbean was not only a breeding place but also a training school for pirates. Those who learned enough about navigation and command to become deep-water pirates headed for richer sea lanes—notably the Indian Ocean, where they preyed with complete impartiality upon the shipping of Britain, France, Spain, Portugal, Holland and the Grand Mogul. One alumnus of the Caribbean, Bartholomew Roberts, commanded a whole pirate fleet and boasted of having taken some four hundred tall ships.

Merchants in England had been clamoring for years without result. Now in a concerted effort they put heavy pressure on Whitehall, and Whitehall was forced to act. It accepted Rogers' proposal. He was backed by some of the "most considerable merchants of London and Bristol" as being in "every way qualified for such an undertaking." He was also, and even more decisively, recommended by Addison, then Secretary of State, and so in due course appointed "Captain-General and Governor-in-Chief in and over our Bahama Islands in America." The Crown assigned him, as he had requested, a hundred troops for a garrison and an escort of two men-of-war.

As a final measure, the Crown issued a proclamation dated September 5, 1717, pardoning all pirates, whatever their crimes, who surrendered before September 5, 1718. For those who refused to take the King's pardon and persisted in their disorders after the deadline, a bounty was posted; it ranged on a sliding scale from a hundred pounds for each commander—two hundred pounds if he were actually brought to trial and convicted—down to twenty for "every Private Man."

The first copies of this proclamation were dispatched to the West Indies aboard a vessel which, like almost every other vessel sailing that way except ships of the line, was promptly captured by pirates. As soon as they were able to decipher the document and its legal language, they began to quarrel among themselves. Half of Rogers' work, it would seem, was already done. Moreover, in addition to his force, other punitive expeditions, on a somewhat smaller scale, were being prepared to proceed against Jamaica, Barbados and the Leeward Islands. The word was out: take the King's pardon or die by gunfire, cutlass and the rope.

Rogers sailed from England on April 11, 1718. He had agreed to pay the cost of feeding and maintaining his garrison of a hundred troops on the condition that he be reimbursed by the Treasury at the rate of sixpence per man per day. That was standard procedure. He also purchased from the Lords Proprietors of the Bahamas a lease on the quit rents and royalties there for a period of twenty-one years—a lease which he later assigned to a small group of speculators and investors. Rogers was about to break the back of piracy, establish a pattern for colonial administration, restore British West Indian trade, and ruin himself.

His ship and the two escorting men-of-war dropped anchor off Nassau, capital of the Bahamas, at nightfall on July 25th; and since the pilot decided not to venture over the bar until daybreak, Rogers blockaded the harbor. During the period of waiting it was learned that all of the pirates on New Providence were willing and ready to take the King's pardon, except Vane. Vane, with ninety men, issued an ultimatum of his own. When this was ignored, he launched a fire ship which scattered the men-of-war before she blew up. Under cover of this spectacular diversion, Vane and his men escaped in a sloop. He was caught later and hanged at Jamaica.

The murdering Captain Teach, or Blackbeard, who lit short fuses of sulphur in his tarry hair and beard and sometimes shot down his own officers for no reason except to teach everyone a proper respect, also refused the royal clemency. He had, however, sailed from Nassau before Rogers' arrival and not long after was engaged in Ocracoke Inlet off the coast of North Carolina by one of His Majesty's sloops, whose commander, a young Lieutenant Maynard, boarded him, fought the giant in a prolonged hand-to-hand duel in the best traditional manner, and at last skewered him and cut off his head.

All other captains and companies in the Bahamas took the oath meekly. When Rogers stepped ashore, the brotherhood even had a guard of honor drawn up to salute him. There were still, however, a lot of pirates in the Caribbean who had no intention of reforming.

After a public reading of the royal proclamation and of his commission, Rogers put everybody to work, clearing and repairing the overgrown and disused roads, rebuilding the ruined fort and mounting new cannon. He appointed a governing council consisting of six responsible individuals he had brought with him from London and six of the local inhabitants who, if not responsible, had at least never been pirates. He organized companies of militia to patrol the streets at night, and to encourage settlement offered everyone a free half-acre of ground, provided the settler cleared it and built some sort of house within a reasonable time. And there all promising things ended.

The two men-of-war departed. The Admiralty, it appeared, was not much interested in any really effective attempt to end piracy. Rogers wrote in a letter to Steele: "Every capture made by the pirates aggravates the apparent inclinations of the Commanders of our men-of-war; who having openly avowed that the greater number of pirates makes their suitable advantage in trade; for the

Merchants of necessity are forced to send their effects in the King's bottoms, when they from every part hear of the ravages committed by the pirates."

Rogers was left with his small garrison and an unreliable population of a few hundred people, while some two thousand pirates still cruised the waters around him. The town itself was pestilential at that period and stank with hides stretched rotting in the sun. Rogers and the majority of his officers fell ill. Most of the industrious settlers he had brought with him—Swiss, German, Huguenot—on whom he had counted for the island's development, sickened and died during the first months; nearly all the immigrant carpenters and bricklayers died.

Provisions ran low, and a sloop under the command of a redeemed pirate, John Augur, who had long ago taken the King's pardon, was dispatched to obtain beef, pork and rum. Augur and his crew promptly went on the account, captured two trading vessels and headed for Hispaniola. They were wrecked on one of the uninhabited Bahamas. When Rogers got word of it, he sent an armed sloop after them and appointed as her captain another former pirate and one of the most famous of all—Benjamin Hornigold, under whom Blackbeard had once served. Hornigold could be trusted not to break his oath, and shortly returned to Nassau with his ex-comrades and some loyal sailors they had marooned on a desolate island.

If Rogers allowed the renewal of piracy to go unpunished, all hope of establishing order in the Bahamas would collapse. He convened a Court of Admiralty and after a trial which was noted by one contemporary as conspicuous for it fairness, ten of the pirates were condemned to be hanged. Taken to the gallows, some of them delivered speeches declaring that far from being repentant for not having lived better lives, they were sorry they had not lived even worse ones. They ended on a shout urging the four hundred former pirates who attended the execution to kill Rogers and save them. Nobody stirred.

Rogers had restored order. But his own position became steadily more impossible. He had to pay, out of his own pocket, for all clothing and supplies at extravagant rates. Moreover, some months after he took office as governor, the War of the Quadruple Alliance erupted, and he had to maintain—in addition to the guardship *Delicia,* the fort and the garrison—a sizable force of armed men to defend the island against a Spanish attack. The attack, when it finally came, in February, 1720, fizzled out.

Nevertheless Rogers, in preparing for it, had been compelled to spend what were then enormous sums. During the single year 1720, as he wrote to London, he paid out more than 11,000 pounds just for the maintenance costs of the *Delicia* and the fort. In the course of nearly two years he had received from the Admiralty and the Lords Commissioners of Trade no ships, no supplies, no reinforcements, no funds, no reimbursement for all he had spent, not even any word.

As a last resort, he decided to return to England to plead in person the case of the colony. He arrived at Bristol during the second week of August, 1721, and proceeded to London, deeply in debt and broken in health. He got a hearing and nothing more. In spite of covenants, contracts, agreements and promises, he received no pay and no recompense for all he had spent. He and his partners had sunk some 90,000 pounds in the Bahama venture; his own fortune was gone and the partners were apparently unable or unwilling to reimburse him for anything at all. He had already been superseded in his post as governor of the Bahamas.

His appeals, including a petition to the King, brought no results. The troubles piled up and he was for a time in debtor's prison. Finally, his creditors came to his rescue with a plan to meet the emergency; he obtained from his former partners 1500 pounds as a sort of token reimbursement for his losses; this sum he turned over to the creditors, who, with more generosity than most of his friends had shown, gave him back 400 pounds for the support of himself and family, while they put through an act of bankruptcy to keep him from going to debtor's prison again.

On the allowance from his creditors, plus whatever small sums he was presumably able to borrow, he managed to struggle through the next few years. He was on the beach, as Dampier had been earlier. And then the ebb was over. In 1727 a board of eight generals, reviewing his case and considering that he had been, to say the least, unjustly treated, awarded him a retirement on half-pay, as a "Captain of Foot." The pay did not amount to much, but it was something and, in addition, the board made it retroactive to 1721—so he must have received an accrual that improved his position substantially.

There was another and very promising development. His successor as governor of the Bahamas, a man named Phenney, and the unofficial governor, Mrs. Phenney, conducted themselves in such a way that everyone began howling for their removal. After much petitioning Rogers received his reappointment as Captain-General and Governor-in-Chief, this time with a salary of 400 pounds, and sailed for Nassau on May 26, 1729. On the eve of his departure for New Providence, Hogarth painted a picture of him, his son and daughter, in a family group against a background of the fort at Nassau, behind him a shield with the legend: *Dum Spiro, Spero,* "While I breathe, I hope."

His second tenure of office as governor was considerably different from the first, but not altogether. The pirates were gone, a chapel was built, the motto he gave the Bahamas still stands: *Expulsis Piratis. Restituta Commercia—* and even if there is still some question as to whether the pirates have ever been entirely expelled, commerce was, and has been, unquestionably restored.

He had restored order in the Bahamas; he proceeded to install constitutional government. In place of the former council, he governed with an assembly of twenty-four citizens who were elected by the inhabitants. Unfortunately, the inhabitants had not changed much. The Speaker of the Assembly did everything possible to block all of Rogers' proposals for the improvement of the colony, and at one point proceedings became so disordered that Rogers was forced to dissolve the legislative body he had set up. He died at Nassau on the fifteenth of July, 1732, still some years younger than Dampier had been when Dampier set out with him around the world.

Dampier's long-range contribution through his books and his voyages was the more lasting, as it was probably the more important; but he could never have accomplished the things Rogers did. He lacked Rogers' ability to command men, to plan an action or a campaign and proceed decisively, to exercise authority as an administrator and executive; he did not have in the same degree as Rogers an understanding of, and insight into, the nature of those around him.

As for the "poor South-Sea Sailors," when their case was finally settled and the owners forced to disgorge, the survivors received approximately fifty pounds per man. This for a voyage that lasted three years followed by five years more of litigation. Very few could have been able to subsist ashore long enough to collect.

A contemporary historian, writing at the time of William and Mary, said that soldiers and sailors, together with more than half the working population, were not paid enough to support themselves and their families and had to rely on begging and stealing or poor relief.

12*

Many of the survivors among the crews, crippled by wounds and rheumatism and pulmonary ailments, must have wound up in the jails or on the gallows, since stealing almost anything was a capital offense. Most of the rest must have been driven to ship before the mast again, either by economic necessity or by being clouted on the head.

The press gangs did not depend on getting sailors drunk in taverns or giving them knockout drops. In the quiet of the evening, or often in broad daylight, they stunned and hurried away almost any able-bodied citizen who seemed too humble and unimportant for his disappearance to cause any real trouble; and experienced seamen were, of course, at a premium.

Obviously, however, some of the "poor South-Sea Sailors" must have lived and been around to collect their shares. And even after so long, even as disproportionate a reward as fifty pounds represented something.

But with many of the sailors what money they got went fast; it went on women and punch and flip and gambling, sometimes in a few days. For them there was nothing left but to ship out again; no choice but the sea again and the maggoty food, the overcrowding, the guns jumping and bulkheads painted red, scurvy and broken bones, the darkness and cold and drenching hell of the wooden walls for what time remained.

Among the amphora and marble statues on the floors of another sea lie encrusted skeletons. And in the great depths, at the bottom of the oceans, in the radiolarian ooze, only sharks' teeth and the earbones of whales resist disintegration.

Phlebas the Phoenician, a fortnight dead,
Forgot the cry of gulls, and the deep sea swell
And the profit and loss.

A current under sea
Picked his bones in whispers. As he rose and fell
He passed the stages of his age and youth
Entering the whirlpool.
Gentile or Jew
O you who turn the wheel and look to windward,
Consider Phlebas, who was once handsome and tall
as you.

Captains and officers and men, all of them who made that voyage, are long gone from the seas, of course; but the seas retain them. The land has changed: wildernesses they visited are now inhabited, many landmarks and promontories have crumbled and washed away. But the giant Cape Horn graybeards are still rolling and rising and cresting against the hurrying overcast; the deep upswellings of the cold Peru Current are the same, and the waters around the black, enchanted Galápagos are the same and so are the heaving immensities of the misnamed Pacific. The objects of the pursuit have changed but not the nature of it, not the illusion or the price men pay or what they are finally able to bring home and what comes of it—supposedly attaining the unattainable, ambitiously crossing and recrossing on the strong planks of reason, so to speak, with courage and faith and endurance and intelligence, all that is shifting, unstable and unpredictable, a universe still unknown and perhaps finally unknowable.

There are Alexander Selkirk's last words to Steele, remembering Juan Fernández: "I am now worth 800 Pounds, but shall never be so happy, as when I was not worth a Farthing." He did not mean it in any ordinary sense, and he might have added, if he had known the lines: . . . *la sua volontate è nostra pace,* "His Will is our peace"—something he had found and lost and did not find again in that life.

Sources of Quotations

Bibliography

ADAMS, W. H. DAVENPORT. *Good Queen Anne*. 2 vols. London: Remington and Company, 1886.

ANON. "The Old English Seaman." *Harper's Magazine*, LXVI (January 1883), 231-232.

ANON. "The Most Precious Jewel in the King's Crown." MS report on the Philippine Islands, Manila, 1673. Trans. from the Spanish. As quoted in Catalogue 442, pt. III. London: Maggs Bros.

ANON. "Proposals to Increase Seamen for the Service and Defence of England." Folio broadside, c. 1695. Catalogue. London: Maggs Bros.

ANSON, LORD. *A Voyage Round the World in the Years 1740-1744*, ed. Richard Walther. London: Dent, 1911.

ASHBURN, P. N. *The Ranks of Death*. New York: Coward, 1947.

ASHLEY, MAURICE. *England in the Seventeenth Century: 1603-1714*. London: Wyman and Sons, 1956.

BANCROFT, HUBERT HOWE. *The New Pacific*. New York: Bancroft and Sons, 1900.

BARNETT, LINCOLN. "The Enchanted Isles." *Life*, XLV, X (September 8, 1958).

BEAGLEHOLE, J. C. *Explorations of the Pacific*. New York: Macmillan, 1934.

BEEBE, WILLIAM. *Galápagos: World's End*. New York: Putnam, 1924.

BELL, BENJAMIN. *A System of Surgery.* 4 vols. Worcester: Isaiah Thomas, 1791.

BETTMAN, OTTO L. *Pictorial History of Medicine.* Springfield, Ill.: Charles C. Thomas, 1956.

BINGHAM, HIRAM. "Further Explorations in the Land of the Incas." *National Geographic Magazine,* XXIX, v (May 1916).

BLEWITT, MARY. *Surveys of the Seas.* London: McGibbon and Kee, 1957.

BOLTON, H. E., and H. M. STEPHENS. *The Pacific Ocean in History.* New York: Macmillan, 1917.

——. *Outpost of Empire.* New York: Knopf, 1931.

BONNER, WILLARD HALLAM. *Captain William Dampier.* Palo Alto: Stanford University Press, 1934.

BOSTELMANN, ELSIE. "Monster and Midget Squid and Octopuses." *National Geographic Magazine,* LLXVII, ii.

BOWEN, FRANK C. *Men of the Wooden Walls.* London: Staples Press Limited, 1952.

BOYD, WILLIAM. *Textbook of Pathology.* Philadelphia: Lea and Febiger, 1938.

BROOKS, E. ST. JOHN. *Sir Hans Sloane.* London: The Batchworth Press, 1954.

BROWN, ALFRED. *Old Masterpieces in Surgery.* Omaha: privately printed, 1928.

BROWN, BEATRICE CURTIS. *Alas Queen Anne.* Indianapolis: Bobbs, 1929.

BULKELEY, JOHN and JOHN CUMMINS BULKELEY. *A Voyage to the South Seas.* New York: McBride, 1927.

BURNEY, JAMES. *A Chronological History of Discovery in the South Sea.* London: Allen and Unwin and Company, 1803-1817.

——. *The Buccaneers of America.* London: Swann Sonnenschein and Company, 1891.

CALDER, RITCHIE. *Medicine and Man.* London: G. Allen, 1958.

CALLANDER, J. *Terra Australis Cognita: Voyage to the Terra*

Australia, or Southern Hemisphere. Edinburgh: A. Donaldson, 1768.

CARERI, JOHN FRANCIS GEMELLI. *A Voyage Round the World.* Vol. IV of *A Collection of Voyages and Travels.* London: Awnsham and John Churchill, 1704.

CARRITT, E. F. *A Calendar of British Taste from 1600-1800.* London: Routledge and Kegan Paul, Ltd., 1948.

CARSE, ROBERT. *The Age of Piracy.* New York: Rinehart, 1957.

CARSON, RACHEL L. *The Sea Around Us.* New York: Oxford, 1950.

CASTIGLIONI, ARTURO. *A History of Medicine,* ed. E. B. Krumbhaar. New York: Knopf, 1941.

CHARNOCK, JOHN. *A History of Marine Architecture.* London: Nichols and Son, 1802.

CHURCHILL, WINSTON S. *A History of the English-Speaking Peoples.* Vol. III. New York: Dodd, 1957.

COKER, R. E. "Peru's Wealth-Producing Birds." *National Geographic Magazine,* XXXVII, vi (June 1920).

COLLINDER, PER. *History of Marine Navigation.* New York: St. Martin's Press, 1954.

Commonwealth Relations Office: Miscellaneous Documents. *East India Company.* Vol. III. Letter dated August 24, 1711.

CONNELY, WILLARD. *Sir Richard Steele.* New York: Scribner, 1934.

COOK, JAMES. *Voyage of Discovery.* New York: Dutton, 1958.

COOKE, EDWARD. *A Voyage to the South Sea and Round the World.* Performed in years 1708-1712. 2 vols. London: Lintot, Gosling, Bettesworth, Innys, 1712.

CULVER, HENRY B. *Book of the Ship,* illus. Gordon Grant. New York: Doubleday, 1924.

DAMPIER, WILLIAM. *A New Voyage Round the World,* ed. N. M. Penzer, introd. Sir Arthur Gray. London: Argonaut Press, 1927.

DAMPIER, WILLIAM. *Dampier's Voyages.* ed. John Masefield. 2 vols. London: Grant Richards, 1906.

DAMPIER, WILLIAM. *Voyages and Discoveries*, ed. N. M. Penzer, introd. Clennell Wilkinson. London: Argonaut Press, 1931.

DANA, RICHARD HENRY, JR. *Two Years Before the Mast*. New York: Dodd, 1959.

DANIEL, HAWTHORNE. *Islands of the East Indies*. New York: Putnam, 1944.

DARWIN, CHARLES. *The Voyage of the Beagle*. New York: Bantam Books, 1958.

DE LUSSAN, RAVENEAU. *Journal du Voyage fait à la Mer du Sud avec les Flibustiers de l'Amérique en 1684 et années suivantes*. Paris: J. B. Coignard, 1689.

DEWHURST, KENNETH. *The Quicksilver Doctor*. Bristol: John Wright and Sons, Ltd., 1957.

DOVAR [sic] THOMAS. *An Ancient Physician's Legacy to his Country*. Printed from the relict of the late R. Bradley, F. R. S. London: pirated ed., 1733.

DOVER, THOMAS. *An Ancient Physician's Legacy to his Country*. 1st ed. London: A. Bellesworth and C. Hitch, 1732.

——. (Anon., attributed to Dover). *A Gentleman of Trinity College, Cambridge. Encomium Argenti Vivi: A Treatise upon the Use and Properties of Quicksilver*. London: Stephen Austin, 1733.

D'URFEY, THOMAS. *Wit and Mirth: or Pills To Purge Melancholy*. London: J. Tonson, 1719-1720.

ESQUEMELING, JR. *The Buccaneers of America*. London: Swann and Sonnenschein, 1893.

EVELYN, JOHN. *Diary*. 2 vols. New York: Dutton, 1958.

FALCONER, WILLIAM. *A Universal Dictionary of the Marine*. London: T. Caddell, 1769.

FALKNER, THOMAS S. J. *A Description of Patagonia and the Adjoining Parts of South America*. Facsimile of 1774 ed., introd. and notes E. S. Neumann. Chicago: Armann and Armann, 1935.

FITZGERALD, BRIAN. *Daniel Defoe*. London: Secker, 1954.

FORBES, ROSTA. *Sir Henry Morgan: Pirate and Pioneer*. London: Cassell, 1948.

FORESTER, C. F. "Wooden Walled Hygiene." *What's New* (early winter, 1957). Chicago: Abbott Laboratories.

FREUCHEN, PETER. *Book of the Seven Seas.* New York: Messner, 1957.

GAMOW, GEORGE. *Biography of the Earth.* New York: Mentor Books, 1941.

GARRISON, FIELDING H. *An Introduction to the History of Medicine.* Philadelphia: Saunders, 1917.

GIBSON, CHARLES E. *The Story of the Ship.* New York: Abelard and Company, 1948.

GOODRICH, F. B. *A History of the Sea.* Ontario: J. W. Lyon and Company, 1880.

GORDON, MAURICE B. *Aesculapius Comes to the Colonies.* New Jersey: Bentnor Company, 1949.

HAKLUYT, RICHARD. *Voyages and Documents,* ed. Janet Hampden. London: Oxford, 1958.

HARCOURT-SMITH, SIMON. *Alberoni, or the Spanish Conspiracy.* London: Faber, 1944.

HARRIS, JOHN. *Navigantium atque Itineratium Bibliotheca, or a Complete Collection of Voyages and Travels.* 2 vols. London: Woodward, Ward, Birt, and others, 1744.

House of Lords. *Manuscripts of the House of Lords,* x, N. S., No. 3136 (June 17, 1714), 360. London, 1712-1714.

House of Lords. *The Humble Petition of the Poor South-Sea Sailors.* Read in the House of Lords, August 31, 1715. London.

HOWELL, JOHN. *The Life and Adventures of Alexander Selkirk.* Edinburgh: Oliver and Boyd, 1829.

JUAN, DON GEORGE and DON ANTONIO DE ULLOA. *A Voyage to South America.* 2nd ed. rev., vol. i. London: Davis and Reymers, 1760.

JUAN, DON GEORGE and DON ANTONIO DE ULLOA. *A Voyage to South America.* vol. ii. London: William Williamson, 1768.

JOHNSON, CHARLES. (Daniel Defoe) *A General History of the Robberies and Murders of the Most Notorious Pirates,* ed. Arthur L. Hayward. New York: Dodd, 1926.

KENDALL, C. WYE. *Private Men-of-War*, McBride, 1932.

KING, LESTER P. *The Medical World of the Eighteenth Century*. Chicago: University of Chicago Press, 1958.

KRONENBERGER, LOUIS. *Kings and Desperate Men*. New York: Knopf, 1942.

——. *Marlborough's Duchess: A Study in Worldliness*. New York: Knopf, 1958.

LAWALL, CHARLES H. *Curious Lore of Drugs and Medicines*. Philadelphia: Lippincott, 1927.

LECKY, W. E. H. *England in the Eighteenth Century*. London: Longmans, 1878-1890.

LEE, F. H., ed. *The Lure of the Sea*. Boston: Little, 1926.

LESLIE, R. C. *Life Aboard a British Privateer in the Time of Queen Anne*. London: Chapman and Hall Company, 1889.

LITTLE, BRYAN. *Crusoe's Captain*. London: Odhams, 1960.

LOVETTE, LELAND P. *Naval Customs, Traditions and Usage*. Annapolis: U. S. Naval Institute, 1939.

LOWRY, R. G. (Lt. Com., Royal Navy). *The Origins of Some Naval Terms and Customs*. London: Sampson, Low, Marston and Company, Ltd., 1938.

LYNAM, EDWARD. *British Maps and Map Makers*. London: Collins, 1947.

MACKAY, CHARLES. *Extraordinary Popular Delusions and the Madness of Crowds*. New York: Farrar, Straus and Cudahy, Inc., 1932.

MAHAN, A. T. *The Influence of Sea Power upon History, 1660-1783*. Boston: Little, n. d.

MANWARING, G. E. *The Flower of England's Garland*. London: P. Allan & Co., Ltd., 1936.

MASEFIELD, JOHN. *On the Spanish Main*. New York: Macmillan, 1925.

MASON, A. E. W. *Life of Francis Drake*. London: Hodder, 1943.

McDOWELL, WILLIAM. *The Shape of Ships*. London: Hutchinson, 1952.

McEWEN, W. A. and A. H. LEWIS: *Encyclopedia of Nautical*

Knowledge. Cambridge, Maryland: Cornell Maritime Press, 1953.

MELVILLE, HERMAN. *The Encantadas,* from the Shorter Novels of Herman Melville. New York: Grosset, 1957.

MINER, ROY WALDO. "Marauders of the Sea." *National Geographic Magazine,* LXVIII, ii (August 1935).

MOLL, HERMAN. *Atlas Geographus, or a Compleat System of Geography.* London: John Nutt, 1717.

MORGAN, E. VICTOR. *The Study of Prices and the Value of Money.* London: Geo. Philip and Son, 1950.

MORISON, SAMUEL ELIOT. *Admiral of the Ocean Sea.* Boston: Little, 1942.

MOYLE, JOHN. *Chirugus Marinus or The Sea Chirurgion.* London, 1702.

MURPHY, ROBERT CUSHMAN. "The Most Valuable Bird in the World." *National Geographic Magazine,* XLVI, iii (September 1924).

OSBORNE, FAIRFIELD. *The Pacific World.* New York: W. Whorton Co., Inc., 1944.

OSLER, WILLIAM. *An Alabama Student and Other Biographical Essays.* London: Oxford, 1926.

OSLER, SIR WILLIAM. *Thomas Dover, Physician and Buccaneer.* Baltimore: Bulletin, Johns Hopkins Hospital, no. 58, 1896.

POWELL, J. W. D. *Bristol Privateers and Ships of War.* Bristol: J. W. Arrowsmith, Ltd., 1930.

QUENNELL, PETER. *Hogarth's Progress.* New York: Viking, 1955.

QUICKE, ALEXANDER. *Adventures and Explorations in South America.* London: Dent, 1930.

RAPPOPORT, ANGELO S. *Superstitions of Sailors.* London: Stanley Paul and Co., Ltd., 1928.

RIESENBERG, FELIX. *Cape Horn.* New York: Dodd, 1939.

——. *The Pacific Ocean.* New York: McGraw, 1940.

ROBINSON, CHARLES N. (Com., Royal Navy). *The British Tar in Fact and Fiction.* London and New York: Harper, 1911.

RODDIS, LOUIS H. *James Lind, Founder of Nautical Medicine.* London: Heinemann, 1950.

ROGERS, STANLEY. *Sea-Lore.* London: Harrap, 1929.

ROGERS, WOODES. *A Cruising Voyage Round the World.* London, Knapton, 1712.

——. *A Cruising Voyage Round the World,* ed, with introd. Manwaring. London: Longmans, 1928.

ROSS, KIP. "Peru Homeland of the Warlike Inca." *National Geographic Magazine,* XCVIII, iv (October 1950).

ROSSI, MARIO M. and J. M. HONE. *Swift or The Egotist.* London: Gollancz, 1934.

RUSSELL W. CLARK. *William Dampier.* London: Macmillan, 1889.

SCHMITT, WALDO L. "A Voyage to the Island Home of Robinson Crusoe." *National Geographic Magazine,* LIV, iii (September 1928).

SCHURZ, WILLIAM L. *The Manila Galleon.* New York: Dutton, 1939.

SELKIRK, ALEXANDER. *Providence Displayed.* An anonymous contemporary account reprinted in the *Harleian Miscellany,* vol. v. London: 1810.

SHELVOCKE, GEORGE. *A Voyage Round the World by Way of the Great South Sea.* London: J. Senex, 1726.

SITWELL, EDITH. *Bath.* New York: Harrison Smith and Robert K. Haas, Inc., 1932.

SMITH, F. G. WALTON. "Shipworms, Saboteurs of the Sea." *National Geographic Magazine,* CX, iv (October 1956).

SOULE, C. C. *Naval Terms and Definitions.* Princeton: Van Nostrand, 1923.

STATHAM, R. N. *Privateers and Privateering.* New York: James Pott and Co., 1910.

STEELE, RICHARD. *The Englishman.* London: Sam. Buckley, 1714.

——. *The Englishman,* ed. Rae Blanchard. New York: Oxford, 1955.

——. *The Correspondence of Richard Steele,* ed. Rae Blanchard. London: Oxford, 1941.

STRONG, L. A. G. *Dr. Quicksilver, 1660-1742.* London: Andrew Melrose, 1955.

TREVELYAN, GEORGE MACAULAY. *History of England,* vol. 2. New York: Doubleday, 1956.

ULLOA, DON ANTONIO DE. (See Juan, Don George).

United States Navy. *Sailing Directions for the West Coast of Mexico and Central America.* H. O. #84. 8th ed. Washington, D. C.: Hydrographic Office, 1952.

VANDENBOSCH, AMRY. *The Dutch East Indies.* Berkeley and Los Angeles: University of California Press, 1944.

VAN NOORT, OLIVIER. *A Letter from Olivier Van Noort, 1598-1601,* trans. Jan O. M. Van Broek. Minneapolis: University of Minnesota, 1957.

VILLIERS, ALLAN J. "Rounding the Horn in a Windjammer." *National Geographic Magazine,* LIX, ii (February 1931).

——. *Monsoon Seas: The Story of the Indian Ocean.* New York: McGraw, 1952.

——. *Wild Ocean.* New York: McGraw, 1957.

——. "Under Canvas in the Atomic Age." *National Geographic Magazine,* CVIII, i (July 1955).

VIEKKE, BERNARD H. M. *The Story of the Dutch East Indies.* Cambridge: Harvard University Press, 1945.

VON HAGEN, VICTOR W. "The Curse of the Galápagos." *Travel,* LXXXI, i (May 1943).

——. *Realm of the Inca.* New York: Mentor Books, 1957.

WAFER, LIONEL. *A New Voyage and Description of the Isthmus of America.* Reprint of the 1699 edition, ed. George P. Winship. Cleveland: Burrows Bros., 1903.

WALLACE, IRVING. *The Fabulous Originals.* New York: Knopf, 1956.

WARD, NED. *The London Spy,* ed. Arthur L. Hayward. New York: George H. Doran, n. d.

WATERS, DAVID W. *The Art of Navigation in England in Eliza-*

bethan and Early Stuart Times. London: Hollis and Carter, 1958.

WILBUR, MARGUERITE AYER. *The East India Company*. Palo Alto: Stanford University Press, 1945.

WILKINSON, CLENNELL. *William Dampier*. London: Lane, 1929.

WILLIAMS-ELLIS, AMABEL and F. J. FISHER. *The Story of English Life*. New York: Coward, 1936.

WILLIAMSON, J. A. *The Ocean in English History*. New York: Oxford, 1941.

WOODBURY, GEORGE. *Great Days of Piracy in the West Indies*. New York: Norton, 1951.

WYCHERLEY, GEORGE (pseud. George W. Kirkman). *Buccaneers of the Pacific*. Indianapolis: Bobbs, 1928.

Index